HOW LIFE WRITES THE BOOK

How Life
Writes the Book

REAL SOCIALISM
AND SOCIALIST REALISM
IN STALIN'S RUSSIA

Thomas Lahusen

CORNELL UNIVERSITY PRESS
Ithaca and London

Boris Pasternak's poem "Fame" is reproduced by permission from
Boris Pasternak: Poems, trans. Eugene M. Kayden,
copyright © by The University of Michigan 1959.

First published 1997 by Cornell University Press.

Printed in the United States of America

Library of Congress Cataloging-in-Publication Data

Lahusen, Thomas.
    How life writes the book : real socialism and socialist realism in Stalin's Russia / Thomas Lahusen.
        p.   cm.
    Includes bibliographical references and index.
    ISBN 0-8014-3394-0 (cloth : alk. paper).
    1. Azhaev, Vasilii.   2. Azhaev, Vasilii.   Daleko ot Moskvy.   3. Socialist realism in literature.   4. Soviet Union — Social conditions.   I. Title.
PG3476.A98Z77   1997
891.73'44 — dc21   97-19261

Cornell University Press strives to utilize environmentally responsible suppliers and materials to the fullest extent possible in the publishing of its books. Such materials include vegetable-based, low-VOC inks and acid-free papers that are also either recycled, totally chlorine-free, or partly composed of nonwood fibers.

Cloth printing   10 9 8 7 6 5 4 3 2 1

for my mother
for Yao Yuan

CONTENTS

ACKNOWLEDGMENTS

Portions of Chapter 1 have been published in German in *Wiener Slawistischer Almanach* 35 (1995): 219–231, © Gesellschaft zur Förderung slawistischer Studien, all rights reserved. An early version of Chapter 2 has been published in French in *Le Gré des Langues* 5 (1993): 116–140; portions of the same chapter have appeared in Russian in *Poiski v inakom: Fantastika i russkaia literatura XX veka,* ed. Leonid Geller, pp. 175–191, © Lausanne University, Leonid Heller, 1994; as well as in *Rossiia i ATR—Russia and the Pacific,* no. 2 (1995): 105–111. An early version of Chapter 10 has been published in Russian in *Revue des Études Slaves* 66, no. 4 (1994): 777–791, © Institut d'études slaves et Institut de recherche et d'étude des nouvelles institutions et sociétés à l'Est (IRENISE), Paris, 1994; all rights reserved. Portions of Chapter 11 have been published in *Discourse: Theoretical Studies in Media and Culture* 17, no. 3 (Spring 1995): 58–74. I am grateful to the Gesellschaft zur Förderung slawistischer Studien, to Leonid Heller, and to the Institut d'études slaves–IRENISE for permission to use the previously published materials here.

I also thank the Arts and Sciences Research Council, the Center for International Studies, the Center for Slavic, Eurasian, and East European Studies, and the Department of Slavic Languages and Literatures, all at Duke University, for financial support; Irina Leonidovna Liubimova-Azhaeva for giving me access to her husband's archive and permitting me to reproduce some of the documents and photographs I found there; Evgeny Dobrenko, Véronique Garros, and Maiia Turovskaia for their help on many occasions; Katerina Clark, Gregory Freidin, Julia Hell, Stephen Kotkin, Moshe Lewin, and Yuri Slezkine for useful suggestions; Sheila Fitzpatrick and the participants in the University of Chicago history workshop for stimulating discussions; Orest Pelech and Patricia Polansky for bibliographic assistance; and Candice Ward for correcting the first version of my manuscript.

I am indebted to friends and colleagues in the Russian Far East for their help and support, in particular to Pavel Minakir and Valentina Buldakova (Economic Research Institute, Khabarovsk), Valentina Rodintseva and Tat'iana Shevchik (State Archives of the Khabarovsk Administrative Region), Aleksandr Bukreev and Tat'iana Kuznetsova (Far Eastern State Research Library, Khabarovsk), Liudmila Romashko (State Archives of the Khabarovsk Administrative Region, Komsomol'sk branch), Pavel Fefilov, Marina Kuz'mina, and Ivan Panin (Komsomol'sk), Ol'ga Elantseva (Far Eastern University, Vladivostok), Viktor Larin and Elena Chernolutskaia (Institute of History, Archaeology, and Ethnography of the Peoples of the Far East, Vladivostok), and Viktor Remizovskii (Far Eastern Popular Academy of Sciences, Khabarovsk), with whom I read *Far from Moscow* on the shores of the river Adun.

Finally, I thank John Ackerman of Cornell University Press for his searching melancholy, and Xiao Hong for enduring mine all along.

T. L.

SOURCES AND
ABBREVIATIONS

AA	private archive of Vasilii Azhaev
Amurlag	Corrective Labor Camps of the Amur
BAM	Baikal-Amur Main Line
BRIZ	Bureau of Rationalization and Invention
Chekist	employee of the ChK
ChK	see VChK
Dal'krai	Far Eastern Administrative Region
Dal'neftekombinat	Far Eastern Industrial Complex of the Oil Industry
DV	Far East
EPRON	Expedition of Underwater Work for Special Purposes
GAKhK	State Archives of the Khabarovsk Administrative Region
GARF	State Archives of the Russian Federation
Glavlit	Main Administration of Affairs for Literature and Publishing
gorkom	city committee
GULAG	Main Administration of Camps
GULZhDS	Main Administration of Railway Construction Camps
GUZhDS	Main Administration of Railway Construction
ITL	Corrective Labor Camp
KLE	*Short Literary Encyclopaedia*
Komsomol	Communist Youth League
kraikom	regional committee
KVCh	Cultural-Educational Unit
KVO	Cultural and Educational Department
litaktiv	active members of the Soviet Writers' Union
MGB	Ministry of State Security
MUR	Moscow Criminal Investigation Department

MVD	Ministry of Internal Affairs
narkom	people's commissar
Nizhne-Amurlag	Corrective Labor Camps of the Lower Amur
NKVD	People's Commissariat of Internal Affairs
obkom	oblast' (regional, provincial) committee
OGIZ	United State Publishing House
OGPU	United Main Political Administration
OKDVA	Special Red-Bannered Far Eastern Army
OLP	separate camp subsector
raikom	district committee
RAPP	Russian Association of Proletarian Writers
RGALI	Russian State Archive of Literature and Art
RGVA	Russian State Military Archives
RKKA	Workers' and Peasants' Red Army
RSFSR	Russian Soviet Federal Socialist Republic
RTsKhIDNI	Russian Center for the Conservation and Study of Documents of Recent History
Sovnarkom	Council of People's Commissars
TsBRIZ	Central Bureau of Rationalization and Invention
TsK	Central Committee
UFSB	Administration of the Federal Service of Security
UITLK	Administration of Corrective Labor Camps and Colonies
UVD	Administration of Internal Affairs
UZhDS	Department of Railway Construction
VChK	All-Russian Extraordinary Commission Combating Counterrevolution, Sabotage, and Speculation
VLKSM	All-Union Leninist Communist Youth League
VKP(b)	All-Union Communist Party (of the Bolsheviks)
VOKhR	Militarized Guard at Places of Confinement
Zaporozhstroi	Zaporozh'e Industrial Complex
zek	prisoner (from *z/k*, for *zakliuchennyi*)
ZhDSU	Administration of Railway Construction

NOTE ON TRANSLITERATION
AND TRANSLATION

The Library of Congress system of transliteration is used throughout
the book, including quotations from the English version of *Far from
Moscow,* which have been modified for the purpose of consistency.
For a few well-known names (Dostoevsky, Tolstoy, Trotsky, etc.) the
traditional English form has been used. All translations are my own
unless otherwise indicated. Translations of letters and documents attempt to maintain the often faulty style of the originals.

HOW LIFE WRITES THE BOOK

INTRODUCTION

The forest warden guarded his forest out of love for science, and at this hour he sat before some ancient books. He was searching the past for some likeness to Soviet times, so as to discover the further torturous fate of the Revolution and to find some way of saving his family.

His father, also a forest watchman, had left him a library of cheap books, all by the unread, the forgotten, the very least of authors. He used to tell his son that life's decisive truths exist secretly in abandoned books.

The forest warden's father compared bad books to stillborn children who had perished in their mother's womb from the lack of correspondence between their own excessively tender bodies and the coarseness of the world, which penetrated even a mother's womb.

"If only ten of those children could stay whole, they would make man a triumphant and exalted being," the father bequeathed to his son. "But instead the mind gives birth to all that is dull and the heart to that which is least feeling, to suffer in the sharp air of nature and the battle for raw food."

Now, the forest warden was reading a work by Nikolai Arsakov, printed in 1868. The work was called *Second-Rate People,* and the warden rummaged through the boredom of its dry words for that which he needed. The warden held that there are no senseless or boring books if only the reader will seek the meaning of life in them attentively. Boring books come from boring readers, for it is the reader's searching melancholy which works in books, and not the author's skill.

—Andrei Platonov, *Chevengur*

People, their deeds and works, are remembered by History only if they succeed as story. Their lives may be told and retold as legend, altered to fit the needs of succeeding generations, or they may be analyzed, shaped into narrative, and catalogued with the biographies of other notable men and women. The less than "notable" can enter History, too, lending their stories to scholars, who seek to capture such individuals in their day-to-day routine. From the point of view of History, the question whether any of these people actually existed becomes all but secondary; their success as story is what counts in the quest to stave off oblivion. In this book I have attempted to write such a story, constructing it from the shards of an all but forgotten life. Whether my telling will help its hero to survive and enter History is of course beyond my control. That is the reader's business.

I became acquainted with Vasilii Nikolaevich Azhaev's novel *Far from Moscow* in 1988 while studying the literature of the Zhdanov era—that is, of the late Stalin years, the end of the 1940s and the early 1950s—at the University of Lausanne. Despite my scholarly interest in reconstructing the institutional structure of late Stalinist culture, reading *Far from Moscow*, which received the Stalin Prize in 1949, was painful: the endless dialogues, the technical details, the bureaucratic clichés, the predictability of the plot, and all the other attributes of a Soviet production novel conspired dramatically to confirm Marc Slonim's classic judgment: the "landscape" of this literary period indeed looked "like a monotonous plain, with just a few low hills emerging from gray overcast skies."[1] But, as Andrei Platonov wrote, "boring books come from boring readers." And so I started to read carefully, comparing different editions of the novel, an exercise that is always interesting as far as Soviet literature is concerned. Subjected to an endless process of censorship, rewriting, and updating, the Soviet text conceals many hidden strata for the archaeologist of culture and many clues and coded messages for the historical investigator. My boredom vanished with the discovery of Azhaev's "code" in *Far from Moscow*, and this is how my journey into the writer's texts and life began.

The publication of an article titled "The Mystery of the River Adun," first in German and then in English, coincided with my emigration to the

United States.[2] At that time, despite glasnost and perestroika, it still seemed as if the Soviet Union would be there forever; no one was predicting its disappearance from the map of the world. The mystery that I had found concealed in the toponyms of the fictitious map of Azhaev's novel was still worthy of being discovered and revealed because it challenged—at least in my eyes—Soviet and dissident censors alike. But not for long. Shortly afterward, communism vanished as a "problem," and a new generation of scholars started to revise the history that previous generations of Sovietologists had given their lives to scrutinize, reveal, and denounce. The open archive had by now replaced the dissident source in the new market economy of scholarly investigation. In the meantime, while teaching on the neo-Gothic campus of Duke University and getting acquainted with "real" postmodernity in situ, I continued my journey into Azhaev's life and work. "The Mystery of the River Adun" took on *couleur locale,* and gave way to irony and nostalgia. The study of a Soviet literary classic seemed increasingly incongruous after I had crossed the ocean. At the same time, I could not avoid a feeling of loss, but my homesickness was for more than Europe: I was mourning the Perfect Island, the Austral Continent, Utopia, all that the Soviet Union could represent, despite "real socialism." Then, during a trip to Moscow in 1992, I found *my* archive in the apartment of Irina Leonidovna Liubimova-Azhaeva. The discovery confirmed my hypothesis as to the presence of a mystery: according to Azhaev's widow, before he died the writer had requested that his archive not be given to the state. The time would come, he believed, when somebody would be able to work on it. I soon realized that what I had found, if given to the state, would have been broken up into standardized inventories and files, and some of its nonliterary documents would probably have been sent back to the organs that had issued them. In other words, the archive would have lost its unity. The deeper my journey took me into the materials I was given by Irina Leonidovna, the more convinced I became that what I was discovering had its own internal logic. In opening these remarkably well organized files, in reading the typed and retyped documents, the letters received and the copies of replies sent, the manuscripts with their titles, dates, and other classification criteria, I felt that this collection comprised a montage intended for the future archivist of the writer's work and life.

A small office in Moscow agreed to copy (for a very reasonable fee) most of the material given me by Azhaev's widow; it turned out that it was a branch office of the Ministry of Internal Affairs. On 16 June 1992 I was heading back home on a Delta flight from Moscow to New York with several thousand pages copied from Vasilii Azhaev's archive in my luggage. The rest followed a few months later, thanks to a Russian colleague who emigrated to the United States. Naturally, the reality that I discovered in these dusty boxes—in the manuscripts, the letters, the private, official, and even secret documents dating from the time the events of *Far from Moscow* were taking place—gave a new surge and new directions to the story I was writing. Although the find did not reduce the irony or my nostalgia, it intensified my urge to answer a number of questions, all boiling down to this: How should we write the history of this past that seems marked by a trauma that afflicts not only the "patient" but also—by some sort of transference—those who are supposed to observe, to understand, or to cure? After meeting Irina Leonidovna and some of Azhaev's old friends and acquaintances (one of them a "major" Soviet poet), after going myself far from Moscow to look for other documents, listen to other stories, and find other clues, I realized that the rereading of Azhaev's published texts and, more than anything else, the deciphering of the author's handwriting brought me closer to the particular cipher that lies, I believe, at the foundation of everybody's life. Of course, the present montage is yet another encryption, but one I offer with hopes of producing, by its parallels and juxtapositions, some insights into a remarkable life and a remarkable time.

Soviet socialist realism has produced an ocean of critical literature, most of it, if seen from inside, actually a parasitical by-product of the "method" itself, if not its main activity or function. As to the works written from outside or afterward, from Abram Siniavsky-Tertz's "What Is Socialist Realism?" to Katerina Clark's *Soviet Novel: History as Ritual,* Hans Günther's *Verstaatlichung der Literatur,* and Régine Robin's *Socialist Realism: An Impossible Aesthetic,* even Boris Groys's *Total Art of Stalinism,* all of them, without exception, focus on the finished product of the canonical works.[3] Whether seen as an aesthetic failure or as an apotheosis of the "most modern art in the world," the method, it turns out, always stands for something else: for myth, hagiography, the "demiurgic construction of the new world," and so on. My book does not aim to refute any of these views, including the internal ones; but, being archaeological in character, and exposing the fragments pieced together from Azhaev's own montage of life, it could not avoid capturing socialist realism in its very writing, and I could not refrain from discovering that, indeed, "people formed in a nonmarket non-consumer-consumptive society do not think like we do."[4]

And while I was searching for the production of socialist realism, many other topics of "real socialism" surfaced.

Azhaev's Project No. 15 will lead the reader directly into the realm of forced industrialization and reeducation through labor in Stalin's time. We shall see how literature and life intersected with the building of an oil pipeline in the Soviet Far East in 1941 and 1942 and with other projects, such as the construction of the Baikal-Amur Main Line, or the second Trans-Siberian Railway. We shall discover how literature itself became a construction site of sorts, produced directly from the blueprints of a "bureau of rationalization and invention," whose director believed that he could use his experience "as a chemist and a writer" to discover and describe the elements of human grief and the mysteries of love and death. Literary production will also be seen from above: we shall witness the entire process of the making of a Stalin Prize in literature and film. Its highlights will be a "literary" encounter between the commandant of a labor camp and an inmate of the Cultural and Educational Department of the People's Commissariat of Internal Affairs; the life of a provincial branch of the Soviet Writers' Union during the Great Terror; the editorial politics of a central literary journal and the intervention of the highest cultural authorities of the Soviet state during the struggle against "rootless cosmopolitanism" in the late 1940s and early 1950s. Azhaev's archive contains many letters and other material helpful to us in evaluating the feedback of his readers, from base to superstructure: to what extent was this "people's literature" read by the people, and what place did it occupy within the "other" literature? Finally, and most important, Azhaev's construction of his own life through what I came to see as the three "borderlines" of his biography shows us the traumatic experience not only of a human being but of a generation. It may perhaps tell us more about what went wrong in the transference from hope to reality, or, if you wish, from socialist realism to real socialism.

1

PROJECT NO. 15

Aleksei closely examined his handiwork by the light of an electric torch. He looked at the welder with a sudden gleam in his eyes and beckoned to Batmanov, Beridze, and the rest. He passed a finger slowly round the pipe and read aloud:

"Long live our Moscow! Glory to the great Stalin! We shall win the war! January 1942."

With these words, engraved in fire for all time on the metal of the first joint, Umara Magomet, the welder, had laid the beginning of the pipeline.

—Vasilii Azhaev, *Far from Moscow*

A document found in July 1994 in the State Archives, or, more precisely, in the former Party Archives of the Region of Khabarovsk, informs its present-day reader—the specialist on Soviet Far Eastern history of the 1940s, for example—of the circumstances under which Stroitel′stvo No. 15 (Project No. 15) was deemed complete and handed over in January 1943 to the Bureau of Pipeline Operations of Dal′neftekombinat, the Far Eastern Industrial Complex of the Oil Industry.[1]

Our document, dated 28 July 1944, gives a detailed description of the various sections of a pipeline constructed between 1940 and 1942, linking the city of Okha, on the northern edge of the island of Sakhalin, to Sofiiskoe,[2] about 250 kilometers north of Komsomol′sk-on-the-Amur, across the Nevel'skii Strait between Cape Pogibi and Cape Lazarevo, where the island of Sakhalin and the mainland are separated by only 9 kilometers. The total length of the pipeline was 373.8 kilometers; other data relate to the diameter of the pipes, the size of the tubes, and so forth. According to the document, the technical review and acceptance of the project, stipulated by Resolution No. 998 of the Council of People's Commissars (Sovnarkom) in 1939, never took place. The "commercial" acceptance of Project No. 15 — in other words, its transfer to the authorities who were now supposed to operate it — occurred under very unsatisfactory conditions.

Project No. 15 showed serious deviations from the original blueprints, and the consequences for its operation were catastrophic. The pipes were not buried deep enough (below the level at which the earth freezes) and continually burst. Their alignment was often so imprecise that the tubes broke. The welds that joined the pipes were of poor quality, with similar results. The infrastructure of the whole line was a disaster: the power stations supplying electricity to the various technical installations that kept the oil going needed major repairs; at the time of the project's delivery, the boiler houses, reservoirs, and pumping stations were dysfunctional, and the telephone lines did not work; various security devices, including fire-prevention mechanisms, were in very poor condition; and the facilities for the staff (themselves poorly trained and lacking in discipline) were in a deplorable state, where they existed at all. The pipeline continually broke down, and an enormous quantity of oil was lost in the sea and elsewhere along the line. Finally, the Bureau of Pipeline Operations of Dal'neftekombinat complained not only that the builders of Project No. 15 had failed to deliver any specific documents concerning the reasons for and appropriateness of their departures from the initial plan but also that such documents had never been requested.

With the opening of the Soviet archives, these and other documents will probably surface, allowing us to fill in the blanks in the story of Project No. 15. Indeed, several Far Eastern publications have recently dealt with the project's history, quoting various sources to which I did not have access, such as a resolution of the Central Party Committee and the Council of People's Commissars which ordered that the tubes used for the construction of the pipeline be purchased in the United States.[3] Other documents suggest that Sovnarkom commissioned Project No. 15 to the People's Commissariat of the Oil Industry in 1939. The administrative structure of the construction project was organized during the second quarter of 1940, and its headquarters were to be situated in Sofiiskoe.[4] That same year the project was placed under the control of the Main Administration of Railway Construction Camps of the People's Commissariat of Internal Affairs of the USSR (GULZhDS NKVD SSSR). The GULZhDS* itself—at times appearing under the acronym of GUZhDS (Main Administration of Railway Construction)—was created by order no. 0014 of 4 January 1940 of the NKVD of the USSR, and represented the union of two former organizations, the Department of Railway Construction of the Main Administration of Camps of the NKVD of the USSR (UZhDS GULAGa NKVD SSSR)† and the Administration of Railway Construction of the NKVD in the Far East (UZhDS NKVD na DV).‡ This restructuring was part of a more general effort to reorganize the Main Administration of Camps (GULAG) by industrial sectors when the Gulag system was expanded in the late 1930s. The Corrective Labor Camps of the Amur (Amurlag) and of the Lower Amur (Nizhne-Amurlag) were formed on 25 January 1940 on the basis of the reorganization of the Administration of Railway Construction of the NKVD in the Far East.[5]

The construction work of Project No. 15 was assigned to the Camp of the Lower Amur of the GULZhDS in May 1941.[6] A recent account confirms this date on the basis of sources such as a resolution by the Sovnarkom of 7 May 1941, an order by the People's Commissariat of the Oil Industry of 9 May 1941, and NKVD order no. 0250 of 17 May 1941.[7] The reason for building a pipeline from Okha on Sakhalin to the mainland was evidently strategic: the relatively mechanized Far Eastern armies needed secure gasoline supplies. Both the Khabarovsk oil refinery and its supply route from Sakhalin up the Amur were vulnerable to attack by Japanese planes, submarines based in De-Kastri Bay, and torpedo boats at Nikolaevsk. These circumstances suggested the need to construct a second oil refinery, to be located at Komsomol'sk, and an unsinkable pipeline.[8]

But what about the failures of Project No. 15 and the deviations from the initial plan? Another kind of document can compensate for the missing one: it is a work of literary fiction, a now-forgotten best-seller of the late 1940s, *Far from Moscow*, by Vasilii Azhaev (1912/15–1968), which was awarded the Stalin Prize (first class) in 1949 (for 1948). The main conflict played out in this drama, the very events that keep the story going, is the

---

*Acronym for Glavnoe upravlenie lagerei zheleznodorozhnogo stroitel'stva.

†Acronym for Upravlenie zheleznodorozhnogo stroitel'stva Glavnogo upravleniia lagerei NKVD SSSR.

‡Acronym for Upravlenie zheleznodorozhnogo stroitel'stva NKVD na Dal'nem Vostoke.

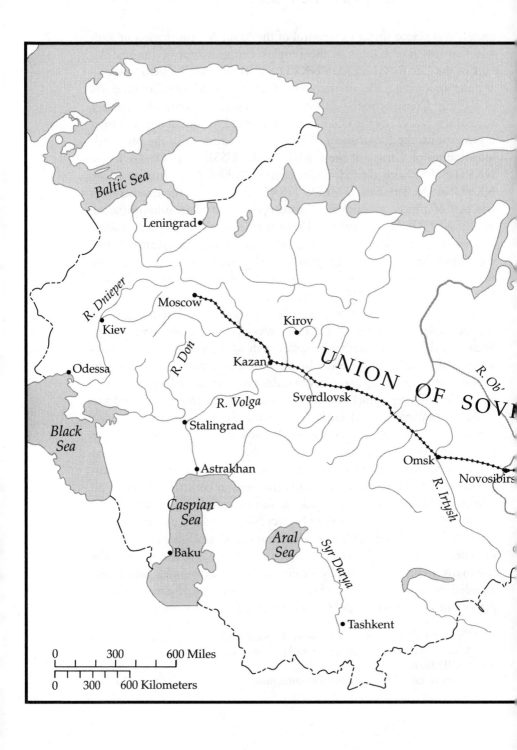

Baltic Sea

Leningrad

R. Dnieper

Moscow

Kiev

Kirov

Odessa

R. Don

Kazan

UNION OF SOVI

R. Ob'

R. Volga

Sverdlovsk

Black
Sea

Stalingrad

Astrakhan

Omsk

Novosibirs

R. Irtysh

Caspian
Sea

Aral
Sea

Baku

Syr Darya

Tashkent

0   300   600 Miles

0   300   600 Kilometers

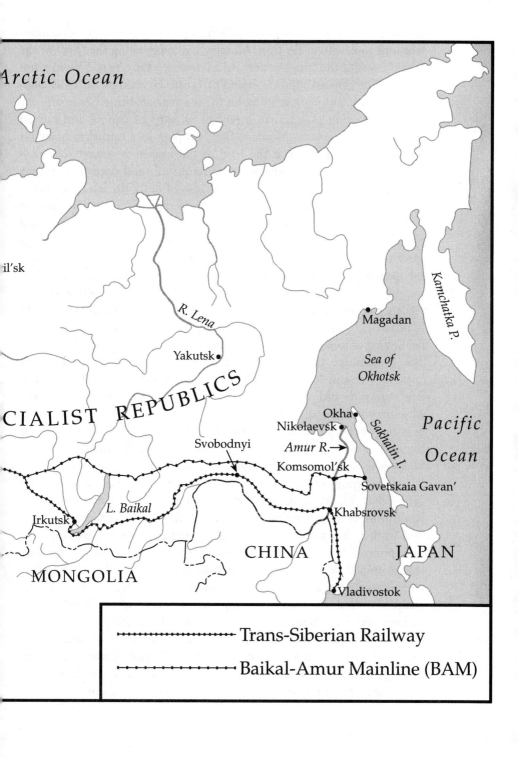

Arctic Ocean

il'sk

R. Lena

Yakutsk•

CIALIST REPUBLICS

Svobodnyi

Magadan•

Sea of Okhotsk

Okha•

Nikolaevsk•

Amur R.→

Komsomol'sk

Kamchatka P.

Sakhalin I.

Pacific Ocean

Sovetskaia Gavan'

Irkutsk•

L. Baikal

Khabsrovsk•

CHINA

JAPAN

MONGOLIA

•Vladivostok

••••••••••••••••••• Trans-Siberian Railway

••••••••••••••••••• Baikal-Amur Mainline (BAM)

controversy over where and how to build a pipeline between two fictitious locations somewhere "far from Moscow": whether along the "left" or the "right" bank of the "mighty river Adun" between the city of Novinsk, not far from Rubezhansk, and the island of Taisin. Devised by the chief engineer, Beridze, who represents Stalin (he is a pipe-smoking Georgian), the new construction plan has to overcome all sorts of natural and human obstacles. Conceived in Moscow, Beridze's plan is nevertheless based on experience and affirmed at the level of the masses: a certain Karpov, a "simple fisherman, true inhabitant of the Adun" (and chairman of a big collective farm), first came up with the idea of using the left bank, but it was rejected by the (reactionary) engineers of the plan. Its final realization is the result of many converging factors: a combination of theory and praxis; active help by the people; nature itself; the radio broadcast of a speech by Stalin, which (in an almost erotic way) cements the collective; the speeding up of time by Stakhanovite work[9] (owing to the new plan, the pipeline is built three times faster than the old plan's schedule); the vigilance of the leaders (above all the head of the construction site, Vasilii Maksimovich Batmanov, and the *partorg* [party organizer] Zalkind); the debunking of some wreckers; and a series of sacrifices, among other things. The competition between the "left" and "right" variants, acted out by "progressive" and "conservative" forces, is predictably resolved in a "positive" way, as the old engineers, who are hostages to Western influences (and who flirt with sabotage), are vanquished by the young. Once again the superiority of the Soviet Union in all domains has been demonstrated. At the end of the novel, the young engineer Aleksei Kovshov departs for Moscow to report on the successful completion of the task.

As Wolfgang Kasack states in his *Dictionary of Russian Literature since 1917,* Azhaev's work "is in complete accordance with the tenets of Socialist Realism in its interpretation of the period: the main characters are idealized in their function as positive heroes, the conflicts are artificial, and their positive outcome is predestined. The fusion of the novel's character into a unified collective is illustrated by the fact that the most important technological ideas always occur to the various characters simultaneously."[10] Indeed, the reader of today needs a good deal of patience, and a perhaps perverse determination, to read through the 456-page Stalin Prize novel (1,430 pages in its three-volume English translation). In other words, what we have here is a typical expression of the "conflictlessness" and "varnishing of reality" that characterized Soviet literature at the depth of its decline during the last few years under Stalin, when representations of the contradiction between the "bad" and the "good" were replaced by depictions of the struggle between the "good" and the "better," and between the "better" and the "excellent." In an article devoted to Azhaev's *Far from Moscow,* the main theoretician of the era, Vladimir Ermilov, reformulated Nikolai Chernyshevsky's famous formula "The beautiful is life" (Prekrasnoe—eto zhizn') to "The beautiful is our life" (Prekrasnoe—eto nasha zhizn').[11]

"This great harmony is the final Purpose of Creation, this beautiful absence of conflict is the future of socialist realism," wrote Abram Tertz (Andrei Siniavsky) in his 1959 pamphlet excoriating the official method that had dominated Soviet literature since 1934.[12] Beyond the lie, which is clearly reflected in Azhaev's fictitious version of Project No. 15, there is another possible reading of "conflictlessness," one in which it is not merely the result of the terror that ultimately paralyzed culture or of the final functionalization of literature in a "totalitarian" society.

Vera Dunham's attempt to understand socialist realist postwar writing in the context of social change is not often cited, perhaps because it poses the problem of literary reflection in almost "vulgar sociological" terms. Her interpretation nevertheless challenges the totalitarian approach, which, focusing on the ideological function of this literature, rarely searches for its mechanisms of production and change. For Dunham, Soviet postwar literature served and reflected the interests of a new middle class, "born out of Stalin's push for the industrialization, reeducation, and bureaucratization of the country, flesh of the flesh of Stalin's revolutions from above in the thirties, and ready to fill the vacuum created by Stalin's Great Purge and by the liquidation of the Leninist generation of activists."[13] There was at least a middle ground where the readers of Azhaev's novel and the interests of the state could meet: the popular success of Azhaev's "conflictless" novel and its message of "the front line and the rear as a single entity" (*edinstvo fronta i tyla*) can be interpreted as the sign of the mass reader's need for (and the state's willingness to help provide) a new symbolic universe after World War II and other horrors: a new shelter. As Peter Berger and Thomas Luckmann stated many years ago, "All societies are constructions in the face of chaos."[14]

The first time we see the left and right bank of the river Adun in the novel it is from a bird's-eye view, when the chief engineer, Beridze, accompanied by the young engineer Aleksei Kovshov, looks down on the site from an airplane. The passage is worth quoting, for it gives a clear sense of the terrain on which the story will unfold:

The route of the pipeline crossed the Adun at two points—at Novinsk and near the small town of Ol′gokhta, also on the river. Slightly below the latter spot the river and the pipeline diverged. The Adun swept on majestically to the right, while the route of the pipeline swung northward to the left. Running down to the sea, it followed the coastline to Chongr Cape, whence it was to cross the stormy twelve-kilometer Jagdinsk Strait at its narrowest point, over to Cape Death on Taisin Island. The oil fields were in the area of the town of Konchelan, at the northern tip of the island, and it was to them that the line was to be laid.[15]

Immediately after completing his inspection flight or reconnaissance (he had already explored these savage regions years before), Beridze rushes to his office and "buries himself in blueprints," reciting a poem by Vladimir Mayakovsky:

> But it seems
> that before the singing can start,
> you toil and sweat with the song's
> fermentation.[16]

Azhaev, too, had explored these savage regions, and what he had seen and lived through had also been fermenting. Bits and pieces of his experiences, principally in the form of rumors, were revealed by dissident voices during his lifetime. The author himself went public, though only posthumously, in *Vagon* (The Boxcar), a novel published by his widow during the era of perestroika. Its highly autobiographical plot centers on the deportation in 1934 of a young worker to the camp called Svobodnyi (Freedom).[17] Azhaev had been arrested on 29 December 1934 for "counter-revolutionary activities" and sentenced to four years in the Corrective Labor Camp of the Baikal-Amur Main Line of the People's Commissariat of Internal Affairs (BAMLAG NKVD), in the Soviet Far Eastern city of Svobodnyi. The Baikal-Amur Main Line (BAM) was the so-called second Trans-Siberian Railway, designed to link Siberia with the Soviet Far East. Its construction, which started in the 1930s within the labor camp system, was not finished until the 1970s.[18] Azhaev was released in 1937, but stayed on at the camp as a "free laborer" and, for some time, head of the TsBRIZ, the Central Bureau of Rationalization and Invention.

Since 1988 I have been trailing Azhaev through the various published and unpublished versions of *Far from Moscow* and other works in his archive, finding in all this material much more than fiction. The trail finally led me to those very places "far from Moscow," where I would discover that the local daily press was at last revealing to its post-Soviet readers the dark secrets of their own past. Today we know that the island of Taisin is in reality the island of Sakhalin, that Novinsk and Rubezhansk are Komsomol'sk-na-Amure and Khabarovsk, and that "father Adun" (*Adun batiushka*) is, like the other toponyms of the novel, a coded name for the river Amur, an anagram for the "hell" (*ad, v adu*) in which Azhaev wrote the first lines of his future Stalin Prize-winner as he worked in the administration of the Lower Amur Corrective Labor Camp, having risen in rank after the job with BAM.

It was here that the free laborer Azhaev also wrote various reports, accounts, and memoranda, some of which dealt directly with Project No. 15, addressed to Vasilii Arsent'evich Barabanov, head (*nachal'nik*) of the camp,[19] to his deputy Figel'shtein; to Grigorii Davydovich Chkheidze, "lieutenant of state security" and chief engineer of Project No. 15; and to Genrikh Moiseevich Orentlikherman, another deputy of Barabanov and head of Project No. 15 in 1942. Meanwhile Azhaev was studying, in his free time, to be a writer: in 1939 he enrolled in a correspondence course of the Gorky Literary Institute in Moscow, where he had been taking evening courses in 1934 before his involuntary departure to the Far East. By 1939 his fellow students had graduated, and some of them now became his instructors, among them the poet Evgenii Dolmatovskii and the writer Konstantin Simonov. They had not forgotten him.

Dolmatovskii's memoirs mention Azhaev's "disappearance" in December 1934 and his 1937 encounter with Azhaev in Khabarovsk, where Dolmatovskii had been sent as the "plenipotentiary" of the Soviet Writers' Union. He avoids going into the details of this mission, which was undoubtedly part of the effort to "cleanse" the Far Eastern branch of the Soviet Writers' Union during the Great Terror, and he also fudges the specific nature of Azhaev's BAM work, with which the literary career of the author of *Far from Moscow* really began: "What these stories were about, and how they were written—I definitely, unfortunately, forgot all of it."[20] When I interviewed Dolmatovskii in May 1993, about a year before his death, he declared that even at that time it was not tactful to talk about those (labor camp) issues. Asked about possible survivors and sources in the Far East, he insisted that "nothing was left there," and that there was "no sense in looking for anything in the Far East."

Azhaev had been published before. His first literary piece appeared in

The Petukhovka region of the Camp of the Lower Amur on the outskirts of Komsomol'sk, 1940s. (Photograph by Ivan Panin, Komsomol'sk; reproduced with permission.)

the August 1934 issue of the Komsomol journal *Smena,* and concerned the class struggle in the countryside during the collectivization drive.[21] Between 1935 and 1937 Azhaev published several stories, plays, and pieces of "documentary prose" on reeducation through Stakhanovite labor in *Putearmeets: Literaturno-khudozhestvennyi zhurnal BAMLAGa NKVD* (The Soldier of the Tracks: Literary-Artistic Journal of the NKVD Corrective Labor Camp of the Baikal-Amur Main Line), and in the various almanacs of the Biblioteka Stroitelei BAMa (Library of the Builders of the BAM). But these works were "not subject to circulation outside the limits of the camp." In Komsomol'sk-on-the-Amur, however, the future Stalin Prize laureate published his work more publicly, in the local journal *Stalinskii Komsomol'sk,* for example. Meanwhile, not far from the camp's headquarters at 47 Vokzal'naia Street, Azhaev was slowly and steadily working out the plot of the novel inspired by Project No. 15.[22]

According to prewar specifications, the pipeline's construction was expected to take many years. When the war broke out, the target date was moved up from the end of 1942 to September 1942, and many aspects of the project had to be modified.[23] Although a report signed by the chief engineer, Chkheidze, testifies to the technical superiority of the "left" vari-

The Petukhovka region today, incorporated within the city of Komsomol'sk. (Photograph by Ivan Panin, Komsomol'sk; reproduced with permission.)

ant, the alternative plan was chosen, and the pipeline was built on the right bank of the river Amur.[24] According to file 35 in the Khabarovsk archives, the discussion whether to lay the pipeline on the right or the left bank of the Amur took place during November and December 1942 and actually concerned the second phase of the pipeline construction; that is, the section from Komsomol'sk to Sofiiskoe.[25] Among the supporters of the "right" variant we find the names of Petrenko and Ianovskii. Since Azhaev seems to have had some problems with Major-General I. G. Petrenko, head of the Camp of the Lower Amur in the fall of 1942 or 1943, the main conflict recorded in *Far from Moscow* probably reflects both these personal tensions and the technical debates among the leaders and engineers of the GULZhDS.

But let us get back to the first phase of the construction; that is, to the year 1941. According to one source, some of its heroes were the *stroibatovtsy* of the day—soldiers who were unfit for duty at the front because of poor physical condition or "moral instability"[26]—but the great majority were ordinary prisoners of the Lower Amur Corrective Labor Camp.

Galina Tkacheva, historian of the Far East, gives a brief description of the labor force used on Project No. 15 and some approximations of the population of the camp, based on various archival sources. According to Tkacheva, at the beginning of 1942, 8,300 people worked at the pipeline construction site. This number was inadequate for the scheduled completion of the pipeline, but only 1,400 prisoners out of a projected 3,000 were available. The problem was solved by shifting to the project first 1,000 then another 4,000 prisoners who had originally been assigned to cut timber. By 1 July 1942, Project No. 15 had a labor force of 11,700. When that number, too, proved insufficient, it was increased by "internal resources."[27] What these internal resources were Tkacheva does not specify; they were probably *trudposelentsy* (deported settlers) working in Gulag-supervised settlements in the region.

The terrain made the pipeline's construction extremely difficult: in addition to the 9-kilometer seabed section of the pipeline, the 376-kilometer line crossed rivers, streams, or swamps at 134 points; it also passed through almost totally uncultivated and nonpopulated regions, if one excepts the rare and fluctuating settlements of Nanai, Nivkh, Oroch, Orok, Udege, and Ul'ch, "small peoples of the North" who traditionally lived by hunting and fishing.[28] It was therefore necessary to build a road 376 kilometers long, including the De-Kastri–Kizi section, which was constructed partly by a local garrison of the People's Commissariat of Defense.[29] The entire project required 447 engineering constructions, including 241 bridges.[30] Concerning the overall labor force, Tkacheva cites the following data: on 1 October 1942 the population of the Lower Amur Corrective Labor Camp included 32,063 prisoners, 8,360 of whom had been sentenced for counterrevolutionary activities, spread out among 125 colonies and zones. Of the 31,099 prisoners listed for construction jobs, 5,148 were assigned to hard physical labor (16.7 percent), 7,676 to average physical labor (24.7 percent), and 11,508 to light physical labor (37 percent). Another 2,022 (6.5 percent) were at that time under medical treatement, while 2,737 (8.8 percent) had been designated invalids. As to the production norms met by this labor force, out of a total of 24,937 people engaged in production, 9,050 met 100 to 110 percent of the norm, 9,643 met 110 to 150 percent, and 2,751 met 151 to 200 percent. There were also 852 "200 percenters," while 2,641 (10.6 percent) did not meet the norm at all. Citations for exceptional work (*knizhki otlichnika*) were awarded to 1,300 prisoners, and after the completion of the pipeline 364 were granted early release from the labor camp.[31]

It is instructive to compare these figures with the national distribution of labor camp workers in respect to physical fitness between 1940 and 1942 (see Table 1).

Table 1. Physical Fitness of Labor Camp Workers,
1940 and 1942 (percent)

	1940	1942
Fit for hard physical labor	35.6%	19.2%
Fit for average physical labor	25.2	17.0
Fit for light physical labor	15.6	38.3
Invalids and weakened	23.6	25.5

Source: "Doklad nachal'nika GULAGa NKVD SSR V. G. Nasedkina.
Avgust 1944 g." (Report of the head of the GULAG of the NKVD of the
USSR V. G. Nasedkin, August 1944), *Istoricheskii Arkhiv* 3 (1994): 67.

The total number of prisoners fit for hard or average physical labor dropped
from 61 percent in 1940 to 36 percent in 1942. Nasedkin attributed this
drastic drop to such factors as evacuation from war zones, harsh conditions during transport, and poor living conditions in the camps. In percentage of prisoners fit for hard labor alone, the Camp of the Lower Amur
lagged behind the overall trend (16.7 percent against the national average
of 19.2 percent). Nasedkin's report details a series of measures that were
taken to improve conditions, including better lodging and medical care,
three days per month of rest from work, eight hours of uninterrupted sleep
per day, and a 33 percent increase in the food rations for prisoners of northern and other remote labor camps.[32] The Project No. 15 labor force seems
not to have benefited from these measures, however, for they were implemented only toward the end of the war. Here is the account of Filipp
Antonovich Andreev, a prisoner who was working in the region of Cape
Chernyi when construction on the second phase of the pipeline (Nizhnaia
Tambovka–Tsimmermanovka) started in September 1942 on the right bank
of the Amur: "We were cutting a trench for the pipeline. At first we lived
in tents. Two kilometers from us they were building barracks. Eight barracks for 60 people each. Only bunks. . . . Mattresses filled with grass. We
were fed very badly. Products were not delivered. We had only what we
had brought with us. Ground flour and water [*zatirukha*]. People were dy-
ing. We ate salt so as to provoke thirst. Then we drank, drank, and drank.
And we swelled up. And died."[33] When Andreev's sentence ended, he was
informed that nobody was allowed to leave the construction site before
the end of the war, by order of the State Defense Committee. So Andreev
remained there as a "free laborer" and was assigned work in the planning

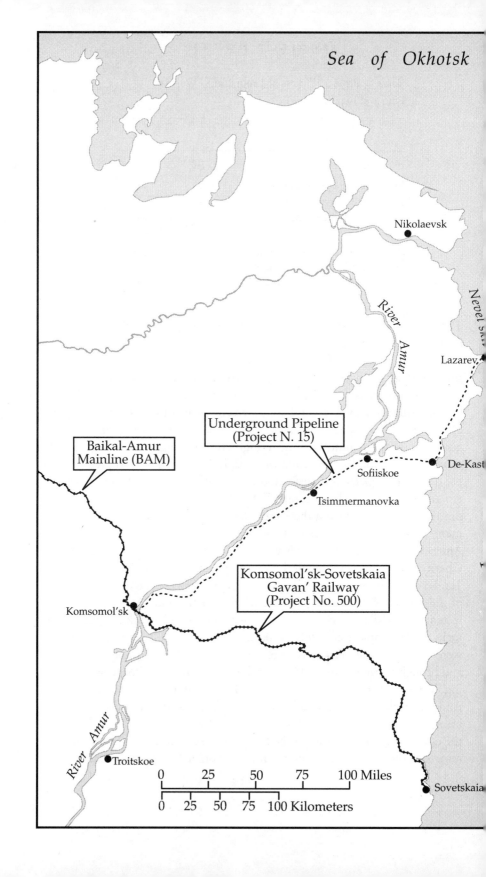

department, headed by one Krupennikov. This name appears in Azhaev's diaries of 1941–42; in *Far from Moscow,* his name is Grechkin. Both names have to do with grains: *krupa* is the Russian word for "groats," *grecha* for "buckwheat."

The bird's-eye view depicted in *Far from Moscow* corresponds to what we can see on a map, except for one detail: it is a mirror image of reality. At the spot where the river and the pipeline diverge, the Adun "sweeps on majestically to the right" and the pipeline "swings northward to the left." In fact the river Amur turns left and the pipeline goes to the right. In other words, Azhaev reversed the topography, undoubtedly for both strategic and "dialectical" reasons. If the novel was even to see the light of day, maps had to be blurred to mislead the enemy, and nature had to be reengineered to allow one of the great Stalinist constructions to go *left.* At the same time, this reversal of direction shows us a way through the looking glass: that is, fiction is useful to history in its *manifold* reflections.

Does the fictitious inversion of Project No. 15 represent another set of codes, in addition to the toponyms of *Far from Moscow,* and if so, what is the relation between the two? In addition to Adun, the "river of hell," and Rubezhansk, the "city on the border," there is Taisin, the "island of secrecy" (from the Russian *taina*) with its city Konchelan, "at the *end* (or *edge*) of the world," and "Cape Death" (*mys Gibel'nyi*). Perhaps the settlement of Ol'gokhta stands for the Golgotha where the prisoners of the real Sofiiskoe worked and died.[34] Azhaev's notebooks and literary works show that code is to reality as Beridze is to Chkheidze the Chekist, or as Batmanov is to Barabanov, or even as Azhaev within the literary montage of his life is to Azhaev "himself." Many clues in *Far from Moscow* and in the novel's prehistory (i.e., the diaries and other material that have surfaced since Azhaev's death) show that life and the novel shared the same realm. Azhaev's doubts and hopes, expressed in his notebooks, his literary conversations with Barabanov, and his debut as a Svobodnyi-reeducated writer, show much more than conflictlessness or the varnishing of reality; they demonstrate a desperate and perhaps unprecedented attempt to create literature and culture from below, almost from ground zero. Azhaev's writings also give us a different angle on prison camp literature and a more differentiated picture of camp life. The author of *Far from Moscow* is far from reaching the level of Swift, Stendhal, or Radishchev, writers whose works he studied at night in Komsomol'sk-on-the-Amur in 1941 as part of the homework for his Gorky Literary Institute correspondence course. If Ermilov's formula—"The beautiful is our life"—was not directly reflected in

Azhaev's book and other novels of that time, it was at least refracted elsewhere, as in the reality that the reader found in them, recognizing in Azhaev's lines his own dreams and aspirations. The following letters, which were found in Azhaev's archive, indicate that postwar Soviet books not only were read but actually saved lives:

> You know that people liked *Far from Moscow;* but what you don't know is that this book was read to shreds in the workers' settlements of the Donbass (there was only one book, and everybody wanted to read it at the same time). Whole pages were copied from it, by people from various professions. . . .
>
> I happened to see this book in the house of a physician. In it was written: "This book is an excellent medicine for many diseases." This book was discussed by Party activists and at workers' meetings. It was compared to the *History of the Party.* It became the most cherished book of the people. You cannot get *Far from Moscow* in any bookshop, not even in Latvian [*dazhe net na latyshskom iazyke*].[35]

> Precious Vasilii Nikolaevich!
>
> How happy I am that I can look at and listen to the living author of the interesting novel *Far from Moscow.* This interesting thought came to mind as soon as you came out on the stage. How much I liked it [the novel] you can judge for yourself. In 1949 I was to undergo a complicated major operation. I had no hope of surviving this operation, and nevertheless I gave my consent. But I confessed to the doctors that I did not want to die without having read *Far from Moscow,* and they postponed the operation till the day I finished the book. I say honestly that this was what happened. I will never forget it. And the doctors told me after the operation that there was never in their practice a case in which they made such a concession to a patient, especially when it was so urgent to treat her and for such a reason. They understood that it was necessary.[36]

One of the most important benefits of a symbolic universe is its "legitimation of death"; that is, the integration of the phenomenon of death within a symbolic universe enables an individual to escape the ultimate terror of anticipating his or her own death, or that of a significant other, and to go on living. On the collective level, a symbolic universe also "orders history." It "links men with their predecessors and their successors in a meaningful totality. . . . With regard to the past, it establishes a 'memory'

that is shared by all the individuals socialized within the collectivity."[37]
The "memory" that *Far from Moscow* established in relation to Project
No. 15 is illustrated by another letter to its author, written in 1952 by a participant in the construction of a new logging enterprise in Lazarev, who
wished "his" writer to know about a memorial desk he had seen on Mysaia
Gora, near Cape Lazarevo, on which was inscribed, "This is the place
where Batmanov ordered the explosion."[38] Batmanov, the head of the construction site in Azhaev's novel, had merged with the historical head of
the Lower Amur Corrective Labor Camp, Barabanov. The year before, the
journalist E. Riabchikov had written an article for the journal *Ogonek*
about an important construction project on the Volga. The highlight of
the article is the reporter's description of his "encounter with Batmanov,"
the hero of Vasilii Azhaev's novel *Far from Moscow*.[39] In real life the hero
was Vasilii Arsent'evich Barabanov, who headed the construction of the
hydro-junction of Tsimliansk. Which is more important for history, the
living legend or any number of Batmanovs/Barabanovs that other archives
might reveal? For there were at least two others.

According to A. Kirichenko, the Batmanov of the novel may have been
inspired by Vladimir Ivanovich Batmanov, head of the Production Department of the GULZhSD.[40] Vladimir Ivanovich had worked before the
Revolution as one of Russia's top railway engineers. Released from labor
camp by Stalin's personal order, he became a deputy to Naftalii Aronovich
Frenkel', head of the Main Administration of the GULZhDS (whom we
will meet again later), and persuaded Stalin and Beria to liberate from the
Gulag a number of other important railway specialists.[41] Another Batmanov, whom Azhaev could have known, was Vasilii Ivanovich Batmanov,
deputy editor of the Khabarovsk newspaper *Tikhookeanskaia zvezda* and
chair of the Regional Radio Committee in Khabarovsk in 1936–37.[42] As
we shall see, this Batmanov played a role in the Far Eastern literary purges
during the Great Terror (of which he himself became a victim), together
with Aleksandr Gai, Piotr Komarov, Mikhail Alekseev, and others who
played important roles in the literary making of Azhaev. Alekseev, for example, was reelected chairman of the Far Eastern branch of the Soviet
Writers' Union in 1937 and was at that time the "responsible editor"
(*otvetstvennyi redaktor*) of the Khabarovsk journal *Na rubezhe*, which published "The Son," a story by our author, freshly released from Camp Freedom in 1937.[43] The journal stood literally "on the borderline" (*na rubezhe*)
between Azhaev's old life and his new one. The story is about a couple of
reeducated (and repentant) criminals whose son is born with a cleft palate.

But Soviet medicine corrects the child's deformity, just as shock work on the Baikal-Amur Main Line had corrected his parents' deviance.[44]

Who is who in this labyrinth of fact and fiction where BAMLAG, Nizhne-Amurlag, Project No. 15, and literature intersect? As our journey extends through pages printed, partly printed, and not printed at all, history becomes a story, context becomes text. Let us remember what Iurii Trifonov said in his story "The Long Goodbye": "Oh, if one could only depict the flow of time, which carries along everything and everyone!"[45] Trifonov and Azhaev shared the same recognition: Trifonov was awarded the Stalin Prize (third class) for his novella "The Students" in 1951, two years after Azhaev received his Stalin Prize (first class) for *Far from Moscow*. Undoubtedly their life experiences intersected. But Trifonov came to terms with both the recognition and the experience through fiction. For him there was "another life," as attested by his novella of that title, which became one of the indisputable literary achievements of the Soviet 1970s.[46] For Azhaev there was no other life. This makes all the difference, at least so far as literature is concerned. To find out why is my purpose here.

UTOPICS: THE "SECOND BAKU" AND THE "OTHER" OF PLACE

It is impossible for me to summarize the great richness of this great novel. The truth, life itself, strikes us in the face like the wind of the taiga. This is how the Soviets fought to win the war, this is how they are fighting to build communism! And their working relations not only reflect the struggle between the old and the new, which becomes a source of epic inspiration, but also reflect the frankness, the uprightness, the human warmth of their fraternity.

Far from Moscow is a book that must be read. It is a strong book, fresh and virile, a book that is the image of the future and of creative passion!

—André Kédros, review of V. Ajaev,
Loin de Moscou, in *Europe*, no. 62 (1951)

When talking about the Perfect Island, the Lunar States, or the Austral Continent, utopia talks less about itself or the discourse it has on the island, moon, or lost continent than about the very possibility of uttering such a discourse, of the status and contents of its enunciating position and the formal and material rules allowing it to produce some particular expression.

—Louis Marin, *Utopics: The Semiological Play of Textual Spaces* (1990)

Everything seems to have been said about the "end of utopia" in its Soviet version, celebrated in the 1950s and canonized by George Orwell's emblematic dystopia *1984*. But it is worth mentioning a paradox: if there is a consensus about the antiutopian or dystopian genre of Orwell's novel, what about the artistic and literary works to which *1984* was a direct response? Considered as the "varnishing of reality," as a "lie," as the "art of pure propaganda," beyond any qualities of literariness, socialist realism of the late 1940s and early 1950s unquestionably contained utopian aspects. Witness the titles of some socialist realist works: *Happiness, Light in Koordi, Light on Earth, Verkhovina Our Light, Light over the Fields, The Knight of the Golden Star, New Horizons, The Future, The Dawn, The Dawn of a Great Construction Site, The Sun That Never Sets, The Moscow Dawns, Far from Moscow*. But none of these works figures in the pantheon of the utopian genre or is ever likely to be included there. The opinions of French Communists such as André Kédros and their fellow travelers did not survive the revelations of the Twentieth Congress (1956), and the literature of high Stalinism remains, in a sense, beyond genre.

How does socialist realism relate to utopia? The classical utopia refers to the perfect place or human community and tends to operate as an autonomous time-space. Utopian thought strives for coherence, simulating the global harmony of an ideal world. But it is also "a hybrid plant, born of the crossing of a paradisiacal, other-wordly belief of Judeo-Christian religion with the Hellenic myth of an ideal city on earth."[1] In the world of socialist realism, this coherence is constantly threatened by the return of the future (or of the past) on the present, and vice versa. The perfection of the "positive hero" of socialist realism is evolutionary, but tomorrow or yesterday is always a function of *now*. This explains the paradoxical openness of high Stalinist literature despite its global and totalizing character. *Far from Moscow* is no exception.

Future and distance presume a marker of present and proximity: the narrative opens in Moscow, where the engineers Kovshov and Beridze prepare for their journey. "Not until the very last moment did Engineer Aleksei Kovshov believe that he was really going out to the East, deep into the country's hinterland." This is the opening sentence of the first chapter, "Good-bye, Moscow!" At the end of the book, in a chapter titled "To Moscow," the transformed engineer/hero prepares to return to the capital: "The plane gained altitude. . . . He almost physically sensed the immensity of his country and of everything that was taking place on its boundless spaces. He experienced such a sense of exultation that he could have sung with sheer joy. Never before had he, Aleksei Kovshov, been so keenly, so palpably conscious, aware of his place in the life of his great Homeland, in her titanic struggle for the future."[2]

On their way to a place "far from Moscow," the engineers pass Kirov and Sverdlovsk, which are merely (dangerous) stages that they must cross in order to get "there." Beyond this point, "real" referentiality ceases. As a place, "far from Moscow" cannot be identified on any map; it is literally *u-topos*, "no place." One might ask whether this division of fiction and reference does not violate one of the basic principles of socialist realism: the "truthful, historically concrete depiction of reality." Not necessarily, because that principle is incomplete without its well-known complement: "in its revolutionary development." Is fiction here the mimetic product of this development? On the one hand, classic socialist realism claims to welcome invention, fiction (*vymysel*), insofar as "it represents in a certain manner the concentration of the writer's experience of the world." The notion is closely related to the concepts of generalization and the typical, or that which is "in accordance with the fundamental characteristics of social relations." On the other hand, socialist realist fiction can also take "forms that are distorted, absurd, and so on" (*iskazhennye, nelepye i tomu podobnye formy*)."[3]

The published versions of *Far from Moscow* that were aimed at the Soviet reader offer no explanation for the novel's fictitious geography: one can easily understand that there were strategic reasons for not mentioning the real location of a pipeline. But whenever Azhaev's book was expected to cross the border, its Soviet publisher felt obliged to explain its geography to the English, French, or German reader, as in the introduction to the English translation, made in the USSR: "Azhaev does not give the actual geographical location of the construction site. Neither the river Adun nor Taisin Island can be found on the map. The names of the builders of the pipeline too are fictitious. Everything else in the novel, however, is based on fact. The writer did not observe his characters from the sidelines, he lived among them, he was one of them."[4] Within the Soviet world, apart from issues of taboo or secrecy, such an explanation was redundant: the representation of space followed the same rules as the representation of socialist realist time. It was determined by an ever-shifting referent: what was considered based on fact or observed from the sidelines depended on the current definition of what was typical and general, or, on the contrary, of what was considered distorted, absurd, and so on. Not unlike the "utopic schema" described by Louis Marin in his *Utopics,* the socialist realist organization of spatiality was a "producing product," an "activity of fiction" engendering "a plurality of spaces in the totality of one project."[5]

One way to take literally the plural conditions of production of *Far from Moscow* is to consider the novel's institutional referent. This referent was nothing other than the official geography of its time, a geography that changed "in accordance with the fundamental characteristics of social relations." *Nad kartoi rodiny* (Across the Map of the Homeland) by Nikolai Mikhailov, published in 1947 by Molodaia Gvardiia, is one such official geography.[6] It provided the Soviet reader with a historical, political, economic, and sociological almanac of the Soviet Union. The book was awarded a Stalin Prize (third class) in 1948.[7]

Mikhailov's book is abundantly illustrated. On the first page, for instance, we find an illustration of a man who, in a heroic gesture, hangs a map on some bookshelves surmounted by an escutcheon representing the arms of the Soviet Union. The map itself is covered by a huge "CCCP" (USSR) oriented toward the east, "far from Moscow." On the cover of the book we find the same arms of the Soviet Union above the inscription "1917–1947." When Mikhailov's book was reissued in 1949, the "revised and completed" edition underwent some interesting shifts.[8] First of all, the supreme consecration (the Stalin Prize) has left its imprint: the 1949 edition is much more sumptuous than the first, with many color illustrations, one of which represents a series of oil derricks on the bank of a river. The first edition had only one color plate, a reproduction of a painting by A. Andreev, *V. I. Lenin and J. V. Stalin Discuss the GOELRO Plan.** In the 1949 edition the map of the USSR itself takes on color (red on a pale blue background); since the first edition, where it was a first-page illustration, it has grown to overrun the margins of the book, with Moscow at its center. As for the text, or at least those pages that deal with our topic, the 1949 edition takes the road "far from Moscow." A chapter of the 1947 edition, "Novye bogatstva zemnykh nedr" (New Riches of the Bowels of the Earth), enthusiastically describes the creation of a "second Baku." That is, the re-

*GOELRO: acronym for the Plan for the Electrification of Russia.

gion of Moscow is on the brink of becoming a second center of the Soviet oil industry, after the capital of Azerbaijan. "Oil may also be found on the Oka-Tsna divide east of Moscow; another likely spot is the underground ridge that lies buried between Moscow and Leningrad. . . . Drilling has been started there. Perhaps we are on the eve of new discoveries—Moscow may eventually become the center of an oil region."⁹ This passage is missing from the 1949 edition. Were the Moscow drillings unsuccessful? The question is answered by means of displacement, by the projection of the present, of reality, onto the future: whereas the island of Sakhalin is simply mentioned among other place names in the first edition, it replaces Moscow in the archipelago of the "second Baku" in the 1949 version. And indeed, there is oil on Sakhalin. With this reality, utopia is transferred "far from Moscow" and enriched with a classic Soviet dream, the transformation of nature and control over climate:

> When the great writer Chekhov visited Sakhalin at the close of the nineteenth century and found himself confronted with a gloomy picture of exile that considerably darkened his impressions, he wrote: "The climate and the soil in the upper (i.e., northern) third of the island make it altogether unsuitable for settlement. . . ." But a new age has dawned, all traces of exile have disappeared, Sakhalin has become a land of free Soviet citizens—and the attitude toward nature has changed. It is no longer an inaccessible wilderness; man has mastered it. And at the northern edge of Sakhalin the great city of Okha has appeared, living an intensive cultural life, in a region that once filled men with despair. The taiga has been cleared and the soil allowed to dry. Even vegetables are grown in Okha. Old-timers say that with the town's growth and with the development of the region around it there has been a decrease in the number of foggy days.¹⁰

The plural organization of Mikhailov's text does not end here: upstream of our two editions of *Nad kartoi rodiny* we find a brochure that he published in 1946, *Prostory i bogatstva nashei rodiny* (The Wealth and Vastness of Our Homeland).¹¹ Mikhailov's brochure can also be found downstream, as part of a 1953 collection published in Moscow titled *Nasha velikaia rodina* (Our Great Homeland).¹² In 1964 the space becomes more national with Mikhailov's *Moia Rossiia* (My Russia), a work marking the forthcoming fiftieth anniversary of the October Revolution.¹³ The year 1967 saw the appearance of *Po stopam ispolina* (On the Traces of the Giant), in which Mikhailov assesses the spatial result of fifty years of the Soviet

Union, "from west to east," "from north to south," "through the deserts, the oases and the mountains of Central Asia."[14] In these last two volumes Sakhalin receives, once more, a chapter of its own—and this time the author mentions not only the construction of a pipeline between the island and the continent, but also the fact that this construction was the principal theme of Azhaev's novel.

As to the motif of a "second Baku," certain passages of *Far from Moscow* were evidently inspired by Mikhailov's work. Or did the novel serve as a model for the geography?

> Dudin and Pisarev flew out to the island the same day, taking Batmanov, Beridze and Kovshov with them.
>
> The frozen desolate taiga stretched monotonously under the wings of the plane. There was not a sign of human activity to be seen anywhere.
>
> "A writer visited this place at the end of the nineteenth century and came to the sad conclusion that the northern part of Taisin Island would never be of any use to man. Just a worthless bit of planet," said Dudin, shifting his gaze to Batmanov. "I'm very glad that the honour of upsetting that notion has fallen to our lot. Little did the writer suspect what a wealth of black gold there was here. By next autumn oil will be running through these jungles along your pipeline. Think of it!"
>
> The taiga came suddenly to an end as the plane approached the northern extremity of the island. The landscape underwent a sharp change. On the right stretched the boundless gray expanse of the strait, on the left a ridge of low hills densely wooded with evergreen trees, and in the middle, all along the coast as far as the eye could reach, rose a forest of oil derricks. From above they made a curious lace work pattern surrounding the town of Konchelan that lay spread on the shores of the bay.
>
> "Far Eastern Baku!" Dudin said in a pleased tone with a jerk of his head towards the derricks. "I prefer that forest to the taiga any day."
>
> The visitors walked over the oil fields and adjacent town till nightfall. Oil filled the huge reservoirs in the harbour and on the foothill. Oil seeped through the black earth. Oil spurted from borings. The very air smelled of oil. The houses, the people and even the food they ate seemed to be saturated with it.[15]

Here are the "objective conditions of production" of Azhaev's novel: the future (utopia) and its discourse are rewritten under the influence of the present; this present reality, in turn, conforms to its "revolutionary development." But what about this "new age" in which "all traces of exile have disappeared"? Most of the pioneers and organizers of the oil-extracting industry on northern Sakhalin, including the entire leadership of the Sakhalinneft' Complex, fell victim to the repressions of 1937–38.[16] Azhaev's "hellish" code shows us, too, that the "foggy days" have not vanished from the present. On the one hand, his fiction clearly conforms to the epic of the "second Baku"; on the other hand, certain fragments relate to another world as subterranean and Homeric as the conquered underground ridges of oil. But this time that world is a "vague, a shadowy place inhabited by shadows."[17] The way to Hades, the kingdom of the dead of the *Odyssey*, "leads over the edge of the world across Ocean."[18]

> The pipeline builders knew that some thirty kilometers down the coast, on the right, there was a fishery and a settlement, and ten kilometers farther, a Nivkh village. But there, at this spot where they had crossed the strait, there was not a sign of human life. The rocky promontory of Cape Death towered desolately over the flat dead shores of the island. Its forbidding name sounded as a warning reminiscent of the fate that met a handful of nameless Russian people who perished on this coast a century before in their unequal struggle with the elements. The granite cliffs stood as a monument to their heroism.[19]

The geography of this underworld is as complex as the world of the living above. What is "father Adun," Azhaev's river "in hell"? Is it the Styx, the river of the unbreakable oath, or the Lethe, the river of oblivion? To what do these nonplace names refer? Let us listen again to Louis Marin:

> Utopian proper names contain their own negation. U-topia, An-ydrus, A-demus, etc. . . . The negation does not affect the name's referent but does affect the name itself, which designates an "other" referent. . . . Utopia is this nonplace where names do not properly or "correctly" designate; there is nothing proper in the name. They designate the "other" of proper. There is disappropriation in their naming function, an absence in their power to indicate presence. There is metaphor within the proper; this is the deconstructive power that utopic names realize. As they are uttered, they create the other of place, of the river, city, wisemen, or meaning. It is their dispossession and denunciation at the very moment language would take hold.[20]

This "other" of place is the writer's ultimate destination in a journey that takes him not from Moscow to the river Adun but in the opposite direction, in which he heads with such a sense of exultation that he could have sung with sheer joy, to paraphrase the end of the novel. As we shall see, this was Azhaev's own and ultimate utopia, his homeland, his principle of hope. But first we have to go back to where it all started. And, once again, we encounter the same activity of fiction, the utopic schema that engenders a plurality of spaces and of times: what happened before *Far from Moscow* will be articulated in the future, in Azhaev's novel *Vagon* (The Boxcar), published twenty years after his death.

3

THE BEGINNING

To the Secretariat of the Board of the Union of Writers of the
USSR
Dear comrades!

At the end of 1965 Vasilii Nikolaevich Azhaev presented to
our journal his new work, the novel *The Boxcar*. The editors
treated the manuscript with appropriate attention. Many members of the editorial board read it and, in general, evaluated it
positively. After this, the board considered it suitable to draw up
a contract with the author and invited K. M. Simonov to act in
the capacity of editor, because he was well versed in the work
of Azhaev. K. M. Simonov accepted our proposition, edited the
manuscript, and wrote a preface to the novel. Thus, over several
months a serious degree of work was accomplished on the manuscript, which was thoroughly edited, prepared for publication and
planned for issues no. 7 and 8 of 1966. The novel was set and
positioned in the issue. However, when the novel passed through
Glavlit,* some serious complications surfaced. For two months,
the main editors of the journal conducted oral negotiations with
the comrades from Glavlit. The novel was postponed from issue
to issue, but failed to be cleared for publication. Finally, at the
suggestion of Glavlit, the manuscript was sent for a reading to the

---

*Acronym of Glavnoe upravlenie po delam literatury i izdatel'stv (Main Administra-
tion of Affairs for Literature and Publishing), the central government censorship office.
Glavlit also had local subdivisions, such as Krailit (regional) and Gorlit (municipal).

Department of Culture of the Central Committee of the CPSU. Two years have already passed since the novel was given to the journal, but the fate of the manuscript has in fact not been decided until now.

We are deeply convinced that V. N. Azhaev's new novel is a significant contribution to Soviet literature, an honest, principled work evaluating the events of 1935–37 from a Party-minded position. This is not cheap speculation on this topic, but a truthful narration of the strength and beauty of the spiritual world of the Soviet people—Communists and non-Party alike—who went through the great trials of life.

The editorial board of *Druzhba narodov* requests the Secretariat of the Board of the Union of Writers of the USSR to raise the question of Azhaev's *Boxcar* during one of its sessions, to take the appropriate decision, and thus to give the journal the opportunity to publish this work in the near future.

Sincerely,

A. Salakhin

First Deputy to the Editor in Chief

[Added by hand] 20 December 1967

The publication of Vasilii Azhaev's *The Boxcar* did not arouse good feelings in me. . . . Perhaps, a few years ago, I would have reacted to *The Boxcar* with understanding. But now, after having read Grossman, Pristavkin, Tendriakov, Shalamov, this is impossible. . . . I recall how my parents were forced to read *Far from Moscow* and to participate in the mandatory readers' conferences. Among other things, I remember when my young parents—she was a physician and he an engineer—made spiteful remarks about this novel while pulling out Chekhov or Tolstoy from the book cases—it irritated them very much at that time. . . . In my opinion, the publication of *The Boxcar* in *Druzhba narodov* comes too late.

—Tat'iana Ivanova, "The Star of Neighbor
Mitrofan's Wife" (1988)

A 1974 edition of *Far from Moscow* contains an afterword by Konstantin Simonov headed "This Is How We Remember Him"—"him" being Vasilii Azhaev, who had died in 1968. Simonov recalls the year 1948, when he was in charge of the journal *Novyi mir* (New World), one of the most prestigious Soviet literary magazines. Azhaev had been working "intensively and passionately" that summer under his direction to complete the "final" version of his novel. He had come to the capital from "far from Moscow" with an earlier published version that had appeared in installments between 1946 and 1948 in the Khabarovsk literary journal *Dal'nii Vostok* (Far East).[1] Simonov himself died in 1979, and his afterword was reprinted posthumously as the much belated and considerably expanded preface to Azhaev's likewise posthumous novel *The Boxcar*. Simonov had actually written his commentary on Azhaev's novel many years be-

Vasilii Azhaev, c. 1939.

fore, in the early 1960s. It was rejected for publication then, like many other accounts of the times of terror which flooded the publishing houses and editorial boards of Soviet journals after the publication in 1962 of Solzhenitsyn's *One Day in the Life of Ivan Denisovich*.[2] The subsequent fate of Solzhenitsyn—and of prison camp literature—is well known: driven underground, or sometimes into exile and fame. Azhaev's novel went nowhere, if one excepts the rumors, and when it finally appeared, it came too late.

The shifts in time and space marked by Simonov's preface correspond to an analogous plural organization of the text(s) that it attempted to interpret: language does not "take hold" in *The Boxcar;* time is "dispossessed." "I Cannot Find a Beginning" is the title of the first chapter. And indeed, on the fourth page of the novel, the narrator expresses his difficulty with setting the temporal borderlines of his story:

> The beginning. . . . Where is the beginning of my bitter story? Once upon a time there was in Moscow, Sretenka Street, Sukharevskaia Lane, a young boy; he worked in the factory and was studying in the Theatrical Institute. He was proud of having time for everything: for his work, his studies, and dating Masha. . . .
> So this is the beginning. Or is it already the end? I don't understand.[3]

"Once upon a time there was in Moscow a young boy" (*Zhil-byl v Moskve parnishka*): because he cannot find a "beginning" to his story, the narrator situates it in the circular time-space of the fairy tale, where end and beginning merge. To this "other" of time corresponds a curious dispossession of voice: a narrator living and remembering during the 1960s addresses himself from the very outset to a female "you," but the story does not devote much space to her, who, as we find out later, happens to be the narrator's wife.[4] The rare appearances of this narrative addressee emerge as a (not always convincing) rhetorical device, serving to actualize the narrator's present thoughts:

> Did you ever see prison carriages? These are ordinary boxcars with small barred windows. Behind them, the pale faces of prisoners. . . .
> —What are you imagining? There is no need for this, I beg you. . . .
> —I'm not imagining. I just don't tell it the way I should, forgive me. I kept silent for so long. I don't understand, why did I start with the carriage?
> —Don't think about it. To start with the carriage or not, what's the difference?
> Yes, of course. It's dark in the boxcar, even during the day. . . .
>
> Why do I undertake this long and painful journey? . . . So that I can tell it to myself and so that it will not be distorted by others. Oh, I know how malicious and unjust other lips can be.[5]

As the story unfolds, dispossession increases: time, space, and narrative voice seem to search for an order—from dialogue to monologue, from third person to second (mainly addressed to the narrator's self), from present to past and the other way around—without ever being able to find this order. The cancellation of time and space, whereby the accounts of memory merge with the questions of the present, seems to correspond to a traumatic dispossession of narrative itself. What Cathy Caruth writes about the traumatic experience that cannot become or has not yet been transformed into a narrative memory is strikingly applicable to Azhaev's last novel:

> The history that a [traumatic] flashback tells—as psychiatry, psychoanalysis, and neurobiology equally suggest—is . . . a history that literally has no place, neither in the past, in which it was not fully experienced, nor in the present, in which precise images and enactments are not fully understood. In its repeated imposition as both image and amnesia, the trauma thus seems to evoke the difficult truth of a history that is constituted by the very incomprehensibility of its occurrence.[6]

In *The Boxcar,* Mitia Promyslov recalls his arrest in the early hours of the morning "three days before the New Year [of 1935]"; the Butyrki prison in Moscow; the transit prison; his "comrades in misery" in the boxcar, their names, their professions, the paragraph of the penal code that dictated the "social" distribution of the boxcar's population between "political offenders" (those who were sentenced under article 58 of the penal code, "counterrevolutionary crimes") and "thirty-fivers" (article 35, "professional crimes"); the conflict between the two groups of convicts and the lengths of their sentences. All this amounts to both more and less than standard Gulag literature: more by virtue of the rawness of the facts, presented as a series of flashbacks, and less because these facts are not integrated into a coherent narrative. Scenes such as the one in which a party cell is formed among the inmates of the boxcar, who elect a chairman "with applause," "as in a decent collective"; the present thoughts of Mitia, searching the newspapers from 1935 for an explanation of the crimes committed during the era of the cult of personality; the statement that he and his colleagues in misfortune "never ceased for one minute to be Communists," or that behind article 58 there always stood "a good Soviet human being" (*khoroshii sovetskii chelovek*), or Mitia's dream of "rationalization" in the chemical plant where he was working before his arrest—all sound wrong, mere half-truths from today's perspective. It is as if the author had tried to blend two fundamentally irreconcilable types of discourse: the narration of the dramatic events that his "double" Mitia Promyslov lived through, and some sort of pompous textbooklike Soviet bureaucratese. For many readers this discrepancy arouses only "bad feelings." But we must still try to understand why this story was not told the way it "should" have been. Caruth writes about the "danger of speech," of "understanding too much." This is precisely, according to Caruth, what Claude Lanzmann understood when he made his film of Holocaust testimony, *Shoah*. In "refusing to understand," he created "listening"; in resisting the "platitudes of knowledge," he gained access to testimony "that can speak beyond what is already understood."[7] As we shall see, Azhaev had reason to understand too much.

Before Mitia arrives at his place of detention, time, once again, is reversed. What came before takes place afterward: Mitia's release from Camp Freedom anticipates his incarceration. The dream of being a Soviet citizen in full possession of his rights once more seems about to come true when Mitia is released, but he soon realizes that Moscow and other important cities are closed to him and that he is one of those who must live in the archipelago beyond the hundredth kilometer.[8] When he is offered the option of remaining "on the construction site as a free-hired laborer," he refuses, but not for long. After a short (and semilegal) visit to Moscow, where he learns that his father has met the same fate as himself, he returns to where he has come from. He stays for fifteen years in the Far East *na stroike*, "on the construction job." Five years after his liberation from the corrective labor camp, his record is clean, but Moscow remains closed to him. When the war breaks out, he wants to be sent to the front, a desire that was expressed ahead of time in *Far from Moscow*:

> "But can't you see my point of view? I want to go to the front, I want to be in the thick of the fighting. Weren't we taught from childhood in school and in the Komsomol not to run away from hardships, that our place is where the danger is greatest?"
>
> "Weren't you also taught to be disciplined? After all, you've got to listen to older comrades," Zalkind put in sternly. "Weren't you taught not to set yourself apart from the common effort?"[9]

Mitia's request is rejected (as was Aleksei Kovshov's in the earlier novel), so he continues to work on various Far Eastern construction projects: an airport, a pipeline, ammunition factories, railroads. In the meantime he takes correspondence courses in civil engineering and writes his thesis on the conditions for building on permafrost. "Where did the strength to endure all this come from? I don't know. Certainly, the consciousness of one's personal innocence, the consciousness that a mistake had happened, fateful for many, a terrible mistake: only this gave strength to go on living, to hope and work. And not to be an outcast." [10] But the mark of the outcast is permanent. In an earlier passage, a flashback to 1952, Mitia submits his application for party membership, but despite good recommendations, he is rejected. So he will be "a Communist without a party card for the rest of his life." [11]

The description of Mitia's arrival in Svobodnyi "after forty-five days and seven thousand eight-hundred fourteen kilometers" again does not arouse "good feelings." The guards, the frost, the barbed wire, the bedbugs, and Mitia's doubts as to whether "it is true that people are arrested and transported here only because the construction needs them as a necessary work force" all sound wrong when woven together with passages describing the newcomers' "collective" sense of organization, their enjoyment of a steam bath and a good meal upon arrival, the distribution among them of sugar and *makhorka*,* and Mitia's conversation with the Chekist commander of the camp, who offers him a chance to "earn points"—that is, to shorten his sentence by counting one day of good work as two. Mitia's technical qualifications put him in the category of "specialists," and he is therefore exempt from hard labor. His assignment is to supervise construction work in a laboratory beyond the zone, and the work performed there, under the supervision of a "Moscow professor," is "not meaningless" but rather "useful for the country" because "*we* are building the Trans-Siberian Railway . . . the BAM, the Baikal-Amur Main Line" [my emphasis].[12] This "we" signals a point of departure, an initial crack after which language does not hold and the narrative is out of joint. Once this "we" has been spelled out, it will be difficult to take it back; hence the continuous and never resolved shifting of voices in *The Boxcar*, the discrepancy between drama and bureaucratese, and all that fails to arouse "good feelings."

Personal pronouns are well-known oscillographs of the soul in its conversations with the real, as they belong to the peculiar category of linguistic signs called "shifters." The choice between the third person of history or fiction, in which the event speaks—and must speak—for itself, and the "I" and "you" of a never-ending present signals a fundamental shift of attitude. The latter pronouns are "pseudo-signs" of language because they

*A kind of cheap tobacco, often rolled in newspaper.

refer only to the instance of enunciation in which they are produced; they have little to do with fiction.[13] The third person, whatever linguistic guise it may take, embodies the very possibility of literature. In *The Boxcar* this choice is blurred, the weight of the instance of enunciation is much too heavy, and "literature" is not written the way it "should be." As the narrator recalls, he had other concerns. In Svobodnyi, he says, "you will learn not to ask the most important question of your comrades, you will get used to not displaying your troubles in any way." After all, "the boxcar was only the beginning of the 'journey.' The year 1934 had just struck at the watchtower. The heart runs cold at the thought of what happened here, at the same place, a few years later, when I was already beyond the zone."[14]

4

CAMP FREEDOM: THE OATH;
OR, ON TRANSFERENCE-LOVE

Smiling, the Sun took off his crown of burning light so that the lad
could look at him without distress. "Come here, Phaëton," he
said. "You are my son. Clymene told you the truth. I expect you
will not doubt my word too? But I will give you a proof. Ask anything you want of me and you shall have it. I call the Styx to be
witness to my promise, the river of the oath of the gods."

No doubt Phaëton had often watched the Sun riding through
the heavens and had told himself with a feeling, half awe, half excitement, "It is my father up there." And then he would wonder
what it would be like to be in that chariot, guiding the steeds
along that dizzy course, giving light to the world. Now at his father's words this wild dream had become possible. Instantly he
cried, "I choose to take your place, Father. That is the only thing
I want. Just for a day, a single day, let me have your car to drive."

The Sun realized his own folly. Why had he taken that fatal
oath and bound himself to give in to anything that happened to
enter a boy's rash young head?

—Ovid, "Phaëton," retold by Edith Hamilton in *Mythology*

The Chekists are the golden fund of the great Party of Lenin-
Stalin, the most precious capital of all capitals in the world. The
country of socialism is proud of the people who bear this hon-
orific name, the country is proud of its Chekists because the
word "Chekist" has become the epithet of strength, discipline,
organizational skill, valor, higher consciousness, brilliant mind, and
a truly humane great heart.

—Vasilii Azhaev, "Materials for a Novella on the Chekists"

Not all the materials found in Vasilii Azhaev's archive pertain to literature. Among the manuscripts, revisions, critical articles, notebooks, readers' conference materials, and personal correspondence, one set of documents authenticates the events described in *The Boxcar* and beyond.

Many of these pages bear the seal of state organs, such as a certificate (*spravka*) dated 16 March 1937 and issued by the NKVD, Administration of the Corrective Labor Camp of the Baikal-Amur Main Line, city of Svobodnyi. It certifies that Azhaev was "sentenced on 17 January 1935 by a special board of the NKVD of the USSR for 'counterrevolutionary agitation' to four years' imprisonment in the Baikal-Amur Corrective Labor Camp, starting 29 December 1934 and ending 29 December 1938." The document also records that Azhaev was released on 16 March 1937 after he had served 643 working days, and that he was expected to register at the administrative office of the Workers' and Peasants' Militia and the People's Commissariat of Military Affairs of the city of Kimry, Moscow Administrative Region. The certificate was to be "exchanged after arrival at the location of residence for a common civil document—an identity card, inasmuch as the present certificate [could] not serve as a residence permit." A superimposed stamp attested that "a passport was issued."[1]

Did Azhaev go to Kimry? Whatever the case, a series of other documents show that, like Mitia Promyslov, he came back. A character reference (*kharakteristika*) of 30 December 1939, signed by one Bakin, chief engineer of the Main Administration of Railway Construction Camps of the NKVD in the Far East, credits Vasilii Nikolaevich Azhaev, head of the Central Bureau of Rationalization and Invention of the same administration (Nachal'nika TsBRIZ'a UZhDS GULag'a NKVD na DV), for proposals, advances, and cost-cutting measures that yielded savings of 2,225,000 rubles in 1937 and 7,615,000 rubles in 1939. Furthermore, Azhaev is characterized as "a very good organizer, a very persistent and purposeful leader, a very conscientious worker, and a very modest man."[2] Azhaev's activities as head of the TsBRIZ in Svobodnyi are mentioned in a book by Ia. Kharon, who was also an inmate of the BAMLAG in Svobodnyi. Kharon recalls Azhaev's correct and humane conduct toward the prisoners. In hiring specialists and intellectuals for the bureau he headed and thus saving them from hard labor, he took considerable risks. Any "complications" would undoubtedly have sent him back to the "zone."[3] But, as other certificates and character references show, there were no such complications. Documents signed by the same organs—some of them additionally stamped "top secret" (*sovershenno sekretno*)—refer to bonuses awarded for outstanding work, initiatives of rationalization, and other decisions. One of the references is signed by Barabanov, head of the Lower Amur Corrective Labor Camp of the NKVD. This undated document states that "Com.[rade] Azhaev Vasilii Nikolaevich, Senior Inspector attached to the Head of the Administration of the Lower Amur Corrective Labor Camp of the NKVD," started work in the NKVD camp system as

Vasilii Azhaev at the Corrective Labor Camp of the Baikal–Amur Main Line (BAMLAG), Svobodnyi, 1940.

a free laborer on 16 March 1937 (i.e., the same day he was released), first as an inspector for the Cultural and Educational Department of the BAMLAG of the NKVD, then as an inspector attached to the senior engineer of the same camp; in December he became head of the Central Bureau of Rationalization and Invention of the Administration of the Lower Amur Railway Construction Camp. On 24 October 1940, by order of the Administration of Railway Construction of the NKVD, Azhaev was transferred to the Administration of the Lower Amur Camp, "where he has worked up to the present in the capacity of Senior Inspector attached to the Head of the Administration." The *kharakteristika* emphasizes among Azhaev's positive qualities his sense of initiative and the fact that he was "well disciplined." It also stresses that Azhaev achieved "a number of valuable technical improvements" and took an "active part in the literary life of the province and in the local press," which brings us back to literature.[4]

Along with music, theater, fine arts, and other cultural activities, literature was part of life in the Corrective Labor Camp of the Baikal-Amur Main Line. Even if *Putearmeets* (The Soldier of the Tracks) and the almanacs of the Library of the Builders of the BAM were not permitted to circulate beyond the camp limits, they reflect the well-known schema of contemporary Soviet cultural production with their division into central and peripheral organs, their artistic contests and literary prizes, their hierarchy of values, and their critical articles celebrating "socialist competition" and "Stakhanovite production" or denouncing "sabotage" and "wrecking." The central newspaper of the BAMLAG, *Stroitel' BAMa* (Builder of the BAM), started publication in January 1933: 95 issues appeared that year, the same number in 1934, and 63 in 1935, with a print run varying between 3,000 and 10,000. There were peripheral or specialized sectors of the BAM press, such as *Stroitel' BAMa na vtorykh putiakh: Organ shtaba KVCh* (Builder of the BAM on the Second Tracks: Organ of the Staff of the Cultural-Educational Unit); *Stroitel' BAMa na lesozagotovkakh: Organ KVCh OLP "Ledianaia" BAMLAGa NKVD* (Builder of the BAM on the Timber Cutting [Operations]: Organ of the Cultural-Educational Unit of the Separate Camp Subsector "Ice" of the BAMLAG of the NKVD); or *Stanem gramotnym* (Let's Become Literate), published to increase literacy on the BAM. The commanders, political workers, and riflemen of the militarized guard (VOKhR) had their own periodicals: *Chekist na strazhe BAMa* (Chekist on Guard for the BAM), *Na strazhe udarnogo shturma za lesozagotovitel'nyi plan* (On Guard for the Shock Work Assault for the

Title page of *Putearmeets*, No. 3 (October 1935).

Timber Cutting Plan), *Zorkii strelok na strazhe BAMa* (The Vigilant Rifleman on Guard for the BAM), and so on, with their own restrictions ("not subject to circulation outside the boundaries of the VOKhR").[5]

Mitia Promyslov's doubts about whether "it is true that people are arrested and transported here only because the construction needs them as a necessary work force" are challenged by the reality of the Cultural and Educational Department of the Corrective Labor Camp of the Baikal-Amur Main Line.[6] "Reforging" (*perekovka*)—to use the established metaphor for reeducation through labor—and production targets were intrinsically related to each other in the BAM.[7] A report (*ocherk*), "Montazh zhizni" (The Montage of Life) by Aleksandr Medvedev, published in the fourth issue of *Putearmeets* in December 1935, not only illustrates the tension between economic factors and reeducation but does so from the point of view of the work force, showing how this tension was internalized. In "The Montage of Life" the human body, its gestures, and life itself become a synecdoche for Stakhanovite production:

> Stakhanov has put the emphasis on the mechanism. Our principal mechanism is the hands. Which is to say that one has to organize the hands. To make certain that, in the brigade, one pair of hands does not interfere with another: everybody should be assigned his place. Material has to be delivered to these hands with precision, so that they do not move aimlessly. As to the rationalization [of the effort], each worker in the brigade should execute one type of work, using a predetermined type of tool. . . . When I try to explain it to my guys, I talk about the montage of life: "You are assembling a sewer? Just a sewer and that's it? No, that's not all of it. It's life that you are assembling." [8]

Beyond life and literature, organized as one construction site, Azhaev seems to have organized his future readership as well, drawing up lists or inventories of his published (and sometimes unpublished) works and material relating to their critical reception. And here again we encounter the "plurality of spaces in the totality of one project" that we have already seen at work on many levels of Azhaev's production: composed by the author himself, these lists were updated from year to year, with additions but also deletions, where the "new" related not only to the present and the future but also to the past.

A manuscript inventory, headed "Spisok proizvedenii V. N. Azhaeva, napisannykh na Dal'nem Vostoke" (List of V. N. Azhaev's works, written

МОНТАЖ ЖИЗНИ

ОДНО время я не очень доволен был своей работой. Строительство вторых путей — это звучит знаменито. И если представить себе, голова закружится: три тысячи километров. А если вдуматься: второй, новый путь жизни, путь в будущее. Почему же я, Медведев Александр Александрович, не этот прямой путь строю, а какие-то водопроводы протягиваю и склепываю разные машины? Как это вообразить? Канализация будущего? Конечно, тоже нужно: и водопровод, и монтажи, и даже канализация, спору быть не может. Но великая трасса — это другое. Если, скажем, ребятишки спросят, какой-нибудь шустрый представитель счастливого поколения: „Дядь, а ты вторые пути строил?" Я, выходит, честного ответа дать не смогу (нельзя же ответить: „Я, мол, по водопроводу. Не строил").

Такие печальные размышления оказались вздором. Был возле меня один неглупый человек. Я ему пожаловался, он ругнул меня: „А ты что думаешь? — сказал он. — Машину монтируешь? Жизнь свою ты заново монтируешь, Медведев".

Он мне Горького читать приносил. Горький тоже кого-то приблизительно так ругает в статье: „Труд сапожника не хуже труда летчика. И тот и другой — нужны, полезны. Кто этого не понимает, тот вообще ничего не понимает. Надо любить и уважать любой труд, если он полезен.

Приказ Народного Комиссара — сто семьдесят второй — окончательно все уточнил для меня. Второй стальной, новый путь — это и дома, это и водопровод, это и станция. Одним словом, не разочаровывайся, бригадир Медведев.

Я про уважение и любовь к труду нарочно вначале завернул. Ведь если свой труд не любить и не уважать, тогда о чем и разговор?

Я человек вполне здоровый, — бессоннице быть у меня не полагается. А вот была у меня бессонница. Так получилось, когда я про Стаханова все подробно из газет разузнал и запомнил речи вождей.

Можно, конечно, подумать, что меня стахановский рывок поразил: нормальный человек, а такую могучую выработку стране подарил. Меня поразило другое. Озарение, я б сказал, упало на меня. Я всю свою работу с другой какой-то стороны увидал. Вот именно — сразу метод работы отчека нился.

Разве об улучшении процесса, о том, чтобы скорее дело шло, не горело сердце? Разве не думалось? Думалось. И разве я не пытался сберечь время, глаже работу завернуть?

Водопровод устанавливали в депо — начальство отпустило времени в обрез. Ребята-энтузиасты подняли галдеж: „Кончим вовремя, как задано!" Всякие восклицательные знаки. А мне такое дело невыгодно: не поспит парень две ночи, измотается, — какой из него

ударник? Отменил эту горячку. Взял карандаш и рассчитал точно — сколько часов, сколько людей, сколько работы. Терять минутки па ерунду очень обидно. А что делать? Материала нет, надо искать, выхлопатывать — начинается бег бригады „с эстафетой". Вот так из трех дней один светлый денек уронишь — обратно уже не подымешь, — до слез его жалко.

На водопроводе я для „бега с препятствиями" особых парней выделил — они материалы обеспечивали. Остальные — в полезном деле остаются. Расставил так, чтобы в работе, как в часах колесики, друг за друга цеплялись. Вышло красиво: водопровод к сроку — выработка по бригаде 312 процентов!

Обдумываю теперь — смешно становится: рассуждал я о стальном и прямом пути, о трассе, а ведь водопровод и всякие машины не бросил бы. 300 процентов-то, они разве получились бы, если бы я по водопроводные трубы не любил и не уважал? Не получились бы.

Стаханов, если вдуматься и понять, прост и хорош. Уголь, пыль, грязь — какое удовольствие, какая радость? Для чего 100 тонн рубать, когда семь полагается? Не то. Рассуждение такое — дрянь. Не уголь вырубал Стаха-

15

"Montazh zhizni" (The Montage of Life), by A. Medvedev (i.e., V. Azhaev), in *Putearmeets*, No. 4 (December 1935).

in the Far East), lists those works under four headings: number, title, date of creation, and "note on publication or other explanation." The works are listed in chronological order, starting with those written in 1935 and published as individual booklets by the Construction of the BAM under the direction of the NKVD (in a 1954 list the writings of 1935–37 bear the note "Dal'nevostochnoe izdatel'stvo" [Far East Publisher]).[9] The list ends with a novel titled *Daleko-daleko ot Moskvy* (Far, Far from Moscow) and dated 1944. The note reads "in progress" (*v rabote*). From the same list we learn that the author of "The Montage of Life" was Azhaev himself. Medvedev was a pseudonym; it was his own life that Azhaev was assembling.

The journal in which "The Montage of Life" appeared bears the mark of its time, for plural organization was already at work: half of the names on the editorial board are crossed out by the strokes of a thick black pencil. Could the printer not keep up with the pace of terror, or did the owner of the journal cross out these names a posteriori? We know that the latter practice prevailed widely, far beyond the camp boundaries. An examination of other scored names in the pages of *Putearmeets* and other publications of the Camp of the BAM shows that the purge took place later. In an October 1935 issue of *Putearmeets,* for example (i.e., the one that immediately preceded the December issue in which "The Montage" appeared), the name of the head of the GULAG NKVD, Berman, is crossed out. The People's Commissar for Internal Affairs (Genrikh Iagoda) was subject to even more radical treatment: his name is cut out.[10] Both Berman and Iagoda were still functioning in those roles in 1935.

Azhaev's name appears for the first time as the coauthor (with P. Zhagir, a name encountered more than once in Azhaev's archive) of an eight-page "comedy in one act" titled "Chuzhoi kalendar'" (An Alien Calendar). It was published in May 1935 in the sixth issue of the *Bulletin-Repertoire of the Press Sector of the Cultural and Educational Department* in Svobodnyi.[11] "An Alien Calendar" is a slapstick comedy on the theme of "reforging." "Antonov the first," a typical "refuser" and "trickster," believes that his liberation is imminent on the basis of something he has read in the camp's wall newspaper. The misunderstanding (in which only he believes) is resolved by the arrival of the positive shock worker "Antonov the second," who decides to stay on the construction site as a free laborer, to the great satisfaction of the commandant-educator and his Stakhanovite comrades. This issue of the *Bulletin* contains analogous materials, such as "Veselye povara" (The Merry Cooks) by B. Puretskii and A. Mulenko, a "hellish" musical farce in which malingerers, refusers, drunkards, wreckers, and

В. Ажаев, П. Жагир

ЧУЖОЙ КАЛЕНДАРЬ

◉ *Комедия в 1 действии* ◉

Действующие лица

АНТОНОВ ПЕРВЫЙ,— неряшливый, косолапый.
СИМА ⎫
ПЕТРЕНКО ⎬ ударники
КОЛЬКА ⎭
ВОСПИТАТЕЛЬ
АНТОНОВ ВТОРОЙ,— выгодная внешность, хорошо
  одет.

Действие происходит в одной обстановке. Помещение воспитателя: стол, скамья, несколько стульев, шкаф. На стенах — пара лозунгов, плакатов (один из плакатов изображает отказчика). Доска об'явлений. Над столом—новый отрывной календарь.

Музыка играет: „За морем синичка не пышно жила“.

Комната пуста. Чуть приоткрыв дверь, просачивается Антонов первый.

Фигура жалкая. Обнаружив, что в комнате никого нет — смелеет, выпрямляется.

АНТОНОВ ПЕРВЫЙ. Вот народ беспокойный! Сидят, придумывают. Хорошенькое дельце сочинили! И неужели гражданину воспитателю не скучно такими мелкими делами заниматься? Не понимаю! Я бы никогда и не пришел, но каждый день почему-то есть хочется. А без талончика на обед сытым не будешь. (Оглядываясь). Бюрократы! Я понимаю—пятый усиленный выдавали бы. А то—штрафной! Каждый день теперь за штрафами приходить! Тьфу!

(Освоившись, Антонов шляется по комнате. Ему скучно. Нескладно напевает: ‹За морем синичка пышно жила... Пышно... жила›).

❉

First page of "Chuzhoi kalendar'" (An Alien Calendar), from *Repertuarnyi Biulleten'*, No. 6 (May 1935), published by the Press Sector of the Cultural and Educational Department, BAMLAG, Svobodnyi.

other negative elements are (literally) fried by the camp's chefs. The name of the "responsible editor" of the issue must have met a similar fate: his name is crossed out so firmly that the pencil has made a hole in the paper. (He is replaced in later issues by B. N. Kuznetsov, lieutenant of State Security and deputy commander of the Camp Administration of the NKVD.)

During that year of 1935, Azhaev's literary career was taking off within the space of the press sector of the Cultural and Educational Department. Volume 7 of the Library of the Builders of the BAM, *Simple Stories of Heroic Deeds,* contains three of his essays: "How Umara Magomet Lost His Hat," "The Interrupted Meeting," and "A Great Thank You." [12] All three are devoted to life "on the tracks," as might be expected. The first tells the story of a prisoner who, at the risk of being cut to pieces, prevents a passenger train from being blown up. When Umara Magomet was reincarnated in *Far from Moscow* as the unforgettable welder who "laid the beginning of the pipeline," he would bear little relation to the character here, except for his name (and his heroic moral qualities and skills). In Azhaev's second story, a meeting is interrupted by the news that a line of boxcars filled with precious cargo has come unhitched and threatens to derail. The catastrophe is avoided by a courageous and self-sacrificing group of prisoner-workers, who resume their meeting after their exploits, about which "Comrade Frenkel' will be informed."

In real life Naftalii Aronovich Frenkel' represented one of the most famous success stories of "reforging" in Soviet history. Even some literary accounts contain elements of Frenkel''s biography, including Solzhenitsyn's *Gulag Archipelago* and a novel by B. Shiriaev, *The Unextinguishable Icon Lamp,* published in 1991 by the journal *Sovremennik.* The fullest information, however, is given by Ol'ga Elantseva in her book on the BAM, *The Doomed Track.* [13] Frenkel' started his professional life at the age of fourteen, well before the Revolution, working on various construction sites. After a period of study at a technical college in Germany, he returned to Russia and participated in the building of several housing projects. From 1919 to 1923 Frenkel' worked as inspector of industrial goods and private shipping companies on the Black Sea and in Turkey. Arrested and convicted in 1923 or 1924 for embezzlement and illegally crossing the state border, Frenkel' was sent to the Solovki forced labor camps. It was there that he demonstrated his skills and his career took a turn toward the highest offices and honors in the corrective labor system. Released in 1927, he became head of the production department of the Solovki camps, then head of the Moscow-based bureau of the same camps. From 1931 to 1933 he directed the Department of Production of the Gulag, after which he became deputy to the commandant of the Belomor Canal (the Stalin White Sea–Baltic Canal).[14] There he received the Order of Lenin for his good work. Elantseva cites as an example the construction in record time of a public bathhouse during a typhus epidemic. "Using the feeling of solidarity between different generations of Russians, their potential for compassion, not yet shattered in these times," Frenkel' was able to take advantage of "immemorial Russian traditions" to achieve his goal. The bathhouse was built in twenty-four hours by a brigade of young prisoners and invalids.[15]

There are, however, less appreciative accounts. According to Jacques Rossi, Frenkel', "a prisoner, trickster and subsequent MVD* general," had invented the system of differentiated food rations that eventually "spread from Solovki to all other labor camps in the country, with a simultaneous systematic reduction of the caloric level."[16] In any case, the same day he was awarded the Order of Lenin (15 August 1933), Naftalii Aronovich was promoted to the post of head of the BAM by the Politburo of the Central Committee.[17] In Azhaev's time, Frenkel' was head of construction for the BAM of the OGPU (Nachal'nik stroitel'stva BAM OGPU); that position is confirmed by a 1935 publication "not subject to circulation outside the limits of the camp," *Falangovaia sistema na rabote* (The Phalanx System at Work).[18] In an issue of *Putearmeets* of the same year, Frenkel' was identified as the "head of construction of the Second Tracks" (Nachal'nik Stroitel'stva vtorykh putei).[19] In a 1937 issue of *Putearmeets,* a photograph captioned "NSTR [*Nachstroi* = head of construction] com. Frenkel' N. A." appeared in a montage created for the celebration of the Day of the Woman, 8 March, together with a photograph of the Presidium of the Third All-Camp Congress of Women.[20] There is no doubt that Frenkel' served as the supreme model for the "builders of the BAM."

But let us return to *Simple Stories of Heroic Deeds* and Azhaev's literary production in 1935. "A Great Thank You" tells a story analogous to "The Interrupted Meeting," but this time from a woman's point of view. Two prisoner-laundresses are heading home to the camp by train at night and realize at the last minute that the train is traveling on a track that is still under construction. Owing to their vigilance, a catastrophe is avoided. An epigraph informs us that "according to an order by the Head of the Gulag, com. Berman, Meshkova and Kostiuchenko are to be released ahead of

*Ministry of Internal Affairs.

schedule," leaving the reader to assume that these are the names of the two heroic laundresses.

While "reforging" understandably remains the main topic of Azhaev's BAMLAG stories, the theme allowed for some variation: "Predislovie k zhizni" (A Foreword to Life), published in volume 8 of the Library of the Builders of the BAM, also in 1935, is based, according to the preface, on the autobiography of Evgeniia Vinogradova, ward of the Commune of Female Juveniles of the Cultural and Educational Department of the NKVD (*Vospitannitsa Kommuny Maloletok KVO BAMLAGa NKVD*).[21] As we shall see, Azhaev considered this novella one of his first literary achievements and tried to publish it outside the camp. Perhaps this is why "A Foreword to Life" resurfaced in 1961, but, again, with its contents utterly changed.

The 1935 "Foreword to Life" is the BAMLAG version of Anton Makarenko's "pedagogical poem" *The Road to Life*.[22] Published serially from 1933 to 1935, *The Road to Life* depicted Makarenko's educational experience as a director of the Gorky Colony for juvenile delinquents. The book became the cornerstone of Soviet education for years and a classic of Soviet literature. With "A Foreword to Life," it became formally part of Camp Freedom.[23] Here is a brief summary of the story. A young woman, Evgeniia, recalls her childhood and teenage years, marked by poverty, fatherlessness, prostitution, and petty crime. She ends up in the corrective labor camp of Svobodnyi, resists reeducation, and escapes. But "freedom turns out to be bleak," and she returns to the camp. The rest of the story could be titled "Reforging through Art Therapy." The stern but, as it happens, profoundly humane head of the cultural department discovers artistic talent in the young criminal and tells her the story of Paul Gauguin, who was "searching for another life in colors, but wasn't able to find it." Evgeniia decides to "succeed where Gauguin had failed" and to paint the future that is "already in reach." Among her projects is a portrait of the camp commandant and a "family gallery" of the great fathers—Gorky, Vladimir Il'ich Lenin, and Stalin, "the pride and joy of the workers of the whole world, the teacher and friend of the people."[24]

The next year Azhaev published "The Rally Goes on in the Factory" and "Polikarpov's Organ," both of which appeared in the fifth issue of *Putearmeets* (August 1936). "Life has become better, comrades, life has become happier," announces the title page, against a background composed of a semaphore signal indicating that the way is clear, a flag of the "Stakhanovite phalanx," and three smiling faces, one of which looks Asian and another that resembles, say, Cary Grant. In addition to belles lettres, the issue contains an appeal for increased production by Comrade Lazar Kaganovich, People's Commissar of Communication and Transportation, "to the Bolsheviks of the Far East," as well as poems in his honor, a report on art in the camp, another report on a theatrical performance of Pushkin's *Mozart and Salieri* at the Theater of the Culture and Education Department (in preparation for Pushkin's centennial), and drawings illustrating various "sports games in the camp."[25]

It appears that the works found in Azhaev's archive by no means exhaust the writer's impressive output during those two years of "corrective labor." Other works of 1935 mentioned in his list include *Samootverzhennyi Klobuk* (Selfless Klobuk), *Noch' v vyemke* (A Night in the Groove), *Aleksandr Dovgal', Podvig* (The Feat), and *Pervoaprel'skii pobeg* (Escape on April First), all five published as booklets by the Culture and Education Department of the BAM; "Rasskaz o prikaze Narkoma" (Story about an Order of the People's Commissar), published in the newspaper *Stroitel' BAMa* (Builder of the BAM); "Pereklichka geroev" (The Heroes' Exchange of Views), "Chistota i akkuratnost'" (Cleanliness and Tidiness), and "O zhelezno-betonnykh rven'iakh i o molodosti" (On Ferroconcrete Zeal and Youthfulness), reports published in various issues of *Putearmeets,* often under a pseudonym. The following titles are mentioned in Azhaev's list for 1936: "Chest'" (Honor), "Ochen' prosto" (Very Simple), "Moe edinolichnoe znamia" (My Personal Banner), "Voditel' paravoza" (The Locomotive Conductor), "U zhizni pervaia rech'" (Life's First Speech), "Uverennost'" (Self-Confidence), and "God zhizni piatidesiatyi" (The Fiftieth Year of Life), all reports and essays published in various formats by the BAM. Another story worth mentioning is "Nevynosimyi promakh" (The Unbearable Blunder), published in *Builder of the BAM* and performed on the stage. Finally, a play titled *Vtorye Puti* (The Second Tracks) "was staged in the theater in the city of Svobodnyi." The performance took place in 1937, the year of the writer's release. Azhaev's "authorship" often seems to have been limited to editing various materials, which explains the discrepancies between his lists and the actual works.[26] Nevertheless, his participation in the creative process was probably important enough to support his claim to authorship of some of those works.

At the beginning of 1937, Azhaev rose in rank. The sixth issue of *Putearmeets* (February 1937) not only included his report titled "The Cordial Speech of the Contemporary"[27] but listed him as the journal's editor in chief, replacing one Laskin. Among the contents of *Putearmeets* no. 6

was an article on a satirical camp "manuscript journal," *Taezhnyi krokodil* (The Crocodile of the Taiga), which was devoted to castigating the lazy, the wreckers, the "twenty-six percenters" (*dvadtsatishestiprotsentniki*)— that is, those who met only 26 percent of the norm. Although praised by the editors of *Putearmeets, Taezhnyi krokodil* incurred some criticism from them as well: the satire "sometimes seems too trite," is "not always con-crete enough," and, most notably, is not always "typical." [28]

The same issue also announces the results of a competition and the journal's awards for the best literary, artistic, and musical works. The jury felt that none of the 298 works submitted deserved first, second, or third prize because none of them met the specified artistic criteria. But the jury was nevertheless eager to reward certain works that deserved to be pub-lished and positively evaluated, among them the play *Stroiteli mostov i peregonov* (The Builders of Bridges and Stages) by V. N. Azhaev and L. K. Lisenko, which won fifth place (a prize of 200 rubles). The jury added, however, "Before its publication, this play will be subject to major editor-ial changes." [29] Perhaps these changes explain why only the title of the work survived revision, as printed on the jacket of volume 19 of the Li-brary of the Builders of the BAM, *Na nashei planete* (On Our Planet). The work is absent from the author's subsequent lists and inventories. In any case, Azhaev now had other venues to explore: after 16 March 1937 his literary works were no longer forbidden to circulate beyond the camp boundaries. As we know, in 1937 the Khabarovsk journal *Na rubezhe* pub-lished Azhaev's story "The Son." In the archival copy of the story, the title has been crossed out by the author and replaced by the words "I am a hu-man being!" (*Ia chelovek!*). Since writing his "Foreword to Life," Azhaev had crossed the borderline it represented. Before we can go on with our own journey, however, we must return to Camp Freedom for a moment in Azhaev's creative output—and inner life—that was to determine, I be-lieve, everything that followed.

Azhaev's archive contains a number of unfinished essays, reports, and other writings; some of them were eventually published, others not. "Ma-terialy k povesti o chekistakh" (materials for a novella on the Chekists) be-longs to the second category. Consisting of something between an outline and a loosely written story in two parts, these "materials" depict the work of an employee of state security at various stages in his career, from learn-ing and growth to maturity. Here again, plural organization is at work: the Chekist not only passes from one stage to another but also changes his name. Moreover, what happens inside the story is later reflected outside:

many elements found in these writings appear in other texts. Some of them have already been described in my discussion of "The Foreword to Life" and other stories on "reforging"; others appear in *The Boxcar* and in *Far from Moscow*. But here, in the "materials for a novella on the Chekists," reforging is described from another point of view; to paraphrase a passage from Slavoj Žižek's *Sublime Object of Ideology,* it is described from the point of view of the "Big Other." This perspective is the ideal point from which the hero-to-be-reeducated views himself, so that he appears to himself to be worthy of the Chekist's love, thus making his way from "imaginary" to "symbolic identification," from personal fantasy to a higher order of social recognition.[30] At the same time, one could say that the object of reeducation is shifted to its subject through some sort of transference, as a psychoanalyst would put it. These materials are of paramount importance for our story because they reveal the trace of the peculiar "fantasy object"[31] by which reforging is made possible; that is, by which coercion becomes desire.

The first set of materials[32] is devoted to the biography of Semen Latyshev, inspector of the Moscow Criminal Investigation Department (MUR). Latyshev's *Bildung* begins as he chases delinquents and bandits through Moscow, then moves on to "political" work in the security organs against the "internal enemy." The passage from one stage to the other, via the catharsis of the Revolution, happens "naturally," in accordance with the "law of history":

> Latyshev's passage to the Chekist-type of work was completed naturally [*zakonomerno*] and almost imperceptibly. Factories, plants, telegraph offices, villages, banks, publishing houses, even hospitals and schools became positions on a huge front in the struggle against the counterrevolution. [By] open banditry and sabotage, impudent resistance or quiet wrecking, with all possible means, but always spitefully and maliciously, the enemies interfered in the developing and creative labor of the workers. From the Latvian border to Central Asia, this was the range of the front on which the Chekist Latyshev operated, under the instruction of the Party.[33]

In 1922 Latyshev is promoted to investigator (*sledovatel'*). His new work is described as "a subtle affair, demanding intelligence," for it is necessary to uncover the "filaments and roots of the crime," leaving "no trace of decomposition . . . in the black earth of the fatherland." Latyshev works hard and successfully. At night he even writes a book, *Methods of Investiga-*

tion, which is published and widely "circulated all over the country." Laty-shev then becomes the assistant prosecutor in a region whose name is crossed out to the point of illegibility. Sometimes there are "festive days" when he comes home all smiles because "in this or that factory nobody is going to disturb the proletarians anymore." Latyshev's work is so exhaust-ing that he reaches a physical breaking point. His doctors prescribe a radi-cal change of regimen: "physical work, simple and healthy, such as work at the [factory] bench." For a whole year Latyshev works in one of Moscow's metallurgical factories, "falling in love with the metal." When his fellow Chekists come to visit him, he gives them a detailed report on the strict routine by which he organizes his days: gymnastic exercises, cold showers, lunch at a fixed hour, dinner at a fixed hour, sleep at a fixed hour. Latyshev, in other words, has become a Rakhmetov of the 1930s and has learned to assemble his life.[34] During his spare time he reads books, goes to the movies, or goes hunting. He likes adventure stories and action films, and he loves to stroll through the forests with a gun. When Latyshev leaves the factory after a year, the workers do not want to let him go: "Who will teach us political education?" they ask.[35] After "cleansing several of Mos-cow's neighborhoods"—"the underground world knows him and respects him"—Latyshev joins the Main Administration of Camps (GULAG) in 1930, and in 1933 earns the distinction of "Honorary Chekist." During a hot summer day in 1934, Latyshev packs his suitcases and tells his wife, "Wait for my telegram and then come and join me." This time his journey will take him far away, a distance of about ten thousand kilometers, almost to the other side of the planet, and he knows that he will not see Moscow for many years: "Somewhere in the fabulous Far East there is a legion of builders—through the taiga, the crags, and the swamps, in the heat and the unbearable cold, the tracks of steel lead toward the ocean. The Party gave the Chekist the order, 'Your place is there.' And the Chekist went there forthwith."[36]

What then follows is a treatise on "class struggle in the labor camp" and reeducation through labor. Latyshev and his comrades are part of a Chekist collective on a huge construction site, in comparison with which the White Sea–Baltic Canal vanishes into the background. Latyshev works intensely: "Different paragraphs, different lengths of sentences, dif-ferent crimes, different class membership. . . . Not one transport escapes the vigilant eye of Latyshev and his aides, not one person goes through without having been examined and scrutinized." By mixing with thou-sands of camp inmates, the Chekist has acquired an "amazing skill": a brief interrogation, a glance at the almost cryptic data of the personal file, and the conduct of the former kulak, bandit, or counterrevolutionary becomes "transparent through and through."[37]

Latyshev's biography ends with a series of "pedagogical" successes, including his extermination of "parasites" in a colony,[38] his redemption of a former counterrevolutionary through directed reading (Stalin's *Problems of Leninism*), and his encounter with a bandit whose vows of vengeance are transformed into expressions of gratitude and overachievement on the production front.

The second set of "materials for a novella on the Chekists" takes up the life of the hero at the zenith of his career. Renamed Filippov and now wearing the uniform of a lieutenant, he watches a parade of gymnasts in a stadium.[39] The sun is shining as the gymnasts perform in honor of sixty new winners of the "Ready for Labor and Defense" badge. Also honored is a group of record-breaking cyclists who tour the USSR (the part of the tour they like best is the "Second Tracks"). A former thief promises to produce 500 percent over the norm. A competition is held between the sportsmen of the BAMLAG and those of the Amur Railway.

Filippov is next seen proofreading the BAMLAG journal. He criticizes the editorial board for not having included enough poetry ("the tables collapse from the weight of the poems received") and wonders why there are no accounts of heroism, since every day he signs dozens of orders for production awards. No one has the right to keep silent about heroism. Furthermore, why hasn't he heard anything about the literary competition? Next comes a description of the tableau of Filippov's office, on one wall of which hangs a "portrait of STALIN and Kaganovich," painted by an artist in the camp.

Filippov has great responsibilities and directs a huge enterprise. What he lacks most is time. But he manages in those rapidly passing hours and minutes to solve several problems at once with a single complex solution. During meetings he deals with three issues at a time. Every day he must wade through an enormous volume of correspondence and other paperwork. There are all sorts of letters: former inmates write to express their gratitude ("the BAMLAG opened the road to real life"); workers who have achieved Stakhanovite standards but have received no award write to complain; inmates send dirty, crumpled letters from their cells in solitary confinement ("I agree to go back to work. But please allow me to join an agitbrigade. I feel in myself the talent for acting"). Filippov's office is a vast reservoir of energy.

Some of these "materials" were to reappear in *Far from Moscow:*

"I'm guilty, I understand that. I'm prepared to face the music. Only please
help me, Comrade Batmanov."

Seregin broke off in confusion. Batmanov's interest was aroused.

"How can I help you?" he asked.

"Don't drive me away from here! Let me go on working. I'll swear I
won't run away. My whole life's now in the pumping station. I see those
machines working in my dreams. Let me see them started, then I'm prepared even to face the firing squad."

"I believe you," Batmanov answered. "I believe you, because a man
must be a hopeless case if, after having worked in a good collective, he
fails to realize the difference between the rich life of an honest toiler, an
equal member of our society, and the miserable lot of a criminal, a social
outcast. You've received a harsh lesson in all respects, but I think it will be
to the good. You can't just lightly dismiss the past. You must actively fight
its manifestations in yourself and others." Batmanov paused. "I think I'll
let you stay on the construction job, I'll vouch for you. And remember
this—a man's future nearly always lies in his own hands."

Seregin lay with his face buried in his hands, and his shoulders
shook.[40]

We return to the original materials. It is night. Filippov is sitting in his
office, humming a song about the frost, the taiga, and the laying of the
steel tracks to the ocean. His secretary announces the arrival of two writers
(*literaty*)[41] who are scheduled to meet with him at this time. Filippov
grumbles something about people taking up his day (or rather night) off,
but finally asks that they be sent in. The writers have diametrically opposed
biographies. One is a "contemporary of the Symbolists"; the other is young
enough to be a member of the Komsomol.

"So, what's up?" The commander addresses himself to the older one but
watches the younger, curiosity in his eyes. "I read the play attentively and
remained unsatisfied," says Filippov, and in his voice one can perceive the
disappointment. "You didn't write what you were supposed to. Creation is
a subtle matter [*tvorchestvo—delo tonkoe*], I understand, and the conversation that you are having with me certainly won't make it easier. But I
will speak frankly; our construction is an exceptional one. The jobs and
the men. . . . Here, even in everyday life there are no everyday jobs. Just

9.

—Там пришли два этих литератора, докладывает он.

— Какие литераторы ? — всплескивает руками начальник. — У меня выходной день, наконец.

— Они говорят, что вы им назначили именно сегодня, именно ночью, — улыбается секретарь.

—У меня выходной. Ну, пусть войдут.

"До конца, сквозь мороз и туманы,
Мы стальную ведем колею,
Проходя по тайге, к океану,
Мы кончаем работу свою".

У литераторов — полярно-различные биографии. Один современник символистов, второй — комсомольского возраста.

—Ну, что у вас ? —Начальник обращается к тому, что постарше, но смотрит на молодого. Любопытство в его взгляде.

— Я внимательно прочитал вашу пьесу и остался недоволен ею, — говорит Филиппов и в голосе его слышится досада. —Не то написали вы. Творчество — дело тонкое — я понимаю — и от разговора со мной — возможно писать вы очевидно лучше не будете. Но я буду говорить прямо. Стройка наша необыкновенная, если откровенно говорить. ... и люди и мысли... Нет ведь будничных дел, даже в буднях вы почитайте хотя бы телеграммы. А в пьесе... Все на месте, верно.. Приходят, уходят. Завязка, развязка. Неужели мы будем в жизни так скучны? Если бы пьесу [illegible] на сцене — у других бы [illegible] будет [illegible].

Typescript page from "Materials for a novella on the Chekists (II)," relating the encounter between Commander Filippov and two writers ("But I will speak frankly; our construction is an exceptional one . . .).

read the telegrams. And in your play . . . everything seems to be in order and truthful. People come in, people go out. Opening, closure. But can life be so dull? What will happen if this play is performed?" The old writer's face is distressed.

"I'm not very strong in literature." Filippov's voice softens. "Perhaps I am not right. I will have your play read by somebody else."

"No, you are perfectly correct," says the writer with emotion. "Everything in me is corroded, Citizen Commander. I have come to love the construction, and I have got a feeling for it, I am a bookworm who is afraid of life's drafts! I have no voice. But soon I will find it, my voice. I will reeducate myself to speak. I will write a play with which you will be pleased and that can be shown on the stage."

The old writer leaves, the young one stays.

"Tell me your story," says the commander.

The theme of the novella, given to the young writer [*literator*] by the commander three days before, had ripened. He lays it out. With gleaming eyes, flushed with excitement, the young lad describes the plot of the novella.

The Chekist lowers his eyes, so that he who stands before him will not read in his eyes the kindness and the joy; the love of the Chekist lifts up the one who has fallen, no matter how low, but this love is always stern, severe, and does not display itself outwardly.

The young lad speaks.

"I want a lot. . . . I want to write, as you said, exceptionally [*neobyknovenno*]. I want to write in a way that would be more interesting than reality. This is very difficult. Somebody once said that to depict reality accurately is as difficult as outlining the shadow of the thunderstorm's cloud skimming over the fields."

The Chekist glows with emotion. The young lad had arrived in the camp all pale and flabby. At that time he did not even think of creativity. Alien influences had almost destroyed him.

"Now listen," Filippov lectures the young man sternly, "I can and must ask much from you. This one" (he points toward the door through which the old writer vanished) "there is nothing to be expected from: he'll crumble to pieces. But you will do me the favor of getting the work going in a clear-cut and organized fashion. There is no time to be lost. The construction will be finished, and what will you have written? You won't want to be ashamed of yourself. You have to learn, that's it. Systematically and profoundly. Read and read, otherwise, pffft, at once. Emotion is good, but it has to be filtered by the silvery filter of reason. Think more. There is no need for green fruit. Things have to grow, so that the mind is captured, everything has to be first-rate. You should grow as grows [illeg.], for instance like [illeg.]. I won't say anything else. Write a novella and come back. But come back within a year; the construction is close to completion."

The young lad bows and turns to leave the room. The voice of the Chekist (he smiles) stops him on the threshhold.

"In other words, keep up the good work." [42]

As we already know, the author of *Far from Moscow* "kept up the good work." What we see here in detail is the site, the origin, the very moment of utterance of the "unbreakable oath" pronounced by transference through the words of the Chekist and the lad's unspoken promise to write a novella. As we shall see, the bond between the young lad and Filippov—the emotional coloring of the scene, the "gleaming eyes" and the flushed face of the former, the lowered eyes of the latter, concealing "kindness" and "joy" and "love"—and the other residue of this particular moment of *jouissance* would reappear in the later novel.

"Materials for the novella on the Chekists (II)" ends in "plurality" with Filippov's biography (which basically recapitulates Semen Latyshev's); with a laconic version of Evgeniia Vinogradova's artistic confession, but with a different ending (she leaves for Moscow after her liberation); and with some excerpts from an "autobiographical novella," *The Fairway of Life* (*Farvater zhizni*), a naval equivalent of "A Foreword to Life." As the hero of this work, Iosif Morozov, foreman of a leading phalanx,* is making a speech at a meeting when he is interrupted by the camp commandant, who announces Morozov's liberation two years ahead of schedule. The story was actually published (in the February 1937 issue of *Putearmeets*) under the name of Iosif Moroz. With its publication, the name of the commandant also changed, shifting from fiction to real life. He became the "distinguished commander of the second tracks of the Far Eastern Region," Lieutenant of State Security B. N. Kuznetsov, deputy commander of the BAMLAG Camp Administration. [43]

---

*Synonym for "colony." Here the chronology of the term seems not to work. See note 38.

5

PERSONAL FILES

"Please give me back my memorandum." . . .

Batmanov picked up Aleksei's memorandum from the desk, glanced at it, and put it into the safe with a laugh.

"I happen to be more persistent in my rancor. I'm not going to return your memorandum. It is a hobby of mine to collect curious documents. This memorandum will make a nice addition to my collection. The time will come when it will be particularly embarrassing for its author to acknowledge his literary effusion; I shall wait for that moment to produce it from the collection and return it."

—Far from Moscow, book 1, chapter 4

We hereby certify that Com. Azhaev Vasilii Nikolaevich, head of the TsBRIZ of the ZhDSU, continually assists the Culture and Education Department of the ZhDSU by organizing literary work. . . .

—People's Commissariat of Internal Affairs, Administration of Railway Construction of the GULAG of the NKVD in the Far East (15 December 1938), Evstigneev

"Time, Forward!" Let us use this title of one of the classics of socialist realism to jump to the future.[1] Various documents found in the summer of 1994 in the State Archives of the Region of Khabarovsk and dating from 1946–47 (i.e., when Azhaev became a member of the Soviet Writers' Union) give conflicting information about the author's literary debut. According to Azhaev's personal Writers' Union file (*lichnaia kartochka*), opened on 10 March 1947, the author of *Far from Moscow* started his writing career in 1935.[2] Another personal file, opened three months later on 23 June 1947, postpones this event to 1937.[3] Azhaev did not become a professional litterateur, however, until April 1946, as stated on the personal registration form of the personnel department (*lichnyi listok po uchetu kadrov*), filled out on 22 April 1946. That date coincides with the beginning of his job in the editorial office of the journal *Dal'nii Vostok*. Finally, an "autobiography," also dated 22 April 1946 and evidently submitted with the registration form, mentions that Azhaev graduated in 1945 from the Gorky Literary Institute's Department of Correspondence Studies, in which he had enrolled in 1939. These four sets of documents give different years for some reason: according to the personal files Azhaev was born in 1915, but both the registration form and the autobiography give the year as 1912, while another form, filled out on 21 January 1940, gives 1913 as the year of his birth.[4]

From Azhaev's personnel department autobiography we learn about the writer's childhood and family, his school years and studies, his first job in a Moscow factory, and his "passion for literature, starting at the school desk." Concerning his early childhood, we find some of the same gloom and doom depicted in several of the pieces written in Svobodnyi. As in "A Foreword to Life," we read that Azhaev spent his early years without a father and in "extreme poverty." Contrary to "A Foreword to Life," however, his father—a Moscow furrier—came back from the "great imperialistic war" in 1919, then went off to fight with the Red Army from 1919 to 1922, remarried (Azhaev's mother died in 1922), and, unlike the father in *The Boxcar*, was never arrested. Personnel departments usually do not allow a lot of narrative in the autobiographies they request, and Azhaev's is no exception. Nonetheless, it contains useful information about the prologue

The certificate of Azhaev's release, issued by the NKVD Administration of the Corrective Labor Camp of the Baikal–Amur Main Line, Svobodnyi, and dated 16 March 1937, states that Azhaev was sentenced on 17 January 1935 by a special board of the NKVD of the USSR for "counterrevolutionary agitation," was released after serving 643 work days, and was expected to register at the administrative office of the Workers' and Peasants' Militia and the People's Commissariat of Military Affairs of the city of Kimry, Moscow Administrative Region.

to the writer's life and beyond: he makes note of a special interest in chemistry during his high school years; his first job in the Factory No. 2 "Vokhimfarm" in Moscow, where he directed the BRIZ (Bureau of Rationalization and Inventions); his second job as chemist on duty in a Moscow gas factory; and his conviction by the NKVD in January 1935 and his transportation to the BAMLAG of the NKVD in the Far East, where he remained from March 1935 to March 1937. The following excerpt not only confirms the various "certificates" and "character references" found in Azhaev's private archive, but also tells us what happened later, and what Azhaev's specific duties were from 1937 to 1946:

> From March 1937 to 1 April 1946 I worked without interruption in the organs of the NKVD (MVD) in the Far East, in the Administration of the BAMLAG of the NKVD (city of Svobodnyi) from 16 March to 1 December 1937 as inspector of the KVO (Cultural and Educational Department), and after this as inspector attached to the senior engineer.

Diploma issued by the Commander, the Political Department, the Party Committee, and the Local Party Committee of the Administration of Railway Construction of the GULAG of the NKVD of the USSR in the Far East, 6 November 1939, to V. N. Azhaev on the occasion of the 22d anniversary of the Great October Socialist Revolution for his successful work and active participation in the community life of the Administration.

Х А Р А К Т Е Р И С Т И К А.

АЖАЕВА Василия Николаевича Начальника ЦБРИЗ"а
УЖДС ГУЛАГ"а НКВД на ДВ.

Тов. АЖАЕВ В.А. в конце 1937 года был выдвинут на
должность Начальника ЦБРИЗ"а Управления Железнодорож-
ного Строительства, Культурно-Воспитательным Отделом,
поддержанным Партийной и Профсоюзной организациями УЖДС.

Со вступлением тов. Ажаева в должность Начальника
ЦБРИЗ"а дело изобретательства на строительстве сразу же
дало значительное улучшение по всем показателям и продол-
жает интенсивно развиваться.

Количество поступивших предложений, их реализация и
суммы экономии по ним составили:

Г о д ы	Количество поступивших предложений	Количество реализованн. предложений	Сумма эко- номии от реализации	ПРИМЕЧАНИЕ:
1937 :	700	368	2.225.000	
1938 :	2034	822	3.899.000	
1939 :	3475	1210	7.615.000	

Тов. Ажаев В.Н. проявил себя как очень хороший орга-
низатор, очень настойчивый, целеустремленный руководитель,
очень добросовестный работник и очень скромный человек.

30.ХП.1939г.   (Б А К И Н)

НКВД на ДВ

АХО

ным верно:

Character reference for Vasilii Azhaev ("a very good organizer, a very persistent and purposeful leader, a very conscientious worker, and a very modest man"), 30 December 1939, signed by Bakin, chief engineer of the Main Administration of Railway Construction Camps of the GULAG of the NKVD in the Far East.

In the Administration of the Railway Construction Camps in the Far East (city of Svobodnyi) from 1 December 1937 to 24 October 1940 as head of the TsBRIZ.

In the Administration of the Lower Amur Camp of the NKVD (city of Komsomol'sk) from 25 October 1940 to 10 May 1943, successively, as head of division, head of inspection attached to the Head of the Administration, assistant to the Head, deputy head of the inspection attached to the Head of the Oversight and Planning Department, and head of the Industrial Department.

In the Administration of Camps of the NKVD of the Khabarovsk Region (city of Khabarovsk) from 10 May [1943] [5] to 1 April 1946 as, first, senior inspector and then head of the control inspection attached to the Head of the Administration. The passages from one post to the other occurred by means of transfer on the orders of the Central Directorate or the Head of the Administration of the Regional NKVD.

From 1 April 1946, by order of the Head of the MVD (Ministry of Internal Affairs), I was transferred [*otkomandirovan*] to the editorial office of the journal *Dal' nii Vostok*.

The conviction, with all its attendant restrictions, was expunged by petition of the commanding authorities and the political department of the Lower Amur Corrective Labor Camp of the NKVD and the senior engineer of the GULZhDS-NKVD, by resolution of the Special Board of the People's Commissariat of Internal Affairs of 7 July 1941. [6]

Between Azhaev's liberation from Camp Freedom and his "transfer" in 1946, almost ten years had passed, enough time for the "novella" to have grown into a novel. Azhaev's new appointment coincided with the publication of *Far from Moscow* in *Dal' nii Vostok*.

6

---•·◄∞►·•---

BORDERLINE I: RUBEZHANSK

Everything is quiet in the Far Eastern branch of the Writers'
Union; one cannot feel the full-blooded life of creation. No one
knows what happened to the group of novice authors from the
enterprises and schools, who still visited the branch last year and
participated in creative discussions. The board alienated them
because of its idleness, its bureaucratic methods.

. . . The work of the board of the Far Eastern Writers' Union
produced poor results in the last half year. All the writers will
have to answer for these results, but first of all the leader of the
board, Com. Alekseev.

—"Everything Is Quiet on the Board of the Writers' Union,"
Tikhookeanskii komsomolets (22 November 1936)

$\mathbf{A}$ meeting of the enlarged board of the Far Eastern branch of the Soviet Writers' Union on 26 November 1936 in Khabarovsk was devoted to
discussing an article that had appeared four days earlier in the newspaper
Tikhookeanskii komsomolets.[1] Its title, "Everything Is Quiet on the Board
of the Writers' Union," and the context in which it was published were
enough to alarm the board members, who responded with a combination of defensive counterarguments and self-criticism.[2] Dal'krai (the Far
Eastern Region) was preparing itself for its great "cleansing," to use John
Stephan's term. In a passage on the "destruction of the Far Eastern intelligentsia," Stephan writes about the repression of the founding editors of

the region's leading literary journal *Na rubezhe* and about the arrest and execution of, among others, Te Men Khi, head of *Na rubezhe*'s Korean department.[3] On 26 November 1936, however, Te Men Khi was still alive and participating in the meeting of the Writers' Union board. What was said at this meeting, and at those that followed, helps us better understand the context in which Azhaev's literary career began to extend "beyond the limits of the camp."

While acknowledging that the Far Eastern branch had demonstrated a "lack of literary mobilization of the masses" in its work, the chairman of the board, Mikhail Alekseev, refuted some of the newspaper's more specific criticisms. He denied, for example, that the Chinese and Korean writers of the region had been neglected. On the contrary, said Alekseev, the board "had called for the Korean writer Te Men Khi to work permanently in Khabarovsk." He continued: "We have educated this comrade, we have given him the opportunity to work creatively, we have studied with him. The same goes for the Chinese writers Borit and Tin'-Shan',[4] and for other Korean colleagues." Alekseev referred to the branch's positive publication record: the two-volume collection *Dal'nii Vostok* (Far East), "edited by Comrade Fadeev and sent to Moscow with the best works of the Far Eastern writers and poets," and a chapter in the volume *Nasha rodina* (Our Homeland), to be published by Molodaia Gvardiia. Alekseev also pointed to the Far Eastern branch's "important work with the young writers of the region," its system of "literary consultations," which had helped to identify "three hundred novice writers who published their works in the regional [*kraevye*], provincial [*oblastnye*], and district [*raionnye*] newspapers of Dal'krai." "A written and oral consultation with novice writers and poets is organized daily," he added, although he admitted that "despite our rich reserves, our active members [*aktiv*], the work that aims to attract [young writers] is proceeding too slowly." One of the major problems that the branch faced with young authors was "graphomania" ("too much ambition, not enough ammunition"); indeed, some of Alekseev's fellow literary consultants had even been "beaten up by novice authors for their sound criticism." He complained that many of the works received were written by people so uncultured (*malokul'turnye*) that "they didn't even know the alphabet, let alone the fundamentals of literary creation." Alekseev accused the regional press of not having recognized the pretensions of these graphomaniacs and of having failed to "boost the authority of the literary consultants conducting such colossal work with young authors."

Continuing in the same vein, Alekseev defended the editorial board of the journal *Na rubezhe* as "meeting the political standards stipulated by the Regional Party Committee and in part by Comrade Lavrent'ev."[5] Concerning the journal's goals and achievements, he pointed out that its sixth issue was devoted to "national" (i.e., ethnic) authors—Chinese, Korean, and Jewish—and to the poets of the construction of the "Second Tracks."[6] "Massive work" had been done in Vladivostok, Komsomol'sk, and Birobidzhan, but other locations, such as Sakhalin, Blagoveshchensk, Nikolaevsk-na-Amure, and Kolyma, had yet to be reached. "Unfortunately," he continued, "and to our great shame, we did not devote ourselves to the countryside." Alekseev's speech concluded with expressions of appreciation for the great help given to the branch by the Regional Party Committee, followed by some organizational complaints and an enumeration of his colleagues' recent publications, including *Radost'* (Joy), a play by the "BAM writer" Sergei Fedotov about "the reeducation of people working on the construction of the Second Tracks."[7] All things considered, the Far Eastern branch of the Soviet Writers' Union was "healthy, in principle." Negative aspects were being corrected, "formalism" or "transmentalism" (*zaum'e*) was being overcome, and Viacheslav Afanas'ev (who exemplified these tendencies), "with whom we work a lot and unyieldingly," was "successfully restructuring himself" and had already written a series of remarkable works. Alekseev concluded that their healthy organization was looking to the future and counted on articles such as the one published by *Tikhookeanskii komsomolets* to help it with its own restructuring (*perestroika*).[8]

Other members of the board and representatives from other organizations agreed with what Alekseev had said, with some exceptions. For example, board member Elpidifor Titov noted some "weaknesses on the theoretical and critical front," in which he was supported by the deputy editor of the journal *Tikhookeanskaia zvezda*, Vasilii Batmanov. Batmanov also regretted that *Na rubezhe* had failed to publish Aleksandr Fadeev's *Last of the Udege* and Petr Pavlenko's *In the East*, and "wondered" why Titov and Kulygin's play *Sergei Lazo* was good enough to be performed "somewhere in Moscow" but not to appear in *Na rubezhe*.[9] Several speakers were more critical of the branch's record in working with young authors. Anatolii Gai, another member of the board, confirmed that many of these authors were not part of any association and that hardly anything was known of them. He also voiced concern over the fact that local literary circles (*literaturnye krushki*) had sprung up spontaneously, and he proposed, among other improvements, the creation of "superior" or "enhancing" bodies, such as "literary-theoretical studios," in which "questions of Marxism-Leninism" could be studied. The representative of the regional committee of the Komsomol, Orenbakh, complained that for reasons of "unfamiliarity with the topic," the Writers' Union member Semen Bytovoi had refused to lecture on Pushkin at some collective farms: "What does this say about a poet who cannot even make a speech on Pushkin?" he expostulated. Bytovoi, who was present at the meeting, replied that indeed "literary studios of a superior type" were needed, and that the union's work with the Komsomol was by no means satisfactory.[10]

The Regional Party Committee representative, Kholodov, had the last word. According to him, the *Tikhookeanskii komsomolets* article had stimulated a serious restructuring effort within the Far Eastern branch, which was a great step forward. The real work of the Far Eastern writers lay ahead, however. Declarations and promises would not be enough as they prepared for the twentieth anniversary of the Great October Revolution and the fifteenth anniversary of the Sovietization of the Far Eastern Region, and tried to give the country "these full-grown works that the Party, the working class, and the mass reader of the region were waiting for." Kholodov continued: "We have no need for Arsen'ev's exotics, the primeval forest, the tigers, the polar bears, etc. We need, so to speak, a different, Soviet exotics, made of what we have built here, of what we conquered." Promising to help the Far Eastern writers in their pedagogical work with young authors, Kholodov ended on a "personal note," addressed to Alekseev, about the dearth of literary works by him: "Mikhail Alekseev is an important writer, and we have the right to request from him new and important works."[11]

Only a few such minutes of the meetings of the board of the Far Eastern branch of the Soviet Writers' Union seem to have made it into file 1738 of the archives of the Khabarovsk Administrative Region, but those that did help us to reconstruct, if not a history, then an atmosphere, and some events. The fourth meeting, held 10 March 1937, with Vasilii Batmanov as the main speaker, was devoted to the issue of the party's banning of Ivan Shabanov (one of the founding members of the Far Eastern branch of the union in 1932 and a delegate to the union's first congress in 1934) as a "double-dealer" (*dvurushnik*) and "Trotskyite enemy."[12] Gai, Bytovoi, Komarov, and Alekseev, all of whom participated in the debate (with the other members present, Vorob'ev, Baturin, Kravchenko, and Shestakova, remaining officially silent), expressed their "total solidarity with the decision of the Party organs." The board decided to ban Shabanov from the

Far Eastern branch of the union and to note for the record the political shortsightedness of the editorial board of *Na rubezhe,* which had allowed the publication of his novella "Lakirovka" (Varnishing).[13]

The board met again on 19 April to (re)elect its chairman and its "responsible secretary."[14] Present were M. Alekseev, I. Rabin, Tin'-Shan', V. Afanas'ev, A. Gai, G. Kobets, Te Men Khi, S. Bytovoi, Volosevich (from the regional party committee), and V. Batmanov. Alekseev was reelected by secret ballot, while Anatolii Gai, who had asked to be dropped as a candidate for reasons of "ideological and organizational unpreparedness," was nevertheless elected "responsible secretary."

"Cleansing" gained momentum during the next, "extraordinary" meeting of 23 April: the program and scope of the meeting (and of those that followed) show that literary life was no different from the other "great Stalinist construction projects" of the era.[15] This time, the board met along with the active members (*litaktiv*) of the Writers' Union. Following a lecture by Mikhail Alekseev on the "Fifth Anniversary of the Historical Decision of the Central Committee of the All-Union Communist Party (of the Bolsheviks) [TsK VKP(b)] on the Restructuring of Literary Organizations"[16] and several "declarations," the board drew up a six-point resolution. The first point responded to the plenum of the Central Committee of 25 February–5 March with a "decisive restructuring" (*perestroika*) of its ranks and its work.[17] It read: "Throwing off all that is worthless, ossified, bringing to light and eradicating the class enemies, the Trotskyites, the spies, the saboteurs, overcoming the resistance of the bureaucrats, the smug, those who have been struck by the political blindness and idiotic disease of those leaders who thought that they would be safe—Soviet literature is cleansing its ranks."[18]

The next four points of the resolution underlined, respectively, the great significance of the decision of the TsK VKP(b) "On the Restructuring of Literary Organizations"; the educational and unifying result for the cadres of Soviet literature of the liquidation of the former Russian Association of Proletarian Writers (RAPP); the exceptional role of the late Aleksei Maksimovich Gorky in gathering the literary forces of the proletariat and the progressive intelligentsia under the leadership of the party of Lenin and Stalin; and the necessity of participating in the forthcoming All-Union "Gorky Plenum" in Moscow with completed books or works ready for publication, and not merely works in progress. These goals mandated "the efforts of all creative forces, a great development of critical work, a critical reconsideration of already completed literary production."[19]

"Reconsideration" was also the subject of point six. A regional meeting of the Far Eastern branch of the Soviet Writers' Union, held a few days before (15–18 April), had judged the work of its board "thoroughly unsatisfactory." The branch board and the editorial board of *Na rubezhe* were both accused of being less than vigilant, of having failed to expose Japanese spies and Trotskyite counterrevolutionaries, and of having allowed a series of Trotskyite works to be published. It was decided that the "working part of the board" was to take a series of measures within the next three days. These measures included ordering the *litaktiv* and other literary circles of the region to study the speeches made by Stalin and Zhdanov during the February plenum of the Central Committee, as well as the Stalin Constitution and the history of the party.[20] They were also ordered to conduct a review of the editorial board of *Na rubezhe;* review the composition of literary consultancies; organize a system of support for the *litaktiv* of Komsomol'sk; create departments, to be accountable to the board, for poetry, criticism, and defense literature (*oboronnaia literatura*); establish general ties between all writers and the masses; establish specific ties with literary circles, in particular Korean and Chinese writers and the peoples of the North and writers in other languages; and provide individual tutorials in Russian language and literature to the Chinese and Korean writers Te Men Khi, Borit and Tin'-Shan'.[21]

Five days later, on 28 April, another board meeting was held with the participants including M. Alekseev, A. Gai, Tin'-Shan', Te Men Khi, and the "invited members" Emi Siao,[22] Tiutiunik, Tislenko, Potapov, Kon, and Titov.[23] Although the meeting was officially devoted to the "organization of political studies of the writers and the *litaktiv*," it aimed to implement a real structure that would incorporate ideologically and "professionally" the literary life of the region and its "spontaneous" manifestations. A new "circle devoted to the study of the speeches Stalin, Zhdanov, and Molotov had made during the February Plenum, and of the new Stalin Constitution" was attached to the board of the union. Together with another "circle" devoted to the study of the history of the party, it represented the apex of this structure. Analogous study circles were to be organized in Birobidzhan, Vladivostok, and other locations, with one or more personalities in charge of each. Moreover, the board recommended that unaffiliated writers (*pisateli-odinochki*) and the *litaktiv* join the political circles of the enterprises and social organizations where they resided. The unaffiliated writers could then be identified by name and place of residence, including Blagoveshchensk, Kolyma, Komsomol'sk, Voroshilovsk,[24] and the region of Ussuriisk. A letter of invitation was to be sent to them "no later than 3 May 1937." The board also came up with its own "Bureau of Rationalization and Inventions": at this meeting it was decided that further work with "young authors" would be rationalized through a network of literary circles from center to periphery and by "departments" (Russian, Chinese, Korean, Jewish, etc.).[25] Selected members of the board were put in charge of systematically tracking down the "new" literature published in all the region's journals and newspapers. Finally, a "Cabinet of the Novice Author" was to be organized in association with Dal'giz (the Far Eastern Publishing House) and Dal'kraiprofsovet (the Soviet of the Far Eastern Trade Union). The board of the Writers' Union was to put its library, with the exception of its archival materials, at the disposal of novice authors. At the same time, a new literary archive was to be organized.

Many other items were on the agenda of the 28 April meeting, and many other decisions and resolutions were taken. Mikhail Alekseev became "responsible editor" of *Na rubezhe,* and the journal's editorial policies were "restructured" in the spirit of collegiality and "vigilance." Elpidifor Titov was appointed tutor in Russian language to Te Men Khi and Tin'-Shan' and was assigned to assist "Comrade Leshak in the rewriting of his book."[26] Special measures were taken in regard to the "young writers" residing in Komsomol'sk-na-Amure: two brigades would be sent there to identify "young talents" and provide them with "literary consultations." Later, a ten-day visit to Khabarovsk would be organized for the most promising of them.

Much of this "restructuring" never saw the light of day, but Vasilii Azhaev was to benefit directly from some of what did. An addendum to the minutes of the 28 April meeting[27] includes a list of works in progress and a thematic plan of publication for 1937 of *Na rubezhe:* works by Batmanov, Titov, Te Men Khi, Bytovoi, and others, as well as an issue devoted to the creation of the Special Red-Bannered Far Eastern Army (OKDVA), with a portrait of Vasilii Blücher, the legendary commander of the People's Revolutionary Army and Special Far Eastern Army, on its cover. Azhaev's story "The Son" was not included in this plan, but for reasons that were not documented it appeared, as we already know, in the fourth (July–August) issue of 1937. This issue was devoted largely to poems and stories by newcomers, with the exception of an article by Iuliia Shestakova on "working with the novices," and several poems by Viacheslav Afanas'ev, N. Shalyi, and I. Kratt.[28] Obviously the Far Eastern branch of the Soviet Writers' Union was under formal (and actual) sus-

Vasilii Batmanov, chairman of the Far Eastern Radio Committee, 1937–38. (Photograph courtesy of the Federal Security Service of the Khabarovsk Region.)

pension during that time, when, as the minutes of July 1937 state explicitly, "all assets and responsibilities [were] handed over to the journal, including the work with the novice authors."[29] The fifth issue (September–October) of 1937 lists only an unnamed "editorial board" (*redkollegiia*).[30] From November 1937 to April 1939 *Na rubezhe* itself was suspended.[31] Khabarovsk and its writers in 1937 represented Azhaev's first borderline (*rubezh*). In *Far from Moscow,* as we have already seen, the city is named Rubezhansk.

Te Men Khi was arrested in 1937 and executed on 11 May 1938.[32] He was only one of the thousands of Soviet Koreans and Chinese who were targeted for "ethnic cleansing" in the Far East during this period.[33] Neither Vasilii Batmanov's agreement with Titov about "weaknesses on the theoretical and critical front" nor his "regrets" that Titov and Kulygin's play *Sergei Lazo* had not been published in *Na rubezhe* prevented Batmanov from bringing to the attention of the City Party Committee (Gorkom) Titov's suspect acquaintance with a poet and former employee of the Chinese Eastern Railway from Harbin.[34] Batmanov, himself the chairman of the Far Eastern Radio Committee, was arrested on 24 April 1938, sentenced to death on 8 September, and executed the same day.[35] Semen Bytovoi's denunciation of Titov in a letter addressed to the Party Committee of the newspaper *Tikhookeanskii komsomolets,* accusing him of collaboration with the Kolchak regime and other counterrevolutionary crimes, led to Titov's arrest on 5 August 1937 and his execution on 14 January 1938.[36] His wife, the physician Mariia Titova-Tumanova, was sentenced to ten years in a corrective labor camp.[37] Petr Kulygin, Titov's coauthor of *Sergei Lazo,* was shot on 7 August 1938.[38]

Lavrentii Lavrent'ev, first secretary of the Party Committee of the Far Eastern Region from 1933 to 1937, to whose "political standards" Mikhail Alekseev had referred "in part" on 26 November 1936, was removed from his post in January 1937 and executed in 1938. He had been close to Ian Gamarnik, chief of the Red Army's Political Administration and Politburo plenipotentiary to the Far East, who allegedly committed suicide on 31 May 1937.[39]

Marshal Vasilii Blücher was arrested on 22 October 1938 and died 9 November.[40] So did many others.[41]

THE NOTEBOOKS OF
KOMSOMOL'SK

Interestingly, I work as head of inspection, which means: organizer, administrator, investigator [*sledovatel'*], economist, technician (production and distribution), writer [*literator*], on special
assignments—from the preparation of lectures to qualified preparation of materials for the People's Commissariat, etc., cultural
and educational worker [*kul'tprosvetrabotnik*].
—Vasilii Azhaev, Komsomol'sk diary (19 March 1941)

While the Far Eastern branch of the Soviet Writers' Union was "cleansing" its ranks, "new talents" were on the rise. Azhaev was one of them. But
few traces survive from the three years and seven months (March 1937
to 24 October 1940) that he spent after his liberation as a free laborer of
the BAM. Among these traces are two letters from Azhaev found in the
Khabarovsk archives. They show how a young writer's career was linked to
personal connections. On 20 October 1939, Vasilii Azhaev informed the
Far Eastern writer Semen Bytovoi of his acceptance by the Gorky Literary
Institute in Moscow and of the fact that Bytovoi's intervention had not
produced the desired results. Azhaev was hinting at his efforts to be allowed more time for writing: his work as inspector of the Central Bureau
of Rationalization and Invention was time-consuming. One of the reasons
for the failure offered in the letter was that "Frenkel' [head of construction
of the Second Tracks] was absent." Azhaev asked Bytovoi to intervene
again. His letter also included a detailed plan for a volume of fourteen

stories and essays (some of them completed, others in progress) and requested the writer's help in getting them published at the Far Eastern Publishing House (Dal'giz). His second letter, dated 15 December, requested Bytovoi's assistance again, this time for a recommendation that would enable Azhaev to travel to Moscow, and for some advice. Worried about the fate of the region's journal,[1] the young author wondered whether he should send his new work to Moscow or Khabarovsk. The central office of the Writers' Union and *Pravda* had encouraged him "to strengthen his ties with the regional branch of the Union."[2] Azhaev had no other choice.

Azhaev's archive contains only a few works that clearly were written during this period: his story "The Son," which appeared in the July–August 1937 issue of *Na rubezhe,* and "Tarakany" (The Cockroaches), a novella to which Azhaev refers in his letter to Bytovoi but apparently never published.[3] Whereas "The Son" illustrates the blessings of reeducation, "Tarakany," written between 1938 and 1939, can be interpreted as Azhaev's own fantasized return to Moscow "by correspondence." At the beginning of the novella, the young protagonist, Leonid, wakes up in the middle of the night, his body literally covered with cockroaches. He is staying in the room of "Aunt Fedosia," an old acquaintance of his father's. Before the Revolution, Fedosia had worked as a nanny in the family of a rich manufacturer while Leonid's father was laboring like a convict in the same manufacturer's brick factory. The father had resented Fedosia's eating at the "bloodsucker's table" and had even accused her of "betraying the working class." During the Revolution, the manufacturer had fled abroad, and Leonid's father had testified to Fedosia's "class purity," compassionately declaring that she was a member of his own family. Now she returns the favor by lodging his son, who has come to Moscow for his studies. But the dark side of her past crawls out at night. The next morning Leonid leaves Aunt Fedosia's apartment and finds himself on the streets of Moscow. The contrast is overwhelming: Red Square, the Mausoleum, the Kremlin, everything is bright and clean. In his first classes at the institute Leonid outshines all the other students.

On 25 October 1940 Azhaev started work in the Administration of the Lower Amur Corrective Labor Camp in Komsomol'sk. His arrival coincided with the reorganization of the city's writers' association in the same spirit of "restructuring" and working with "novices" discussed by the Khabarovsk writers a few years before. In an article that appeared on 26 October 1940 in the newspaper *Stalinskii Komsomol'sk,* titled "To Educate the Writers of Komsomol'sk" and signed by Anatolii Gai and Nikolai Shalyi,[4] the Far Eastern branch of the Writers' Union, together with the local social organizations, were once more accused of failing to deal effectively with young writers. The production of these literary novices "depicted our reality in too superficial a manner"; their works represented "underdeveloped artistic mastery," "suffered from plagiarism," and were "sometimes simply illiterate." In order to give these new literary figures the support, advice, and political orientation they needed, the Party City Committee had decided to create a new writers' association (*literaturnoe ob"edinenie*), attached to the editorial board of *Stalinskii Komsomol'sk*. Azhaev would take all the advantage of this new opportunity he could.

"Smert' cheloveka" (The Death of a Human Being), found in the author's archive (and published in *Na rubezhe,* according to the "List of V. N. Azhaev's works, written in the Far East"),[5] seems to be one of the last essays written "far from Moscow" in which he attempted explicitly to overcome the trauma of his past: a man who killed his wife by accident is pardoned by her brother, who then leaves his sister's funeral to defend the project on which he has worked for many long years. The manuscript ends with a signed note: "Azhaev Vasilii Nikolaevich, senior inspector attached to the head of the Administration of the Lower Amur Camp of the NKVD, Komsomol'sk-on-the-Amur, 1940." A document bearing the same signature, dated 29 December 1940 and titled "Method of Acceleration and Price Reduction for Drilling Hard Rock by Means of Firmness Reduction," can be considered the real-life enclosure of the brother's project.[6] The hope of leaving the construction site for "literature" had turned out to be as illusory as that of regaining the status of a Soviet citizen in full possession of his rights. Bound by the "unbreakable oath" he had taken a few years earlier, Azhaev carried on with the montage of life and literature that had now merged in a single project.

I found two notebooks in Azhaev's archive, both signed and dated by the author. Because of the very small handwriting and the many abbreviations, they were difficult to read and could not be entirely deciphered. The first notebook, or, to be accurate, forty-five loose sheets of $9\frac{1}{2}''\times 3\frac{1}{2}''$ paper headed "Vas. Azhaev, year of 1940, city of Svobodnyi, Far East—city of Komsomol'sk-on-the-Amur,"[7] contains a series of scattered notes on daily life, details, anecdotes, thoughts, and quotations from readings. There are also several lists of expressions, including "camp vocabulary" and dialogues, songs, and poems; remembrances titled "Encounters, Details,

Four hundred young women disembark at Komsomol'sk in 1937. (Photograph courtesy
of the Museum of Local History, Komsomol'sk.)

Dates" (among them the fateful events of 29 December 1934, 11 March 1935,
and 16 March 1937);* a list of literary topics "realized in part" and "not yet
realized"; and sketches and outlines, some of which were put to use in
works we have already encountered. The stenographic report of a "meeting with the leadership [of the camp] in May '36" is noted as "leading toward an entirely new form" and making possible "the resurrection of the
human being." We understand these notes to refer to "Materials for the
novella on the Chekists" or some later version of it. Others refer to the future, such as the words on page 44: "Teisin in Nanai language means
'Abode of the Gods.' A horribly unattractive and filthy place." That sentence became the title of a chapter in *Far from Moscow* (bk. 3, chap. 6), the
only change an *a* for the *e* in Teisin. Was "Taisin" meant to hint at the island's "secrecy"?† At times the reader feels the breath of life in these notes:

---

*The dates of Azhaev's arrest, arrival in Svobodnyi, and release.
† The Russian word *taina* means "secret."

a passage explaining the origin of the toponym Fleishman's Leap, named after a "spectacled" engineer who fell down a *sopka** on the Komsomol'sk-Urgal line; an incident in the zone during which a criminal "chopped off the head of his comrade"; and a note on "literature" and "love," in which Azhaev says that "as a chemist and a writer," he "should know the elements of human grief."

The second notebook (220 6" × 5½" pages, with the signature of the author on the first page) can be regarded as Azhaev's diary for the periods 1 February to 31 May 1941 and 3 March to 28 September 1942.[8] It gives a very detailed account of his activities in Komsomol'sk, of his truly "poly-phonic" work, in which official duties, such as those of the "head of inspection attached to the Head of the Administration," combined with correspondence studies with the Gorky Literary Institute and, of course, writing.

The very first entry of 1 February 1941 introduces the topic of literature with the casual mention of one of its greatest names: "Trouble with the de-signers. Discussion about every chart, diagram, or map. Even Barabanov is satisfied. Kariakov. Zabolotskii, the poet. Derebenko, a Leningrad archi-tect." Here is what the investigator-technician-rationalize-writer Azhaev noted in his diary a month and a half later: "20 March 1941. Statement by Zabolotskii (poet, reddish face, physiognomy of an accountant). As to his case, he has been sentenced for counterrevolutionary Trotskyite activities. The commandant has ordered that I look into this matter [*Nachal'nik poruchil v nem razobrat'sia*]. He [i.e., Zabolotskii] requests work in his specialty, as a pedagogue. What kind of work should I give him?"[9]

Zabolotskii's letters from "there," published in 1989 in the journal *Znamia,* do not mention this encounter, but they indicate that his request was not granted.[10] In any case, he belonged to the past, like the unsuccess-ful writer, the "contemporary of the Symbolists," in Azhaev's "materials for a novella on the Chekists." What about the present? "People think well of me in Khabarovsk," says Azhaev's entry of 2 February 1941, which at-tributes this hearsay to Agishev, a fellow writer living in Komsomol'sk with his wife, the journalist and actress Serafima Plisetskaia, where Azhaev was a frequent guest. From another personal file, deposited in the archives of the Khabarovsk Administrative Region, we learn that "member of the Soviet Writers' Union of the USSR Agishev, Rustam Konstantinovich," born in 1913, journalist, member of the editorial board of *Stalinskii Komso-*

---

*Mountain or hill of the Far East.

Komsomol workers at a parade in honor of the fifth anniversary of the founding of Komsomol'sk, 1937. (Photograph courtesy of the Museum of Local History, Komsomol'sk.)

mol'sk, "was taken to court on account of the slander by an enemy of the people, but was released and entirely rehabilitated" and "joined the VKP(b) as a candidate member of the year 1941 in the city of Komsomol'sk."[11] The diary entry for 2 February also includes Azhaev's response to the report that "people think well" of him: "Why, I say, do they not publish my book? They say: it bleeds. And that it is naturalism, that one must not write about everyting. If they knew what naturalism was like!"[12]

Naturalism indeed inhabits Azhaev's diary. Here is what he wrote on 7–9 February 1941:

> Snowstorm. Everything is blown away. The cold is unbearable. Barabanov is sitting in his fur coat. The cars don't run and the trains have stopped. No communication. I work the day through, until four. I go home only to sleep. Lists. Regulations. I gave them to Figel'shtein. He liked it. . . . Karapetian told the following story: in the Vostlag,[13] toward Ust'——[illeg.], an old thief hit upon the idea of trying to escape. He stole some

money and documents. He had unrestricted circulation . . . the frightening picture of the foolish struggle of the fugitive with nature. He tried to
make a fire, tore some money to pieces, it didn't catch fire, he tried to do
the same with his documents, that failed too, then he walked away, and
fell. Typically, he was walking around the colony.[14]

For Azhaev, everyday life in the Nizhne-Amurlag administration was
less dramatic but busy. From morning to evening and often until late at
night he wrote endless reports, orders, accounts, completing paperwork
for his boss Barabanov about almost everything on earth, from timber exploitation to increased ventilation, from sanitary services to a speech for a
rally, from disciplinary investigations into some misappropriation of funds
to financial planning or milk ration allotments for the special colonies of
"mothers and children" (*kolonna mamok i detei*). Many events and names
are difficult to decode because the context is missing.

I finished the survey of the materials devoted to the colonies. It amounted
to 100 pages. I am very proud of this work, done for the first time in the
camps. . . . I looked into the matter of the embezzler Zhabrev. Wrote a report to the GUZhDS about the inspection. Worked on the materials concerning the orders on the financial situation of the camp. . . . Signed the
sentence for the rape of 5 women (5 March 1941). Made a report on the
control of the execution of the orders concerning the financial department.
Malen'chikov and Zhun'ko. Krupennikov. Zobnin. Blasorozov. Bol'shov.
Barabanov criticizes the poor utilization of person-days.[15] . . . (Barab-ov):
It is important to talk every day with the colony through the selector ap-
paratus. On the use of women (11 March 1941). . . . The whole day I've
been busy with the prosecution. Merezhko, Gotilev. Gol'denberg. The
hospital janitor [*sanitar*], the medic [*lekpomsha*]. Tunik. . . . Gorskii: the
workers supply the *zeks** with vodka [*rabochie snabzhaiut zekov vodkoi*]
(18 March 1941).[16]

But Azhaev's passion for belles lettres never flags. No wonder, then,
that we find "literature" where we least expect it: in a proposal concerning
the results of drilling tests, "about which I should write a novella, or a passage in a novel" (12 February 1941); in documents such as "regulations,
and principally important orders and memoranda"; in the shared passion

*Prisoners. From the abbreviation *z/k* (*zakliuchennyi*).

Two pages from Azhaev's Komsomol'sk diary. The first page (entry of 19 March 1941) enumerates the various functions that his duty as "head of inspection" entailed, from "organizer," "administrator," "economist," and "technician" to "writer," "investigator," and "special assignments." The entry of 20 March 1941, on the second page, describes his encounter with Nikolai Zabolotskii, whom he describes laconically as "poet, reddish face, physiognomy of an accountant."

(with his boss Barabanov) for "Malenkov's speech," where everything is expressed "to the point" and "is very relevant to matters of the camp" (17 February 1941).[17] A "resolution" (*postanovlenie*) that he composes for Barabanov "turns out to be very interesting: . . . a very concrete plan following the guidelines of the Eighteenth Party Conference, which is very popular in spirit, almost like a short story" (*kotoraia ochen' narodna, pochti kak rasskaz*) (21 February 1941).[18] The style of another resolution is described as "close to what Stendhal said about the Code Napoleon," that is, it reveals "utmost clarity and profoundness of thought" and can be compared to "literature" (*tozhe svoeobraznaia khudozhestvennaia literatura*) (17 February 1941). No wonder the style of Azhaev's duties permeates his own "literature":

7 March 1941. . . . Orders concerning the preparation for the spring and summer period: fire prevention and sanitary services in the camp. Answer from *Literaturnyi sovremennik* [The Literary Contemporary] about "A Foreword to Life": "This is not yet a story, but an abstract; even if it is written competently [*gramotno*], it sounds like a business letter." Signature: Livshitskii [?]. I was saddened: perhaps they are right, I'm not made for this activity, and when I think that something worked out well, it's not suitable. I wrote back with a critique of his "abstract" review. Went to the see the boss: about the organization of thorough verifications concerning questions of production and the fulfillment of the plan.[19]

Against all odds, Azhaev did his homework for Moscow: "I read *Igor's Tale* and Novikov's essay. Rabelais, Stendhal, *The Red and the Black*" (12 February 1941); "During the night I read Mstislavskii's article. Wrote a long letter to Zhenia Dolmatovskii" (23 February 1941); "I wrote a letter to Boris L., to Oleg, to Kuibyshev at the Institute. Worked a little. Letter about 'A Foreword to Life' and literary failures" (16 March 1941).[20]

Azhaev's letter to Dolmatovskii was published in 1982 as part of the poet's "recollections of the past," which included his old friend and protégé Vasilii Azhaev.[21] That same year a shorter version of Dolmatovskii's memoirs appeared in a Far Eastern anthology devoted to the fiftieth anniversary of the creation of the city of Komsomol'sk.[22] According to Dolmatovskii, Azhaev's letter "could have served as a foreword or afterword to the novel *Far from Moscow*, one of the most famous, and perhaps most important, literary works of the first postwar years." Dolmatovskii quoted the letter in its entirety because he "wanted to let the man reveal himself." I will follow his example here. Beyond self-revelation, the letter adds a dialogic component to the intimacy of the diary and, more important, it shows that Azhaev took his organizational work very seriously:

Hello!
You evidently had time to forget Azhaev—so he decided to remind you of him by his own initiative. I wanted to write you long ago, but I somehow couldn't get to it. But today is a special evening—free from duty, thinking about Moscow, remembering friends—I feel like talking, but there is no one to talk to.

In Komsomol'sk I felt depressed in the beginning, and then I got used to it. Let my new home be in Komsomol'sk. It is cold here, the temperature doesn't go above forty degrees.[23] Wind, snowstorms. There is not enough heat, even the stone houses can't keep the calories from escaping.

The wooden sheds are blown away, and the roof of our four-story administrative building was torn off.

The head of the construction, Barabanov, promised me during our first encounter to create suitable conditions for my literature and my studies, but after this he appointed me head of the inspection of the Administration, and my studies, literature, and all that were set aside. And what I expected happened: I found myself involved in exceptionally intense activity in terms of organization and production, the construction placed tons of responsibilities on my feeble shoulders, and nothing was left except work: day, evening, and night.

It is excitingly interesting to work with the construction boss, but difficult. He asks me to do more than anybody else and assigns me what is most difficult. Sometimes it seems that I lack the brains and strength to fulfill his demands. He requests, it is impossible to refuse, and the task is fulfilled (even for me) in the most extraordinary way. Unfortunately, it is difficult to tell you what I am working at, if I were able to, you would certainly envy me! This can be called organizational creation, that is, the aspect of creation that has the greatest direct impact on the world. The most important aspect of it is the fundamental transformation of the entire organizational system of the construction, based on very interesting principles (the project is his and mine). And besides—I participate directly in literally everything.

Due to my activity, and because the construction boss makes me the initiator of large-scale and minor initiatives, I have become almost prominent. True, this is more difficult than pleasant. Don't think that I don't write anything anymore. In my head and my notes the foundations of a novel are laid. The time has not yet come and it has not yet taken literary form, but ultimately it should be carved out as an equivalent of the tremendously active and complicated life that I am presently experiencing, and to which I have long since become drawn, avidly. In relation to this future life of mine, my present production looks nongenuine. I write (inspired by life, of course) novellas on love, and about such eternal topics as death. I have written several novellas; mainly about Moscow, about my Moscow life in principal—in December one wants to write about May. If you wish, I can send them to you.

I participate in the local literary life, it is true, by making partisan raids (the city is 8 kilometers from where I am). I publish stories, reports, and folklore. In Komsomol'sk a fairly strong group has been formed. I bear a grudge against Khabarovsk—they accepted a volume of stories, and now they keep persistently silent.

Here, in honor of the Eighteenth Party Conference, I contributed an interesting technical improvement concerning the accelerated drilling of tunnels and other objects. The experiments proceeded successfully—on the production site and in the laboratory the results showed up to 40 percent more labor productivity. The economists calculated: 4 million rubles in savings. If it turns out to be 10 times less, I'll still be completely satisfied.

The lead team (the heads of departments) don't like me very much because I am for them the source of all sorts of assignments, orders, and requirements that disturb their routine. I do my best to get used to it. I have to break the well-established order, a certain lack of discipline, superficial and shallow work. This team is older than me—there is a lot of hurt pride, grievances, and complaints.

Barabanov is a very complex man, intelligent and talented. A Bolshevik organizer about whom, to tell the truth, a journalist would invoke the term "icon" [*ikonopisnyi obraz*]. For the first time I met in my direct work a leader who profoundly understands his job, the human character, life. In life I'm not a schoolboy and not an American observer, but through him, by the common work we do, I get wiser every hour. I have learned almost not to sleep—I leave at nine in the morning, and I come back (home) at 2, 3, 4 in the night.

So you see that in my present existence I have been able to realize my aspiration to participate in life through three kinds of creativity: the work of an organizer and a leader, technical, and literary labor. I must admit that the last kind of creativity falls short and does not satisfy me, but, with god as a witness, I can say that this is not my fault. My exercises for the [Gorky] institute are in bad shape. I fear that Fedoseev has given up on me.[24] Besides all the rest, I have no books. I am supposed to write a work on Swift, but how can I do this when even *Gulliver* is missing? This depresses me. Oh, my studies—I have become an eternal student!

And the thought of my return to Moscow torments me. If I can prepare for the exams, if the construction lets me go, if the authorities in Moscow will not object, I'll come to Moscow in June.

My good one, I must have bored you by now. If you see Lebedev and Simonov, give them my greetings. Try and write to me, if only from time to time, and at greater length. It would be wonderful if you could come again and see us here. Well, all the best to you. Forgive the handwriting—it's cold here, my hands are frozen.

Your Vasilii[25]

The Petukhovka region of the Camp of the Lower Amur on the outskirts of Komsomol'sk, I

(Photograph by Ivan Panin, Komsomol'sk; reproduced with permission.)

The Petukhovka region today, incorporated within the city of Komsomol'sk. (Photograph by Ivan Panin, Komsomol'sk; reproduced with permission.)

Some of the events described in this letter were directly imported into *Far from Moscow:* "In Novinsk the snowstorm had been raging unabated for nearly three days. It knocked down fences and telegraph poles, tore up the flimsy little wooden sheds and dashed them to the ground. During the night a gust of wind tore off the roof of the four-storied head office building. It fell flat on the loose snowdrifts and looked from afar like a house buried to the roof in snow."[26]

Although the cold of Komsomol'sk caused the handwriting to "freeze" (in the literal and metaphorical sense), there were moments of joy and satisfaction as Azhaev achieved both minor and more major successes on the local literary front: "Varshavskii, and then Zhagir told me that 'Medved'' [The Bear] was broadcast with an introduction, where it was said— shows great promise, distinguishes himself by the originality of his form.[27] Evening, I prepared an order and a letter about timber violations, including prosecution, etc." (10 March 1941).[28] About a month later Azhaev wrote in his diary: "With the rise of the temperature, Komsomol'sk at once turned into the dirtiest place on the entire globe. Everything that was covered by the snow now comes to the surface" (6 April 1941).[29] But it seems that with the spring, "literary consultations" had reached the city: at a discussion of Azhaev's "Girl's Conversation," somebody points out that his "talent as a storyteller" is "close to Esenin's," even allowing for the "insincerity of his dialogue." Azhaev was also clearly among those "most promising young talents" invited to Khabarovsk. On 30 March 1941 one Eselev, evidently vice secretary of the resuscitated Far Eastern branch of the Soviet Writers' Union, speaks "very gently" (*ochen' miagko*) about Azhaev's recent literary production, about his "gift," his "irrepressible force, the talent to arouse emotion and the capacity to find a plot for this." According to Eselev, the young author understands literature "much better than we" and "finds it difficult to say trivial things." But, Eselev tells him, "your stories have not yet given the result that we expect from you" (30 March 1941).[30]

Some of Azhaev's publications on the weekly literary page of *Stalinskii Komsomol'sk* were explicitly devoted to "Soviet exotics": "On the Subject of One Oroch, Who Built a Road to Heaven,"[31] and "A Tungus Tale about the Fox" show the remnants of "superstition" among the natives of the Amur and the necessity of overcoming them in the new Soviet times.[32] "Nani at the Partisans" tells the story of the socialist transformation of a representative of the "small peoples of the North." Thanks to the heroic sacrifice of the Giliak (Nivkh) Taras, influenced by the Oroch Nani, a de-

tachment of Japanese occupiers is ambushed by Red partisans and liquidated.[33] Other works published by Azhaev in the Komsomol'sk newspaper tell the familiar story of heroism and overachievement on various
construction sites.[34]

In "a civilization amidst low literacy"—to borrow the title of a section
of Moshe Lewin's book *Russia/USSR/Russia: The Drive and Drift of a
Superstate*—the system had to produce its own poets, and we know that
Azhaev was a product of this process.[35] From his 8 March 1941 journal entry, we also learn that he actively participated in its reproduction: "I sent
for the prisoner Gusev. He came with some poetry. He is forty-two and
suddenly decided to write verses. Good taste and genuine poetic sense [*so
vkusom i nastoiashchim liricheskim chuvstvom*]. I took the verses, ordered
him to go back, promised some consultation (Dolmatovskii and Khabarovsk)."[36] The consultation seems to have worked: the name Gusev appears among the authors of the almanac *Na rubezhe* in 1946,[37] unless
this Gusev was his namesake from the Camp of the Baikal-Amur Main
Line who, ten years before, had been "responsible for the artistic part" of
Putearmeets.[38]

One who undoubtedly made the journey from Svobodnyi to Komsomol'sk was P. Zhagir, whom we remember as the coauthor with Azhaev of
"Chuzhoi kalendar'" (An Alien Calendar), published in the Camp Freedom press. It turns out that Zhagir was not only one of Azhaev's closest
friends at that time but also his most attentive reader, listener, and uncon-
ditional admirer. After dismissing one of Zhagir's stories as "mere journal-
ism" (*gazetnyi pustiachok*),[39] and challenging him to "do things in a big
way," that is, to aim for "great literature," Azhaev shares his thoughts about
the "great thing" that he himself is contemplating—a novel about himself, now at the stage of a story. Titled "Solar System," it depicts a man
who loses at each step vis-à-vis the other characters, but who wins in the
end. Then he reads Zhagir his "Smert' cheloveka" (Death of a Human Being): "Zhagir remained silent for five minutes. 'Overwhelming. This is
part of a bigger thing.' . . . I told him about the idea of the thing. The
world of emotions and of thoughts. . . . Insurmountable contradiction.
The subtler the feelings, the more difficult and accountable the behavior"
(13 April 1941).[40] Azhaev notes another of Zhagir's responses, after he gave
him "Razluka" ("Separation," not included in the author's lists) to read: "I
haven't read such a thing for a long time; this will never age." To Zhagir's
question whether "Razluka" is an autobiographical piece, our author replies—one could say quite professionally—"the important thing is the re-

sult," and he goes on to share with his friend his literary plans for the future: "I want to write a whole book of stories, novellas, and studies on the theme of love . . . on the dialectics of love (which, according to Rousseau makes the very stuff of the hero)" (20 April 1941).[41] Real friendship, however, can accommodate competition: an entry of 23 April reports Zhagir's triumphant phone call with the news that *Stalinskii Komsomol'sk* will publish his story but not Azhaev's.[42] Azhaev took no offense. As we shall see, he remained Zhagir's mentor long after Komsomol'sk.

Who, then, was Azhaev's mentor? Vasilii Arsent'evich Barabanov, head of the Administration of the Lower Amur Corrective Labor Camp, is present on almost every page of the diary. From a conversation with Aleksandra Ivanovna, Barabanov's wife, reported in the entry of 27 March 1941, we learn that Barabanov was no newcomer to the labor camp system and its construction sites.[43] Here are some highlights from her account. After graduating from the military academy in 1926 with the rank of engineer-economist, Barabanov headed the special department of the Central Asian military district in Tashkent.[44] Back in Moscow, he became plenipotentiary of the special department of the OGPU and then its deputy head. He worked in various camps, including the camp of the Moscow-Volga Canal, where he was head of the "third section" and deputy head of the administration.[45] Owing to "difficult relations" with Firin, Kogan, and Berman, and to his "fierce criticism" of the Gulag leadership, Barabanov was expelled from the party, stripped of all rank, and sent (as administrator) to the North.[46] First came the corrective labor camps, then the coal mines (*ITL, potom ugol'*). He was driven from one place to the other. In 1936 he read about Firin and Kogan. "'Good news,' he said to his wife."[47] At the end of 1937 he returned to Moscow. "For twenty-two days," Aleksandra Ivanovna told Azhaev, "we traveled using reindeer and dogs from Vorkuta with our two daughters (Lena was four)." Frenkel' (head of construction of the second track) offered him work, so Barabanov again left for the Far East as his assistant.[48]

We read in *Far From Moscow*: "Beridze gazed in admiration at Batmanov standing there tall, broad-shouldered in his white sheepskin jacket and a cap in the form of a helmet; in some sense he resembled one of those knights [*bogatyrei*] of an old Russian tale, only the shield and the sword were missing. His gray eyes reflected the fire of the sunset."[49] The distance between Azhaev's "fantasy object" and its Komsomol'sk embodiment can be measured by the shifting forms of personal distance and proximity: "Barabanov is sitting in his fur coat"; "Barabanov came to the rally wearing a new blouse"; "Barabanov added in the margin of the report: 'solitary confinement cell' [*shtrafizoliator*]"; "V. A. [Vasilii Arsent'evich] clasped me in his arms, cried on my shoulder: 'You [*ty*] are the only one here who is close to me'" (the scene occurs after several glasses of vodka); "The boss likes to be comfortable and to have people look after him. He can't stand to be confronted with the details of everyday life."[50]

While it was precisely Azhaev's duty to ensure that his boss was not "confronted with the details of everyday life," Barabanov did not attain Commander Filippov's level of "kindness and joy" in regard to the young litterateur, but his interest in literature cannot be denied. Azhaev recorded in his diary (28 March 1941): "We had interesting discussions. V. A. is very well read and has clear judgment on everything, about our cinema, our literature (shows very often good taste); he was ecstatic about Mstislavskii's article concerning the writer's mastery (where it talks about the necessity of fully participating in life and about how literature turns out to be authentic when it becomes part of life)."[51]

On 14 May 1941 Barabanov granted Azhaev a three-month leave so that he could go to Moscow and take his exams at the Gorky Literary Institute. The entries in Azhaev's diary prior to 14 May consist of increasingly desperate declarations about the importance of this trip and, even more important, his civil status. He was, after all, a "free laborer" who had been sentenced for "counterrevolutionary agitation":

> A sense of injustice weighs upon me. I can have no complaints toward the State, to my State to which I give everything, including my life, but its officials are committing a distinct injustice in my regard. Why must I convince myself that I am evil because I was sentenced in 1934? . . . Everybody is interested: will B-v let me go or not? Nobody knows that no matter what the decision, it won't solve my problems (10 May). . . . I bear no grudge against anybody, I am able to understand everything, but the heart doesn't follow. The more ardently I serve my people and my government, the more absurd, painful, and morally unbearable becomes my situation of half-citizen (14 May).[52]

The diary also mentions some correspondence with the Main Administration of Camps (GULAG), and evaluations written on Azhaev's behalf by people who "love him earnestly" and by others who "hate him." What these letters concerned is made clear in Azhaev's 1946 "autobiography":

"The conviction, with all its attendant restrictions, was expunged by petition of the commanding authorities . . . by resolution of the Special Board
of the People's Commissariat of Internal Affairs of 7 July 1941."

By 22 May, Azhaev was on his way to Moscow: "In the dining car a
Japanese wipes the cutlery with disgust. My country, how huge you are,
it takes the fast train eight days to reach the capital" (24 May 1941).[53] He
thinks about "Valentina," his "beloved Valia" (a name mentioned here for
the first time), and feverishly prepares for his exams: "The most important
thing: not to flunk these exams, otherwise shame on me, better not show
up before Ev. A."[54] Azhaev's diary of 1941 ends with an entry dated 31 May:
"I am back. Father and Valiusha* have come to meet me. She is clinging to
my neck and looks and cannot believe. In her eyes the suffering, immensity, love. They took me by the hand and we walked to the car, amidst the
crowd. Here she is, my Moscow. Hello my dear ones, my city, my family!"[55]

A month later Azhaev's conviction was expunged, but he neither stayed
in Moscow nor was drafted for the Great Patriotic War, which had started
on 22 June. Blind in one eye, he was unfit for service. Moreover, he still
had to keep his promise, the unbreakable oath he had sworn. The first
lines of *Far from Moscow* could not better convey what he must have felt as
he left the city once again: "Not until the very last moment did engineer
Aleksei Kovshov believe that he was really going out to the East, deep into
the country's hinterland. When he was told at the Central Administration
that his appointment had finally been decided upon, he was overcome
by a feeling of depression, and he listened apathetically to the hasty instructions given him in the personnel department as if they did not concern him."[56]

The second part of Azhaev's Komsomol'sk diary also begins with a departure: Barabanov and "half of the administration," including a certain
"F." with whom Azhaev is in love, leave for Saratov on 3 March 1942.[57]
From the scattered archival material to which I had only indirect access,[58]
Barabanov's departure appears to have been an administrative maneuver to
cover up shortcomings through dismissals that had no serious consequences
for the dismissed, who were simply assigned other responsibilities.

What was the shortcoming in this case? In a letter of 30 June 1942 addressed to Grigorii Ivanovich Shatalin, First Party Secretary of the Khabarovsk *kraikom,* from one Mikhailov, "instructor of the Department of

---

*Diminutive of Valia (itself a diminutive of Valentina).

Fuel Exploitation of the Regional Committee of the VKP(b)," Barabanov
and other leaders are accused of being personally responsible for the catastrophic state of work on Project No. 15. According to Mikhailov, the section of pipeline laid on the mainland by the sixth division the year before
was in need of reconstruction, for "the head of the Camp of the Lower
Amur and the head of the political department shifted their responsibilities onto the commanders of the divisions, who in turn gave them to their
own subordinates." Moreover, "Barabanov, the head of the camp, visited
the construction site only once a year (and then only before his report to
the regional bureau and after the resolution of the Council of the People's
Commissars of the USSR)," while the visits of the head of the political
department "resembled those of someone off on a tour" (*nosili gastrol' nyi
kharakter*)."[59] Another document, dated 29 September 1942 and headed
"Act of the Government Committee on the Delivery of the Industrial Exploitation of the Pipeline Okha-on-Sakhalin–Village of Sofiiskoe-on-the-
Amur, and Materials Related to It," identifies G. M. Orentlikherman, not
Barabanov, as head of the Lower Amur Corrective Labor Camp and Project No. 15.[60] What may surprise the reader is that the conclusions of the
government committee are positive overall, totally contradicting Mikhailov's charges as well as the findings articulated by the Bureau of Pipeline
Operations of Dal'neftekombinat on 28 July 1944. According to the committee, "the Lower Amur Corrective Labor Camp, working in the difficult
conditions of the taiga and using accelerated construction methods," completed the pipeline from Okha to Sofiiskoe "ahead of schedule" and at
a savings of "18 percent of the budget allocation." The committee assures
us that the resulting pipeline was of "high quality."[61] One month later, on
30 October 1942, a decree of the Supreme Soviet of the USSR rewarded a
number of "construction workers of special projects." The decree was
printed on the front page of *Tikhookeanskaia zvezda* on 3 November 1942.
Many of the names mentioned there are directly related to Project No. 15,
and help us to identify who was who in *Far from Moscow*. (This document
is reproduced in the Appendix.)

Azhaev's diary entries from 3 March to the end of September 1942 are
difficult to decipher. Does his deteriorated handwriting reflect the increasing complications of his professional and private life? We do not know exactly when Azhaev was "assistant to the Head" or "deputy head of inspection attached to the Head of the Oversight and Planning Department," or
when he became "head of the Industrial Department,"[62] but in March

1942 his routine was disrupted by new responsibilities and some troubles of the heart:

> March 7. Very sad days. Torn feelings. To wait, to leave, or not. A telegram from Buianov,[63] but here [in Komsomol'sk] they don't want to let me go, some answers are being prepared. The question is principally unresolved. . . . B——v's [Barabanov's] maxim: remember everything, manage by yourself, expect no instructions from others. And everywhere, signs of F. Nowhere to go. . . . I cannot visit the places where we walked together, I cannot sit on the riverbank. Pain. Clearly, another image has intruded into F.'s image, undoubtedly much closer, dearer, and larger—that of my bright star V.
> March 8. Report of renewed air attacks on Moscow.[64]

Thoughts about "F." and "V." and news from the war dominate Azhaev's entries for early spring 1942. He thinks of the "great example of Zoia Kosmodem'ianskaia (Tania). . . . The luminous image, elevated by the sacrificial feat" (Zoia Anatol'evna Kosmodem'ianskaia—Tania was her partisan name—had perished as a martyr of the Great Patriotic War on 29 November 1941). "I saw F. in my dream" (12–14 March 1942). On 18 March, however, a telegram from "V." makes Azhaev "scream with joy."

> My star, you are alive. . . . I left you, all that I love most in the world— you, Father, and Moscow. And the three of you were subject to a terrible danger that did not threaten me. Objectively you know that I am not at fault here, but subjectively I was ashamed (and I am still ashamed) when I think about it. When will I see you? Every morning I get up with an intense pain in my soul: perhaps during this night my Valia is no more. What injustice to lose you, my dear one, my young one, my beautiful one, my dear Muscovite. For several months there was no news about you, then I heard where you were. And I was even more proud of you and I worried even more and now you are alive, you exist.[65]

Those who have read *Far from Moscow* will realize that this passage contains the key to understanding, the very origin in reality, of one of the important subplots of the novel: the engineer Aleksei Kovshov's "heroic" struggle to remain faithful to his wife, Zina, who had stayed behind the German lines as a partisan fighter, and not to succumb to his feelings for the sexy accountant in the economic department, Zhenia Kozlova, on the banks of the river Adun. Created out of life's own contradiction, this sub-plot was made up of "V." and "F." and other elements about which we shall learn later.

"As a chemist and a writer," Azhaev knew "the elements of human grief." He also knew, or had learned by now, how to combine these ele-ments in a compound that would hold, in the "plurality of spaces . . . in the totality of one project." As for reality, some passages from Azhaev's in-creasingly sporadic diary tell us about the "difficulty of working with-out Barabanov" (that is, with his successors Orentlikherman and his dep-uty Akimov[66]), increasing problems at the GUZhDS, a second trip to Moscow ("decided by Goglidze[67] and Buianov"), another encounter with Valia, news of Azhaev's marriage (to "F."?), and a reference to the fact that "in the GUZhDS the plan is changed again by a decree of the People's Commissariat" (11 August 1942).[68] Azhaev was probably hinting here at the reorientation to which the Camp of the Lower Amur was subject at that time, namely, the interruption of work on the pipeline from Sofiiskoe to Komsomol'sk and the undertaking of other tasks related to the war sit-uation, such as the construction of Project No. 500, that is, the construc-tion of the Komsomol'sk–Sovetskaia Gavan' Railway.[69]

Dolmatovskii's memoirs again intersect with Azhaev's diary:

> We started to write to each other. From his letters I learned that he went to Moscow, for a session of correspondence students, where he saw his friends Boris Lebedev and Konstantin Simonov; I learned that in Mos-cow, at the institute, there was some sad love story, which quickly came to an end. It would not have cost him much effort to stay at home, but his word, given to the head of the construction, was sacred for Azhaev, and without delay he went back to Komsomol'sk-on-the-Amur.[70]

It may be that Azhaev returned to honor more than one word given. According to later accounts, Azhaev had married a certain Anna Iosifovna in Komsomol'sk. Whether she was identical with "F." cannot be estab-lished. According to the Far Eastern writer Iuliia Shestakova, Anna Iosi-fovna was much older than Azhaev, of Jewish origin, not beautiful "but a very good person." Shestakova also remembers that Anna Iosifovna had some family ties with a "very important commander of the camps."[71] Ivan Vasil'evich Panin, photocorrespondent for the newspaper *Stalinskii Kom-somol'sk* during the late 1930s and early 1940s, recalls that Azhaev's first wife was a secretary to Major-General I. G. Petrenko, head of the Lower Amur Corrective Labor Camp at that time.[72]

In any case, Azhaev's diary indicates that on 25 August 1942 he took another series of examinations at the Gorky Literary Institute. Then, on 20 September, he boarded a train from Moscow to the Far East, asking himself, "When will I write about railway stations, these receptacles of bitter parting?"[73] Indeed, if the "beautiful" was not necessarily part of "life," there was always "literature" to fall back on: the last pages of Azhaev's Komsomol'sk diary, written on a train heading from Irkutsk to Khabarovsk on 28 September 1942, were filled with a list of twenty works he hoped to complete in the future, including *Nefteprovod: Povest'* (The Pipeline: A Novella).[74] The montage of Project No. 15 had begun at the very moment of its interruption in reality.

8

FAR FROM MOSCOW

Not long ago I borrowed some books by local authors from
Zalkind. And would you believe it, nearly all of them wax ecstatic
about the taiga! And it isn't only local writers who gush about it.
You get the same glowing description of wild vines entwining the
tree trunks, of the wonderful birds and beasts, the Gol'd [Nanai]
and Udege with their primitive customs, canoes hewn out of a
single log, cloudberries. . . . Arsen'ev wrote some fine stuff about
all this in his time—why repeat him? Why don't the modern authors write about the Gol'd and the Udege who have graduated
from institutes and brought new life to their settlements? Why
don't they write verses and novels about men like Terekhov, for
instance, and his plant?

"What's wrong with us two as heroes of some novel?"
Beridze asked wickedly and flung his snowball far into the distance.
—*Far from Moscow*, book 2, chapter 1

He liked to think that he and all the other men of the section out
here at the eastern extremity were the first in the country to
greet the dawn of the working day, an honor which they perhaps
shared only with the frontier guards. A strange and wonderful
sense of power swept over him and he squared his shoulders,
barely suppressing a happy laugh. That sense of power came to
him like a warm wind from the whole of his native land. Vasilii
Maksimovich Batmanov, a Soviet man, was no jackstraw without
kith or kin. He was fond of recalling that Russian pioneers had once

been here, and that Nevel'skoi [1] had sailed in these waters. . . .
How much stronger than he was Batmanov, sent out here at the
head of an immense collective and with all the resources of modern science and engineeering at his command!

—*Far from Moscow*, book 3, chapter 2

C ertain questions about the authenticity of *Far from Moscow* were
raised from within, and from the very outset. According to a rumor that
seems to have been limited to the immediate audience of the novel, namely,
the Far Eastern readers in the know, Azhaev had not actually written the
book himself but had used materials by a prisoner from the camp of
the Lower Amur.[2] Ivan Panin, former photocorrespondent for *Stalinskii
Komsomol'sk,* believed this rumor to have been spread by the Komsomol'sk
writer Aleksandr Grachev shortly after the novel was published in *Novyi
mir* in 1948.[3]

One of the original builders of the city of Komsomol'sk, Grachev
came to the village of Permskoe (founded by peasants from central Russia
during the second half of the nineteenth century) in 1932 with the first
Komsomol brigades. The city's first teacher and school director, he was
also one of its first writers, and he may have bitterly resented the awarding
of the Stalin Prize to a newcomer.[4] Azhaev's archive contains a letter in
which Grachev asks the author of *Far from Moscow* to arrange an invitation for him to the All-Union Writers' Congress of 1954, and reports on
the progress of his novel *Pervaia proseka* (The First Breach).[5] Did Azhaev
fail to respond? During my visit to Komsomol'sk in August 1995, I heard
another version of the novel's authorship, according to which a certain
Zhagirnovskii had written *Far from Moscow.* Was this person identical with
Zhagir, Azhaev's admirer and, at times, his competitor?

A series of documents in Azhaev's archive testifies to the various raw
materials that were used to manufacture his novel. Some are manuscripts
relating to earlier stages of writing and were written on long sheets of
paper ($18'' \times 4\frac{1}{3}''$) apparently cut from factory blueprints. Others are fair
copies of these earlier manuscripts, some of which are copies of copies. A
notebook headed "Materialy k 'Daleko ot Moskvy'" (Materials for *Far from*

Moscow) contains the following notes and documents: a report from an expedition "along the Nanai camp sites" by N. I. Riabov;[6] a report by "Belov, Nikolai Maksimovich, former head of the Pogibi division of Project No. 15, on the subject of his work on the construction"; two official telegrams concerning the early completion of the section of the pipeline across the Nevel'skii Strait in March 1942; "G. D. Chkheidze's opinion of and in relation to the novel *Far from Moscow*";[7] notes "on winter landscape," numbered one to forty-seven; notes "on the taiga of the Far East," with different (also numbered) sections on the kinds of forests, their geographic locations, various "routes," and "seasonal changes"; and a last section on "details—situations, portraits, psychological characteristics, examples of dialogues, aphorisms, thoughts, jokes."

The descriptions of nature and people, the geographic and botanical sketches copied from encyclopedias or Far Eastern geographies, the technical details on excavators and suction dredges, an electric welding machine and a "double-handled model of a saw," and the snatches of dialogue from life all give us a unique insight into Azhaev's literary laboratory of "rationalization and invention." These materials are thoroughly written out, well presented, and completely legible, with titles and subtitles underlined and numbered. The pages of the notebook are themselves numbered from 1 to 53 (including a few blank ones), and the first page contains, as in an exemplary school binder, Azhaev's signature and address: "Khabarovsk, Karl-Marx Street 15, apt. 8." It is clear that these materials were compiled and organized in their ultimate version *after* the novel was written. Not everything in Azhaev's archive, of course, could undergo the same treatment; some of it escaped "rationalization." But, together with the novel, these materials "[engender] a plurality of spaces in the totality of one project." In other words, everything was part and parcel of one "montage of life." At the same time, it is precisely here, in the a posteriori preparation of these materials vis-à-vis their literary embodiment, that the montage of life is dispossessed of literature. Or should we say that literature here becomes secondary in relation to its archive? Is it because things were not told the way they "should" have been that the novelist needed to bolster their sources?

In *Arctic Mirrors* Yuri Slezkine writes about the changes undergone by the "small peoples of the North" on the "Long Journey" from ethnic backwardness to communism: "With the leap definitely accomplished by the mid-1930s, the Long Journey became a historical theme, which could be introduced as a series of flashbacks by a triumphant but now serene protagonist."[8] Seen from the standpoint of "Soviet exotics"—those new Soviet men and women forged from "what we have built here, from what we conquered"—the history of the small peoples of the North is yet another instance of the familiar "varnishing" of reality, in which not only a people's way of life but even nature itself has been "reforged." As N. I. Riabov's report on his expedition "along the Nanai camp sites" confirms, "the Nanai embraced the collective farm system very naturally and willingly because they had not developed proprietary instincts. . . . Before, the Nanai had built their *fanzas** collectively, now they collectively build schools and clubs."[9] *Far from Moscow,* in turn, confirms the findings of Riabov's ethnography:

> "Expedition come!" the youngsters shouted. "Expedition come!"
>
> "They mean us—'expedition come,'" Beridze said with a laugh. "By the way, you'll get a chance to see the new Gol'd [Nanai] here. I advise you to observe their life and customs at Tyvlin. It's one of the biggest camps on the Adun. . . . They had to leap from the Stone Age straight into ours, the Soviet Age."[10]

"The first secretary of the District Committee is a Nanai, all chairmen of the collective farms are Nanai. There are Nanai teachers, Nanai veterinarians and physicians, and they even have their own apiarist," wrote N. I. Riabov. Azhaev then applied this information to his novel: "You obviously take us for some expedition or other. We belong to the construction job," Beridze says to Khodzher, the chairman of the village soviet, who was "wearing a sheepskin coat, taller than the rest, with a broad face and high cheekbones. . . . Khodzher and the rest of the Nanai laughed heartily, a laugh that was childlike in its spontaneity." We, like Beridze and Kovshov, are not surprised to discover that this Nanai village, having completed its "Long Journey," resembles "an ordinary Russian village with a long broad street flanked by sturdy log houses" and that there is no sign here of any of "those squat huts and little sheds on piles which the engineers had met in the other Nanai camps along the Adun." The "typical" and space for future progress are nevertheless maintained by the continued existence of certain purely local (i.e., un-Russian) phenomena. For example, "The Nanai took their water from the river, there weren't yet any wells." Other

---

*Ethnic village constructions, also found in China and Korea.

observations from Riabov's expedition, such as the survival of shamanism or the fact that "after the liquidation of the Nanai-language newspaper and the theater during the war years . . . the majority of songs and ditties were translations from the Russian," also found their way into *Far from Moscow*. Chapter 3 of book 2 describes in detail the debunking of a local shaman by a mini–show trial "in camera," during which Khodzher and his villagers display a high degree of "vigilance" and political maturity. Shortly after this scene, a young Nanai student "treats his companions to a performance of the operetta *Sylva,* which he had seen in the Rubezhansk theater of musical comedy."[11] Sometimes the novel resolves some of the contradictions of real life which had surfaced in Riabov's report. "What are the Nanai?" Riabov asked, "Farmers or hunters and fishers? For now, the controversy takes place within the directional-planning organizations, each collective farm holding to its own position. During the war, agriculture progressed. The argument to 'let them be engaged in hunting or fishing' is not unreasonable. Life itself dictates the survival of traditional forms of economy."[12]

In *Far from Moscow,* life has unequivocally completed the Long Journey from primitive forms to Soviet exotics: the engineers are served pickled cucumbers (a traditional *Russian* dish) from the vegetable garden of Katia Khodzher, whose husband explains that "vegetables and livestock yield an even bigger return than fish."[13] Riabov's expedition report and *Far from Moscow* coincide at other, more fundamental points, for example, on the fact that, contrary to what previous explorers had claimed, the Nanai were not "lazy and unfit for work." In *Far from Moscow* they "go out to work as if to a festival," and, above all, they "have become their own masters."[14]

In *Far from Moscow* we see that even the natural environment has taken the Long Journey to become the proper setting for Soviet exotics: Azhaev's images of "suns" and "moons," or of the "hoarfrost" that traces "a multitude of petals on the ice of the Adun . . . like diamond flowers growing out of the river bed," or of "the riot of vegetation," the "sinister dark green or black moss," the elms and Manchurian oaks, and other specimens of Far Eastern landscape and botany, all oppose (symbolically) and proceed (historically) Katia's (Russian) vegetable garden and the Novinsk oil refinery. This reforging of nature, this Long Journey to make it a fit environment for Soviet exotics, involves an "active fight" against the "wild thickets . . . where no living man has ever set foot." For "no one knows

better than the Far Easterners that these huge tracts occupied by the endless taiga are no more than blank patches on the map, terra incognita. They
should be wiped out, not glorified!"[15] The climax of the struggle against
nature in *Far from Moscow* is reached when the builders launch a general
offensive against the taiga on the island of Taisin to cut a breach for the
pipeline. This is a scene of veritable rape, powered by Silin, one of the men
who participates in the operation, and whose name comes from the Russian word for "strength."[16]

> "This, Comrade Chief Engineer, is one of those blank patches on the map
> we have often spoken about and will now have to tackle," Aleksei ob-
> served. . . .
>   An endless chain of trucks with men moved along the ice. Huge trac-
> tors with powerful bulldozers crawled slowly with clanking treads. The
> voices of the men and engines mingled in a single roar, the grim and mar-
> tial music of the assault. . . .
>   The tractors snarled and the trees fell with a defeaning crash. Clouds
> of snow dust shot up in the air, wreathing the forest as if with the smoke
> of a battle. The taiga resounded with a startled hum. Silin, his face burn-
> ing with excitement, looked around and shouted:
>   "Give it to her, give it to the taiga! There. No you don't. . . . Not if I
> can help it! You're coming down. . . . That's the stuff! Go for it, Silin!"[17]

The document in Azhaev's archive that would probably be of most interest to the historian of the construction of the Okha-Sofiiskoe pipeline is
the account by Nikolai Maksimovich Belov, the former head of the second
(Pogibi) division of Project No. 15 on Sakhalin.[18] Belov's recollections were
evidently used by the author of *Far from Moscow* to construct his plot from
the moment the two engineers Aleksei Kovshov and Beridze head out on
their skis to inspect the various sections of the project, from Novinsk to
the "last works section on the mainland," beyond which "lay the strait,
and there, at last, the island of Taisin." This episode constitutes most of
books 2 and 3, with book 1 covering the bureaucratic aspects of the plot
(and the struggle between proponents of the "right" and "left" banks of
the Adun), aspects of which Azhaev had experienced firsthand through his
own work in the Administration of the Camp of the Lower Amur. Here
are some excerpts from Belov's account; together with the corresponding
passages in *Far from Moscow,* they give us further insight into Azhaev's
montage of Project No. 15:

Belov:
I receive an order and travel to the new site. In May 1942, I was called from Pivan'* by the commander of the construction, Com. Orentlikherman, who read me Stalin's telegram concerning the deadline for the construction of 1 September and invited me to travel with him to the construction site if my health was good enough. Despite the fact that I didn't feel very well (I had been sick some time before), I immediately agreed, because I had not been able to go to the front and I wanted to work here, in the rear, on the most serious and difficult section.

Far from Moscow:
It amazed Batmanov that Stalin had found the time to give attention to the report about the pipeline construction at a moment when the terrible Battle of Moscow was raging. Not a single battle at the front or the rear was fought without Stalin's participation—his genius inspired every general and soldier of the fighting army, every leader and worker of the labor army. At the end of August, before the construction chief had left for the Far East by plane, Stalin had also found time to receive him. Before dismissing Batmanov, Stalin had told him what he had probably told other industrial commanders. He had said that it was necessary to wage a ruthless struggle against people infected with peacetime moods, to fight these moods in oneself and in others, wherever they might reveal themselves. Men of such temper would maintain that the pipeline could not be built in even three years. Stalin had made it incumbent on Batmanov to go into that matter himself. The leader held out his hand to Batmanov and concluded the interview with a phrase that often afterwards rang in Batmanov's ears: "I wish you success, Comrade Batmanov!" (bk. 2, chap. 11, pp. 387–388)

The *Dal'nii Vostok* (1946–48) version of *Far from Moscow* does not contain the passage about the "ruthless struggle against people infected with peacetime moods," which was added during Azhaev's rewriting of the novel under Konstantin Simonov's direction in 1948. A manuscript page inserted in the typescript of a previous version of the novel (containing various traces of Simonov's pen) shows that the whole passage on Batmanov's encounter with Stalin was rewritten. The earlier version contained,

*Station on the right bank of the Amur, facing Komsomol'sk, on the Komsomol'sk–Sovetskaia Gavan' Railway line.

among other things, a lengthy explanation by Stalin of the rationale for building the pipeline in one year. By 1948 other priorities had surfaced, such as the campaigns against "antipatriotic" elements in Soviet society launched during the postwar years.

Belov:

15 May, we left Komsomol'sk by the motor launch *Perl,* together with Orentlikherman, Kuchera, Bondarenko, and Badiul.[19] After two days we arrived in Sofiiskoe. There, a meeting of the Sofiiskoe division was called during which the leaders of the construction and the Party organizer put forward new tasks; during this meeting I understood for the first time the significance and the huge scale of the construction. Com. Stalin himself was in charge of it.

The leadership stayed in Sofiiskoe, and I myself, Bondarenko, and Badiul set off on horseback to the strait, where we were to cross over to the island. It was already decided that Bondarenko and I would work there.

During our entire journey, we followed the line. Most of the time there was a log road [*lezhnevka*], but it was very bad. There were no settlements whatsoever, the grass hadn't yet come up, therefore we suffered a lot with the horses. We rode for five days. We took a bath in the river Iai. We forced our way through De-Kastri with great difficulty. The ice was breaking and melting everywhere; at times we had to ford the river.

On the mainland before De-Kastri a breach had already been made, some pipes were strung out, some of them already welded together. There were sections where the tubes were already dug in. After De-Kastri, nothing had been done yet.

Far from Moscow:

The engineers had the sun's company on the second day, too, and on the third and fourth. At first they seemed to think there was too much of it on the river, for its glare dazzled their eyes. But after a while they got used to the unvarying brilliance, as they did to the continuous traveling. They crossed and recrossed the Adun many times and explored all the bends of its arms and channels, its gradients and bluffs on both banks. They dropped in at all the villages and questioned the inhabitants closely about all the river's habits and its fullest flood tides. With the help of the section workers they measured the thickness of the ice, sounded the depths and determined the speed of the current scores and times. The engineers' notebooks were filled with fresh notes and their topographical maps embellished with new lines of corrections. They were now able to measure and inspect every meter of the line, and see for themselves that the builders had settled on the left bank and forgotten about the right. (bk. 2, chap. 1, p. 15)

Belov:
22 May, we reached Cape Lazarevo, settled in to wait for the commander, and looked around. What evidence of the section existed here on the strait? There was a colony of four barracks and two small houses. All around there was the forest, but it was rather sparse. They were digging out foundation pits under the pumping station, two portable power plants were running, the tubes had not yet been delivered. We lodged ourselves in the stable, separated from the common barrack by slabs. On the cape, everything looked strangely disorganized. Discipline was nonexistent, and almost nobody was working. Every day in the club (in the barracks), they showed a movie: *Bogdan Khmelnitsky, Alexander Nevsky,* etc.[20] We stuffed ourselves with *navaga.** Morale was uncertain: we waited for the new leadership, we awaited changes.

On 4 June a terrible storm came up, which covered everything with snow. The whole population of the section was sent out to clear the roads, to dig out the buildings, etc. We were sitting there, waiting and getting nervous, and not knowing our further destination.

Finally, the boss arrived; he said that we would cross the strait at the first opportunity. He got busy with things at Cape Lazarevo, and we continued to wait.

We sat there another couple of days. The ice in the Tatar Strait was still holding firm on the fringes, while it was constantly moving in the middle. The cutters were not yet running, and we were told that the navigation would not start for ten days. But it was impossible to wait any longer, for every day was precious for the job on the island, so the boss and Kuchera gave the order for departure.

Far from Moscow:
So This Is the World's End!
The Adun was left behind. This was the second day that Batmanov and his companions were traveling over Merzliakov's area—the last works section on the mainland. Beyond that lay the strait, and there, at last, the island of Taisin. . . .

*A small fish of the cod family.

There was a good deal at the near sections which had gladdened the eye—the winter road with its strings of trucks and horse trains, the little blockpost houses, the settlements, the pipes lying in stacks and strung out, and the bustling activity of thousands of men. Here there was nothing of the kind: only a clearing in the taiga, and here and there evidence of an attempt to build a motor-car road. The only visible structures were several roughly built sheds intended as stores, but even these were empty. The people here apparently had not yet started to transport foodstuffs, pipes, materials, and equipment from the strait to the interior of the mainland.

"The section is dead and deserted," Batmanov said, worried and indignant. "Where are the men we sent out here?" . . .

They went up to the center of the building, where the foundation for the diesel pumping station was being dug. Workers in padded jackets were breaking the frozen rocklike earth with pickaxes and crowbars. Several pairs of men were removing the earth on handbarrows. Two bonfires glowed at the bottom of the pit, around which another three dozen or so workers were warming themselves. . . .

Inside the barrack—a ramshackle, hastily built log house—it was dark. An oil lamp standing on a long table did not provide sufficient light for the whole barrack. Men in padded jackets, *valenki*,* and fur caps lay on the double-tiered bunks. Several men huddled around a cast iron stove. Sneezing and coughing could be heard on all sides.

"Good evening, comrades!" Batmanov said.

No one answered him. Batmanov touched the stove in passing—it was barely warm. He sat down on a bench before the table, lit a cigarette, and placed his open cigarette case on the edge of the table. He took silent stock of his surroundings. The inmates of the barrack, too, were silent, eyeing him and the cigarettes.

"Well, are we going to keep silent forever? I want you to tell me how you are living," Batmanov said good-naturedly.

"What's there to tell? If you've got eyes you can see for yourself. We're shivering with cold and waiting for no one knows what," said a stoop-shouldered old man standing by the stove. (bk. 2, chap. 12, pp. 424–425, 443–444, 453)

---

*Felt boots.

Belov:

Shipwreck in the Strait

6 June, we set off (Orentlikherman, Kuchera, Bondarenko, Badiul, and I). The cutter made its way with difficulty through the breaches in the ice along the shore and gradually got to the middle of the strait.[21] And there, something terrible happened: the engine died, the cutter stopped. The situation became very serious: our little wooden cutter was surrounded by crushing ice.

While the sergeant was pushing the ice off with a boat hook, he fell into the water. Kuchera: "Man overboard!" We pulled him out.

Then night fell and we drifted in the direction of De-Kastri. The ice was increasingly pressing against the cutter. In this critical moment, everyone reacted in his own way. One was joking ("Let the fellow go under, don't waste your strength for nothing!"), another proposed singing the "International."

Orentlikherman and the Party organizer kept calm, cut short the panic-mongers, and suggested that we struggle with the ice and repair the engine. They organized a roster in shifts.

In the morning we could see land. The engine got started. We touched shore but didn't know where we were, on the mainland or the island. The shore was like a desert, with sparse vegetation, the trees were bare on the north side, without twigs. We entered a small river and went upstream. After 4 kilometers we met some people from the fishing collective farm "Friendship"; they were catching fish with nets. They confirmed that we were on the island. When we reached the village, there was a telephone (the entire shore is linked by telephone—border zone). We made connection with Cape Pogibi, and it turned out that Chkheidze was there; he immediately sent horses. After a ride of 40 kilometers we finally arrived in Pogibi.

On Pogibi there is nothing, a bare spot, a small house dating from the time of EPRON,[22] and several *fanzas*. The leadership was lodged in a circular *fanza*, and we in the EPRON house.

That evening Bondarenko and I were summoned to "headquarters," that is, to the *fanza*. There, the boss, Kuchera, and Chkheidze said, "Now we will divide the island among you." They explained the resolution and the task, and they read the order to us. This conversation took place on 8 June, the pipeline was supposed to be laid by 1 September, and the material was not yet on the island; it was partly on the mainland, partly on the Pacific shore.

According to the order, the line on the island diverged in two directions toward two sections: Laguri and Pogibi. Bondarenko got Laguri and I Pogibi; my assignments were the crossing of the strait and the laying of 80 kilometers of pipeline from Pogibi inland in the direction of Okha.

Chkheidze determined the distribution of colonies: one every 10 kilometers. At that time I had at my disposal only 800 men.

Far from Moscow:

The boat shook and was tossed about so violently that it was difficult to sit in the cabin, even holding onto the bench with both hands. Nevertheless, the walls of the cabin seemed to the engineers a haven from the storm that raged without. Thus does a traveler, caught in a blizzard, see salvation from the snowy whirlwind in a flimsy shanty that he has chanced to run accross. Beridze caught Tania's eye and smiled at her.

"Let us get out of here, my friends," Aleksei said calmly, and began throwing off his raincoat and jacket.

"Take these, just in case," Beridze said, handing Tania and Topolev the life belts.

"What about me—have I got to die! Give me a life belt!" Kondrin shouted down from the ladder in a shrill voice of panic.

"Go on deck, the sergeant will give you one," Beridze said, turning away from him in disgust. . . .

A violent heave of the cutter knocked them all off their feet. There was a loud splintering noise, as if the frail craft had been broken in two. They made a dash for the hatchway. The face of a sailor appeared over the hatch.

"Hurry up! Get out, quick!" he shouted.

Aleksei snatched up the life belts. He put one over Topolev and the other over Tania. The girl clung to him for a moment.

"Aleksei, save Georgii," she whispered, and kissed him affectionately. . . .

Aleksei made an attempt to get in touch with Novinsk from the kolkhoz office—the village line, at the request of Nikifor, had been connected with the construction trunk lines that winter. . . . "Batmanov is coming down by plane," Beridze announced joyfully, as though hoping that Batmanov would find Tania, Topolev, and the sailors.

They were found before Batmanov arrived. One of the Nivkh ran across Polishchuk and brought him into the camp in a state of extreme exhaustion. Polishchuk told them where they could find the others. It appeared that, on coming out of the water, they had struck off from the coast and gone into the taiga in the hope of finding a Nivkh camp, but had lost their way. (bk. 3, chap. 9, pp. 312–314; chap. 10, pp. 331–332)

Belov:

How the Work Started

The next morning I and Badiul went to look over our property. There were no tracks or roads, therefore we went on horseback. The horses got stuck up to the belly in the swamps, fording the brooks and rivers. It took us 5 days to cover 80 kilometers. Then the difficulty of the task became clear to us. In regard to the total absence of roads, one could only move forward by foot. The horses couldn't be used, and we had to transport the food, the tubes, the fuel, the aggregates, and other equipment immediately.

Here and there on my section there was a breach, 9 kilometers from the shore a schist was running, above a person's height; further on, the taiga spread out 60 kilometers, and after this there was a clear plain up to the spurs of a stone ridge.

It was clear—we had to start with the road; if we didn't build a road, we wouldn't achieve anything.

We divided up the section into 12 foreman-supervised distance zones; within each zone we drew boundaries between the line brigades. We spread people out along the whole section and started to transport food and salt by pack [na v'iukakh]; this was the only way. The aim was as follows: to build a road within two weeks. We selected the people, assigned the foremen and the brigade leaders to their zones, and the work started.

We cut out breaches, grubbed out the stubs, felled trees for a log road. Almost all along we had to build a log road. Temporary communication was established by lines attached to the trees: the hooks with the isolators were driven straight into the trunks.

It is impossible to imagine the difficulties and pain related to the construction of the road. Of its 80 kilometers, 65 had to be made from a layer of beams [nakat]. The forest was dense, horses couldn't be used in the marsh, so people had to drag the trunks by themselves 700–900 meters across the swamps. People were falling, stuck in the liquid mud, but they worked in silence. With all this, there was also the difficulty of delivering supplies; they don't bake bread in the taiga, people were poorly fed.

When the road was finished, it was a great joy to all, and for me it was as if a mountain fell from my shoulders.

On 22 May the first truck [polutorka] ran from one end of the line to the other, to the farthest section, and 10 hours later brought back fresh fish and bread. Packhorses would have needed four days minimum, and the supplies would not have been edible, they'd have been spoiled from the sweat of the horses.

This first victory had a great impact on morale. It encouraged the collective; now nobody could say that the island was a murderous place where nothing could be accomplished.

Far from Moscow:
Late one night Batmanov called the chiefs of the three competing sections on the wire—Rogov on the island, Filimonov on the strait, and Kovshov on the mainland.

"Good evening—or rather good morning," Batmanov said. "I have the Party organizer here beside me. We want to check on the results of the last five days' competition. Are you ready?"

"We are," Rogov slipped in quickly.

"Who's that answering for the others? Rogov? Have you such a good view from the island that you can see what Filimonov and Kovshov are doing on their sections?"

"I have, Vasilii Maksimovich," Rogov answered, his husky voice gay. "I know every step they take. I can tell you, for instance, that Filimonov hasn't come out of the pumping station for seventy-four hours, and Kovshov lives in his runabout and has stopped taking food—he hasn't had dinner all week. Labor enthusiasm—please make a note of it. . . ."

"Your collectives have undertaken additional responsibilities," Batmanov went on. "Comrade Rogov, since you're the perkiest, you report first."

"Very good," Rogov rapped out so smartly that he set the receiver rattling. "We undertook to finish pipe transportation to the terminal point of the line, that is, the oil wells, by tomorrow—sorry, by twelve o'clock today. The results are: we have a hundred pieces, more exactly a hundred and two pipes, left to transport. All the pipe carriers of my section are now loaded up and will start out at dawn. Then they'll make a second trip and that will clinch the transportation job."

"By twelve o'clock?" Batmanov queried.

"No, by eleven," Rogov said. (bk. 3, chap. 12, pp. 382–384)

The conjunction of fiction and reality reveals many other correspondences between *Far from Moscow* and Belov's account. In a section titled "Work on Two Fronts," Belov describes an initiative that "came up almost

naturally" (*pochti stikhiino*) during the difficult work on the line. It con-
sisted of laying the tubes from both ends at the same time, which had
the advantage of making it possible to coordinate the organization of the
different brigades and colonies as a means of speeding up construction.
Before the initiative was adopted, it spurred a controversy between the
Stakhanovite practitioners and the "theoreticians," who feared for the
quality control of the work and foresaw the dissipation of cadres and technical resources. "You can divide a barrel of fuel in two, but you can't divide
an engineer specializing in welding or isolation in two," argued one of the
opponents of the intitiative. In the margins of his copy of Belov's account
of the controversial meeting, Azhaev has noted: "See Beridze (Chkheidze)
on the welders." The contradiction was resolved by Belov in favor of coor-
dinating the "work on two fronts." His argument was that the pipeline
must be completed not only on time but "before the deadline," because
"Comrade Stalin was waiting for the pipeline and the front needed the
oil." Belov added that those who associate lack of control with waste and
defective work exhibit a point of view that is "harmful [*vredno*] and an insult to the workers." And so it was decided to entrust the task to the foremen and brigade leaders. The version in the novel not only agrees with
Belov but also anticipates the meeting's resolution: the "inward" laying of
the pipes (i.e., the work on two fronts) is initiated in practice by the
Stakhanovite driver Makhov well before the idea occurs "in theory" to
Aleksei Kovshov (i.e., in the engineer's mind).[23] But nurture, in Azhaev's
version, is enriched by culture and traces of the writer's own history:
Makhov, who is described elsewhere as "a handsome young man with a
delicate girlish complexion,"[24] had "a gift for music" and had started at-
tending a music school. When the war began, he was not drafted because
he was "flat-footed."[25] But he refused to "get stuck in the orchestra,
fiddling with the keys of an accordion and blowing into a trumpet when
[his] comrades were risking their lives at the front." So he joined the
"battle for oil."[26]

Another section of Belov's recollections is titled "On the Problems and
Obstacles during the Work." Project No. 15 suffered from many problems,
one of the most severe being the chronic breakdown of fuel delivery:
Belov depicted workers stealing gasoline "and hiding it in the bushes," and
Chkheidze sending fuel by plane, an event that "filled everybody with
great joy." "I had used up forty-five years of my life," wrote Belov, "but
never had I experienced such emotions and such joy as during my work on
the island." There is no doubt that *Far from Moscow* accurately reflected

"the joy of victory, the joy of good work," as another section of Belov's account is titled, describing the end of the work on 29 August 1942, two days before the deadline. What followed was yet another challenge: the laying of a second section of the pipeline across the strait during the wintertime.

The rest of Belov's account, "On the Technique of Laying the Pipeline" and "How the Second Section of the Line was Laid in the Strait" (in an astonishing twenty days instead of the projected eighty), is full of schemes and diagrams, plus a detailed description of the various stages of the work, much (perhaps too much) of which was used by Azhaev in the third book of *Far from Moscow*. Chkheidze and Orentlikherman's appreciation of the novel, of what was "correctly described" and of what "could have been added,"[27] as well as the telegrams with dates and numbers,[28] provides much information about Project No. 15 and fills in the blanks of what was bothering the Bureau of Pipeline Operations of the Far Eastern Industrial Complex of the Oil Industry and causing complaint in 1943–44.

What remains to be said is that Azhaev's "sources" were themselves products of memory, of recollections that can be evaluated in terms of other, more primary documents, some of which have surfaced recently. The following excerpts from a series of orders and instructions issued by Nikolai Maksimovich Belov between June and September 1942 were copied from a file deposited in the Information Center of the Khabarovsk Administration of Internal Affairs (UVD). They not only offer some additional information on Belov's "emotions" and "joy," but also give us further insight into daily life on the "line."

No. 6. 12 June 1942. Pogibi-on-Sakhalin.
Increase the workday for free laborers working on the welding job. 12 hours.
Belov.

No. 8. 16 June 1942.
On 16 June 1942, because of the criminal negligence of the individual responsible for supplies, Kopytin, the prisoner Klimenko, and the educator [*vospitatel'*]* Novitskii (all of them prisoners), the brigade of fishermen of colony 12 was given a meal with great delay, the food was cold, and the dishes were dirty. . . . They stopped work for a while and reduced the catch.

*The *vospitatel'* (himself or herself a prisoner) was responsible for driving the prisoners to exceed the norm, denouncing and chastising those who did not, and other such duties.

Send Klimenko to colony 8: three months of exceptionally hard physical work. Novitskii: general labor. Kopytin: 3 days under arrest. Belov.

No. 11. 17 June 1942.
Criminal account for the prisoners of colony 10: A. M. Kuznetsov and A. Murza for 14 acts of refusal to work, paragraphs 162, 192 "intentional hiding from work."

No. 18. 24 June 1942.
Put under arrest for 5 days and work under guard the prisoner Kuliaev, for resistance to the VoKhR* and debauchery in drunken condition.

No. 28. 29 June 1942.
Conditions in colony 12: filth, theft, lice, the work force is poorly utilized, a mass of people hanging around. Artemiev established a regime of terror, provoking hooligan-like outbursts directed against higher-ranking authority. Managed to get a health certificate and attempted to go to Okha. Remove from his post and send to colony 6 for exceptionally hard work for three months. . . .

No. 43.
For each truck the norm of laying and stringing out pipes [is] 85 pieces of pipe.

No. 53. 11 July 1942.
Summary of the work for June and July 1942.
The personnel of the VOKhR division joined in the battle to meet and exceed the plan: discussions, increased control for the optimum utilization of the food supply, struggle against refusers. 8 *subbotniki*[†] for digging trenches and centering of the pipes.

No. 71.
Starting on 1 August 1942, reveille will be at 6:30 A.M., 12 hours of work. Lights out at 9:30 P.M.

No. 141. 9 September 1942. On the awarding of bonuses to prisoners.
"For systematic overachievement, for work by Stakhanovite methods,"

*Acronym for Militarized Guard at Places of Confinement.
†Voluntary unpaid work on days off.

acknowledgment of thanks recorded in the personal file, uniform of the first category [*pervogo sroka*],* monetary remuneration; "participants in the all-section rally of record breakers," 65 people from 15 to 100 rubles. Petitioning: 200 people to be released or given shorter terms. Belov.[29]

The same file of the Information Center of the Khabarovsk UVD contains, among other documents, a series of orders relative to an earlier period. These orders were signed on 3 July 1941 by one Mel'nikov, head of the first section of the Lower Amur Corrective Labor Camp (i.e., the first 74 kilometers from Laguri on Sakhalin to Pogibi). Mel'nikov is also mentioned in Azhaev's Komsomol'sk diary. His orders reflected the increased restrictions on the line after the beginning of the war. All prisoners "sentenced for counterrevolutionary crimes and banditry," as well as German and Polish prisoners, were to be sent to severe-regime colonies and brigades for exceptionally hard physical labor. Unrestricted circulation was canceled for 75 percent of prisoners and was totally suppressed for the aforementioned categories. The use of the telephone by prisoners was forbidden, and the delivery of all mail was canceled. The orders also reflect the often chaotic situation in various colonies, such as drinking parties involving prisoners and members of the VOKhR, and close contacts between the population of the camp and the workers of the Japanese Concession in Okha. Here are some further details: "The systematic refuser Sevchugov hit Medvezhev, commander of colony 5, with a stick. The refuser Perov started to strangle Matiushin, commander of colony 7. The VOKhR failed to announce these violations early enough. All criminals and counterrevolutionaries shall be sent to one colony." An order signed by the head of the Lower Amur Corrective Labor Camp, Barabanov, following an order by Lavrentii Beria of 22 June 1941, introduced martial law for the VOKhR: all prisoners were to be systematically searched, and the guards were requested to remain on duty until the work was completed, "independent of location and time."[30]

At approximately the same time, the author of *Far from Moscow* started to fill in the blanks that were still terra incognita for Soviet literature. I found in Azhaev's archive two hand-drawn maps showing the route of the pipeline from Sofiiskoe to Okha, via De-Kastri, Cape Lazarevo, and Cape Pogibi. In the blueprint variants, and in the Far Eastern published version

*New uniforms.

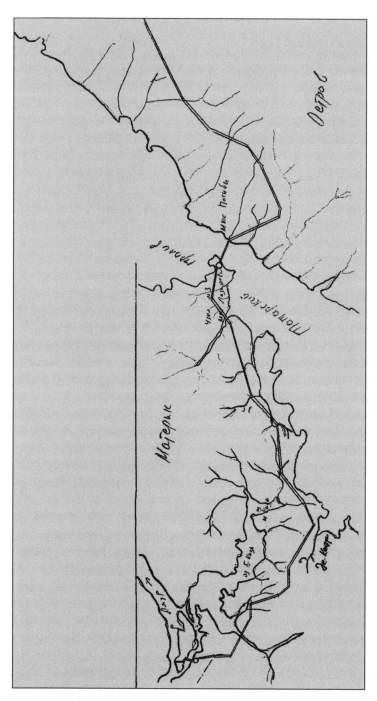

Azhaev's hand-drawn map of the pipeline, sketching its route from past De-Kastri north by east to Lazarev and then across the Nevel'skii Strait to Cape Pogibi, on the island of Sakhalin. Note that in the author's sketch of the "real" Far East, the Amur swings northward to the "left" while the great Stalinist construction sweeps decisively to the "right."

of *Far from Moscow* (1946–48), the place names had already been changed, but the route still corresponded to "real" topography: the river Adun "swept on majestically" to the "left," while the route of the pipeline swung northward to the "right." After he used Belov's recollections and other accounts of Far Eastern geography, Azhaev continued to work on "generalization," that is, on making his map "typical" and avoiding (per the theorist L. I. Timofeev's definition of fiction) any "forms that are distorted, absurd, and so on." When the novel was published in *Novyi mir* in 1948— that is, in its Stalin Prize version—the mirror image was corrected to correspond to the pipeline's "left" reality. As we shall see, it was here that Azhaev's unbreakable oath, taken years earlier, came into conflict with what represented "in a certain manner the concentration of the writer's experience of the world."[31]

9

BORDERLINE II: TO MOSCOW!

The plane gained altitude. . . . He almost physically sensed the immensity of his country and of everything that was taking place on its boundless spaces. He experienced such a sense of exultation that he could have sung with sheer joy.

—*Far from Moscow*, book 3, chapter 14

On 18 December 1944 the regional committee of the Soviet Writers' Union met to discuss the works of Vasilii Azhaev, resident of the city of Khabarovsk.[1] The subject of discussion was to be twelve short stories "of various thematic directions" and the novel *Far from Moscow*, "on which the author is working at the present time." After a reading by Azhaev of several chapters from his novel, the participants launched their discussion. G. S. Fedoseev emphasized the variety of themes contained in Azhaev's stories, which were devoted to issues such as the Great Patriotic War, the collectivized countryside, the city, construction projects, and corrective labor in the Far East.[2] According to Fedoseev, "The Son" attempted to "demonstrate the idea of the theme of reeducation through the topic of motherhood." "The dialogues are Azhaev's strength," remarked another critic. All agreed that one could feel "the breath of reality" in his novel. Some critics complained about the lack of space devoted to the personal lives of the heroes, and one of them, Nikolai Zamoshkin, noted that the novel suffered from the "pressure of the material." Azhaev, he said, "knows too much about what he is writing on, and this constrains him internally."

The chairman of the committee, A. D. Kartsev, understood better than anybody else the nature of this constraint. In order "to help Azhaev improve the condition of his creative work" and "confirm him as a man of letters," Kartsev suggested that "a request be lodged with the NKVD, through Polikarpov," for his transfer to Moscow, so that he could complete his studies in the Institute of Literature and graduate.[3]

Azhaev's "autobiography" of 22 April 1946 indicates that he graduated from the Gorky Literary Institute in 1945 after six years of study "by correspondence." But the publication of *Far from Moscow,* as well as his transfer to Moscow, met some serious obstacles related to the fact that he did in fact "know too much about what he was writing on." In a letter to Petr Komarov of 23 May 1945, Azhaev complained about his problems with the local censor and asked for help.[4] The letter is worth quoting nearly in its entirety, for it reveals not only some of the mechanisms of publishing at that time, but also the author's feelings about crossing the second borderline of his career.

Khabarovsk, 23 May 1945

Hello, dear Petr Stepanovich,

I hope that this letter will find you still in Moscow.

After your departure yet another misfortune [with the novel] has befallen me and I have definitely decided that I belong to this pathetic category of losers, whom I myself despise profoundly.

The novel received unanimous approval from the editorial board, and it was decided to go ahead immediately with its production, as part of the almanac.[5]

However, it came as a total surprise to us that the *Krailit* [regional censor], Com. Byvshev, refused to put his stamp [*zavizirovat'*] on the manuscript, on the grounds that the novel was about the construction of a pipeline, which is listed as a "classified subject." Maintaining an extreme formalist position and safeguarding himself, Com. Byvshev refused to take into consideration our arguments in defense of the novel.

We decided to ask Com. Polikarpov to resolve the question of publication of the novel through Glavlit. For this we are sending with Com. Kovalevskaia a copy of the novel and two letters—mine and Rogal''s. I deliberately didn't include the arguments for publication—they are included in the letter for Dmitrii Alekseevich [Polikarpov].

I am asking you emphatically to push the novel through the Soviet Writers' Union and Glavlit.

The manuscript sent consists of ten chapters (I added two chapters); I didn't manage to finish typing another two chapters, which conclude the first part. It seems to me that the decision by Glavlit can be made entirely on the evidence of the first ten chapters.

If you consider it worthwile to show the novel, after Glavlit, to Com. Zamoshkin at *Novyi mir,* perhaps the journal will find it possible to accept the first part. . . .

I am in a very bad mood but I am still working on the novel from force of habit. If feelings of self-pity get the upper hand, and I don't hang myself, I will switch to writing historical novels and stories for children.

Orentlikherman is adding daily to all these misfortunes and annoyances.

In one word, bad news, brother. I envy you for being in Moscow. Don't forget to pay a visit to my parents,

I squeeze your hand.

Yours,

V. Azhaev[6]

Dmitrii Alekseevich was in fact helpful, although just in the nick of time. After violent complaints about the *orgsekretar'*'s "antidemocratic style of governing" (he was accused, for instance, of having inaugurated a "reign of terror" within *Literaturnaia gazeta,* the organ of the Writers' Union), Polikarpov was removed from his post by order of the Central Committee on 3 April 1946, an action confirmed by the Politburo six days later.[7] It was no doubt a coincidence that on 6 April the Moscow publishing house Molodaia Gvardiia resumed publication of its prestigious series Lives of Remarkable Men. The schedule of forthcoming volumes included a life of Chekhov by V. Ermilov and a biography of the "Far Eastern Chapaev," Lazo, by M. Gubel'man.[8] As for Azhaev, he was "transferred" on 1 April to work in the editorial office of *Dal'nii Vostok* "by order of the Head of the MVD,"[9] and the first double issue of the journal (nos. 1–2 [January–April 1946]) included the first eleven chapters of *Far from Moscow.*

Five months after Azhaev's appointment to the editorial office, on 14 August 1946, the Central Committee of the CPSU passed its famous resolution "On the Journals *Zvezda* and *Leningrad,*" stating, among other things, that "any advocacy of lack of ideological content, political indifference, or 'art for art's sake' is alien to Soviet literature, harmful to the interests of the Soviet people and its government, and should not take place in our journals."[10] As is well known, the scapegoats of the resolution were the poet Anna Akhmatova and the satirical writer Mikhail Zoshchenko. During the Great Patriotic War the Soviet leadership needed to gather all possible forces in order to defend the country against the Nazi invasion, including previously repressed writers. Now that victory had been attained, such ideological concessions became obsolete: the "total mobilization" of Soviet culture after the relative loosening of the war years had begun.

On 15 April 1947 the Committee of the Soviet Writers' Union on Russian Literature of the Regions and Districts of the RSFSR met in Moscow to discuss whether the contents of the newly reopened "organ of the Far Eastern branch of the Soviet Writers' Union" *Dal'nii Vostok* and its authors had responded correctly to the challenge.[11] The session was opened by A. D. Kartsev, presenting the prehistory of the journal from *Na rubezhe,* published between 1933 and 1941, to its renaissance in 1946 under the name *Dal'nii Vostok.*[12] He was followed by the "responsible editor" of the journal, Anatolii Gai, who said that "new forces" had compensated for the departures and losses of the Far Eastern branch's *litaktiv* during the war: about forty writers had joined the organization, six of whom were formal members of the Soviet Writers' Union. All were young, and the harvest was quite impressive. Among the authors and works cited were Nikolai Zadornov and his novel *Amur-batiushka* (Father Amur); Dmitrii Nagishkin and his novella *Tikhaia bukhta* (The Quiet Bay); Nikolai Rogal', who in 1938 had published "Na granitse" (On the Border) in *Na rubezhe*[13] and who was at present working on a "historical novel devoted to the civil war in the Far East" and other projects; and Rustam Agishev, who specialized on military topics and had written a play based on Chukchi folklore. Gai also cited the Far Eastern poets Petr Komarov, Sergei Tel'kanov, Stepan Smoliakov, and Sergei Feoktistov. As for Vasilii Azhaev, he "had come with stories and reports on the construction of the Far East; his stories had been published in *Na rubezhe.* Then he produced *Far from Moscow* and had a novella in progress as well, titled *Vechnaia merzlota* [Permafrost]."[14]

After this positive news, and in accordance with the campaign against the journals *Zvezda* and *Leningrad* and other "resolutions" of 1946, Gai proceeded to criticize the deficiencies of the Far Eastern branch of the Soviet Writers' Union and of their journal, *Dal'nii Vostok.* The Far Eastern writers were still putting too much emphasis on historical topics, he said, and there had been abuses of "our taiga exotics," which represented a "peculiar flight from reality." A great exception in this regard was Azhaev. His work showed that history had resolutely turned its back on Arsen'ev and other promulgators of "regional folklore," and that there were now new places of central importance, such as Komsomol'sk and Magadan. Gai concluded with a report on the "outreach" activities of the branch over the previous two years: 480 authors of 1,500 manuscripts had participated in two competitions (one per year), and the organization had provided literary consultations to 249 writers (in the preceding year). Gai complained about problems related to the Jewish Autonomous Region of Birobidzhan: the comrades from the Khabarovsk bureau of the union "had no knowledge of Yiddish," and several requests for help addressed to the center (Moscow) had gone unanswered.[15] The responsible editor finally presented a publication plan for *Dal'nii Vostok*: it included works by young Nanai and Udege authors, "national" publications on folklore, on Lenin and Stalin, and on "the new Soviet woman," as well as reports and diaries by adventurers, sailors, specialist-administrators, scientists, people from Amurstal' (the iron and steel plant of Komsomol'sk),[16] lumbermen, and oil prospectors from Sakhalin.[17] Judging from this program, Azhaev was in good company. But our author had other ambitions, and these were shared, at least in part, by his critics from the Committee of the Soviet Writers' Union on Russian Literature of the Regions and Districts of the RSFSR.

The verdict of 15 April 1947 handed down by the "center" on the periphery was severe and spared no one, including Anatolii Gai. The Komsomol poet Aleksandr Zharov, for example, criticized the responsible editor for his cycle of poems "Morskaia tetrad'" (Notebook of the Sea),[18] in which Zharov perceived a "deviation from the path of Soviet poetry" and an "escape toward Akhmatovian distance."

The characteristics of these lyrical poems . . . are for me absolutely unacceptable, and they are unacceptable now for the precise reason that they do not conform to Soviet lyricism, and it is very unfortunate that they are still present in Gai's work of 1946, at a time when he himself understands that this is not the path of Soviet poetry, that this is a departure, a tendency to escape toward Akhmatovian distance, or to enter Akhmatova's closed and stuffy world, in which these males toss about in pleasure and in sadness [*v kotorom mechutsia, naslazhdaias' i pechalias', eti samtsy*].

This is how things are, unfortunately, and I felt the urge to tell Gai about this and to warn him that this line can get him into trouble; also, it is easy for the 10–12 talented young guys to be led to deviate from the correct path, especially by Gai, who has authority and a great deal of experience. This is the reason why I felt the need to speak out with such harshness on Gai's work.[19]

Another member of the committee, the literary critic and writer Fedor Levin, who was known for his "polemical style,"[20] simply dismissed the prose that had been published in *Dal'nii Vostok,* concluding that the journal "would do better to concentrate on ethnographic material and wait for literary works worthy of the name to appear."[21] Concerning Azhaev's *Far from Moscow,* Levin recognized that the author (whom he did not know) "knew his topic from the inside." "Some characters are well described," said Levin, "but the novel lacks a great idea." Levin submitted Azhaev's style to a merciless critique: "At times he writes in the language of technical projects or notes for a resolution on a project"; "the heroes speak like a newspaper editorial of average quality"; "Azhaev's characters all talk the same way"; "the author writes in the language of a collective farm secretary who reports on how he organized some travel allowance."[22] For Levin those most responsible for the shortcomings of *Dal'nii Vostok* were its editors, A. Gai, N. Zadornov, P. Komarov, N. Rogal', and so on, though their crime lay not in what they did but what they failed to do. "*Dal'nii Vostok* lacks force," Levin said. "Send something interesting so that it can be reworked [*obrabotano*] here [in Moscow], or better yet, send the author."[23]

Levin's "polemical style" of criticism would be remembered during the campaigns against "rootless cosmopolitanism" and "antipatriotic" elements in Soviet society, which took on a distinctly anti-Semitic coloration. Launched in 1947, these campaigns continued until Stalin's death in 1953. The struggle reached its height during the first half of 1949, that is, in the same year that Azhaev was awarded the Stalin Prize. Like his unfortunate predecessors, the literary consultants of 1937, Levin was "beaten up." In a February 1949 article A. Makarov accused him of being a "arch-hurrah cosmopolitan and aesthete." Before the war Levin had "on the sly" criticized *Chapaev, How the Steel Was Tempered, The Tanker Derbent,* and *The Pedagogical Poem;* after the war he had infiltrated various editorial boards and committees where, in the role of literary consultant, he had slandered—again "on the sly"—B. Polevoi's "volume of short stories"[24] and Azhaev's *Far from Moscow,* accusing the heroes of the latter of "speaking like quotations from a newspaper editorial."[25]

Levin was not Azhaev's only critical commentator, by any means; others pointed out different defects. Valeriia Gerasimova, a specialist on the psychology of careerists, timeservers, and other "unreal people" (from the title of her 1923 novella), disliked the disturbing "adventure" subplot of the *Dal'nii Vostok* version of Azhaev's novel.[26] To her, the wrecking activities of the mysterious Khmara were not "typical," and "only Dostoevsky could write about strange things." The novel, in other words, "was in dan-

ger of becoming a detective story" or something in "bad taste." Gerasimova, too, regretted the lack of a good editor who could correct Azhaev's
"affected stylistic flourishes."[27] Nikolai Moskvin, a holdover from the literary avant-garde of the 1920s who had written a novel on the problem of
the old and the new in early Soviet pedagogy but had later switched to the
theme of the civil war and the Great Patriotic War,[28] wondered about the
concept on which Azhaev's novel was based: "What is the idea? To build or
not to build? Of course, to build, otherwise the author would not have
written 'how we built the pipeline.'" For Moskvin, the idea of simply depicting good Soviet people was not enough on which to organize a successful novel. The same went for the love story in *Far from Moscow*. While
his wife writes him passionate love letters, Pervov (Aleksei Kovshov in the
Dal'nii Vostok version) has only one passion: to go to the front. Moskvin
wondered whether the hero should not be allowed some additional plea-
sures.[29] As we shall see, this problem was not solved in the direction
Moskvin preferred when the novel was rewritten.

Nikolai Zamoshkin, who had been present during the discussion of
18 December 1944 (and had noted that Azhaev's novel suffered from the
"pressure of the material"), was certainly the most senior participant in
this discussion. He had been a member of the literary group Pereval in the
1920s, had planned, with Maxim Gorky, the never-completed "History of
the Countryside," and had founded the journal *Kolkhoznik* (The Collective Farmer) in 1937.[30] Since 1944 he had directed the creative prose semi-
nar of the Gorky Literary Institute. Zamoshkin reproached the author of
Far from Moscow for his clumsy handling of "the art of psychological mo-
tivation." For him, the two main lines of the novel—productional and
personal—never converged, and the characters suffered from a peculiar
form of "split personality": "all are not what they seem"; "in all of them a
kind of crack-up [*nadryv*] can be discovered"; "they all have their personal
grief, they all hide it, but it breaks through." This criticism applied even to
the main negative character of Azhaev's novel, Grubskii (the previous chief
engineer of the construction, a "typical" representative of the old intelligentsia and advocate of the "right variant" of the pipeline). Perhaps the de-
funct theory of the "living man" could accommodate a motive such as
"loyalty to the intelligentsia," said Zamoshkin, but "in life, such a motive
simply does not exist."[31] He continued with a long list of stylistic flaws,
adding that "the editors had not done their job."[32]

Other participants in the discussion were more positive: A. V. Bakov-
nikov, editor of the army newspaper *Krasnaia zvezda,* compared *Far from
Moscow* to the Battle of Stalingrad. It showed the important theme of

"work in the rear, about which the army knew little."[33] The critic Osip Reznik, author of the 1946 *Pobeda i literatura* (The Victory and Literature),[34] noted that Azhaev should not be accused of injecting too much politics into his work, when, some time before in the very same room the Presidium of the Soviet Writers' Union had accused Viktor Nekrasov of doing just the opposite.[35] Despite its "horrible language," *Far from Moscow* demonstrated the Soviet people's love of work; the novel was guaranteed a bright future.[36] The poet Ashot Garnakerian spoke in his "provincial voice from Rostov-on-the-Don," a city that "would welcome a publication such as *Far from Moscow.*" Nevertheless, he agreed that the author was "young, much too young," and that "a good editor would have shown him that a Georgian (Beridze) does not speak like a man from Central Russia."[37]

There was no doubt of the consensus: Azhaev needed further help. Nobody could have expressed this thought better than Evgenii Dolmatovskii, who was also present that day. He declared:

> Concerning the quality of their prose, however, the comrades have not been communicating enough with Moscow. Azhaev's novel was very interesting for me because I have been in the Far East, I know the material, and I know Azhaev. I believe that if a good editor had worked on this thing (an editor like the one who worked with Panova on her *Fellow Travelers,* an editor like the one who worked with Vershigora, with Kazakevich on his novella *The Star*), the result would have been different. I think that there, in the Far East, there is nobody to do this. And I think that it is necessary to send some people there from time to time and, even more often, to let people come here and to work with them on their prose.[38]

Azhaev made a brief response in which he thanked all the participants for their attention and endorsed most of the criticism. His emotional response to Levin's accusation that the novel lacked a "great idea," however, can hardly have satisfied the "polemicist": "This is a novel on our contemporaries, on the people of Soviet society, the most progressive society of the world, on people with special spiritual qualities, on people who, during a quarter of a century of Soviet power, have turned out to be fully prepared for all sorts of experiments."[39]

Many other topics were debated during that long meeting. Dolmatovskii spoke about the "tragic situation" of the Jewish writers of Birobidzhan, "who remained without readers and publishing houses," and voiced his appreciation of the Birobidzhan poet Israel Emiot.[40] Sergei Markov

Дорогой Константин Михайлович!

Если бы знали Вы, как я волнуюсь, передавая для Вас эту рукопись! Даже самому странно — давно ведь вышел я из школьного возраста и слышал немало мнений сведущих людей и читателей о романе. Но почему то Ваш суд для меня очень страшен. Не подумайте только, что это в связи с тем — буду или не буду печататься в «Далеко от Москвы» в Вашем журнале.

Видно очень уж личное у меня связано с этой работой, и Вы, быть может и не вполне представляя себе силу своего влияния на всех нас, своих сверстников, — судья для меня особенный. До сегодняшнего дня мне не верилось, что Вам удастся выкроить время для чтения такой нудной рукописи. А сейчас я рад уже и тому, что в столь трудное для Вас дни, Вы так интересовались моей работой.

V. Azhaev's letter of 12 May 1948 to Konstantin Simonov ("If you only knew with what emotion I am sending you my manuscript").

V. Azhaev, Khabarovsk, 1948.

(who had written "The Russians in Alaska" and "The Russians on the Kuril Islands") praised Iuliia Shestakova's "V khorskikh lesakh" (In the Khorsk Forests) and expressed his desire to see more works that reflected the fusion of ethnography, history, and politics in the Far East.[41] M. M. Gimpelevich of OGIZ (United State Publishing House), who shared Aleksandr Zharov's negative opinions of Gai's poetry, acknowledged the importance of the political theme in *Far from Moscow*. By the same token, he announced the introduction of a new policy concerning "double issues" (of which *Dal'nii Vostok* was an example).[42] Henceforth the publication of double issues would lead to the closure of the journal in question.[43]

After a session that lasted more than eight hours, the Committee of the Soviet Writers' Union on Russian Literature of the Regions and Districts of the RSFSR adjourned. That day Azhaev had emerged a second time from obscurity. In 1937, in the midst of the Great Terror, he had emerged as a "novice author" from Camp Freedom. Ten years later, while Akhmatova, Zoshchenko, and many others were being silenced, Azhaev had risen in "quality." On 12 May 1948 he wrote to Konstantin Simonov: "If you only knew with what emotion I am sending you my manuscript! . . . Obviously, for me, a great deal is invested in this work. . . . I consider literature a serious business and I don't ask for indulgence, but on the human level I want very, very much for this novel to please you!"[44] We know that Simonov was pleased.

10

---•·◦∞◦·•---

BETWEEN ENGINEERS: MORE
ON TRANSFERENCE-LOVE

> To urge the patient to suppress, renounce or sublimate her in-
> stincts the moment she has admitted her erotic transference
> would be, not an analytic way of dealing with them, but a sense-
> less one. It would be just as though, after summoning up a spirit
> from the underworld by cunning spells, one were to send him
> down again without having asked him a single question. One
> would have brought the repressed into consciousness, only to
> repress it once more in a fright.
> —Sigmund Freud, "Observations on Transference-Love" (1915)

> I very much want [to be] with you, Georgii Davydovich. But I
> want even more to go to the front.
> —Far from Moscow, book 1, chapter 1

In the foreword to an unfinished novel found among Nikolai Chernyshevsky's manuscripts, the author of *What Is to Be Done?* described his projected novel as one in which the subjectivity of the author would be entirely eliminated. This is what he wrote about "The Pearl of Creation," as
he was then thinking of calling this work: "The pearl of creation. Story
within the story, a novel or not a novel, a collection or not a collection, written by him or her, or them, unknown, dedicated to Mlle V. M. Ch. by the
author, or the authors, or one of the authors." Farther on we read: "To
write a novel without love—without any female character—this is a very

difficult task, but I felt the need to prove my strength on an even more difficult task: to write an entirely objective novel, in which there would be no trace at all of my personal relationships—and not even a trace of my personal fellow feelings." [1]

Mikhail Bakhtin saw in these lines the quasi-discovery of the "polyphonic novel," [2] and I will return to this issue later. For our immediate purposes, it is interesting to note that Chernyshevsky links his desire to write a "purely objective novel" to the object of writing "a novel without love," one without the presence of a single female character. Chernyshevsky's desire can, of course, be seen as biased, but one can also interpret it as a "gendered" aspect of his revolutionary thinking, that is, a striving for the abolition of property relations in the domain of gender, assuming that we agree, after Gayle Rubin's reworking of Lévi-Strauss, that "patriarchal heterosexuality can be best discussed in terms of one or another form of traffic in women" and that "it is the use of women as exchangeable, perhaps symbolic, property, for the primary purpose of cementing the bonds of men with men." [3]

Socialist realism often claimed Chernyshevsky as one of its forerunners, and it could be argued that to some extent its method realized the coupling of objectivity and the absence of love advocated by the nineteenth-century master. As Katerina Clark has shown in *The Soviet Novel,* socialist realist love is an "auxiliary ingredient in the plot." The "hero's love life is not valuable in itself; it serves only to aid him in fulfilling his tasks and in attaining 'consciousness.'" [4] An entry of 23 April 1941 in Azhaev's Komsomol'sk diary says that the novel he wants to write "will have two lines: a very subjective one—told from the first person—and a strictly objective one." About the same time, as we have already learned, he dreamed of writing "a whole book of stories, novellas, and studies on the theme of love . . . on the dialectics of love (which, according to Rousseau, makes the very stuff of the hero)." Which of the two manifestations of love encountered so far prevailed in *Far from Moscow,* the hero's love for "V. or F." or the "love of the Chekist"? To which line—the "very subjective" or the "strictly objective"—does each belong? Predictably, the second prevailed, "consciousness" was attained, and the romance with "V. or F." and other forms of "traffic in women" served only to build socialist realism. But this outcome was not without consequences for subjectivity itself. Let us take a look at the various forms of this traffic in Azhaev's "pearl of creation."

Far from Moscow has its moments of love and pleasure, including "the pleasure of the text," as in the following scene. The protagonists are the senior engineer Beridze, who says that "all my strength is in my beard" (*vsia moia sila v borode*); the young engineer Aleksei Kovshov, who is deeply disappointed that he was not sent to the front in the Great Patriotic War against the German fascists but instead has been assigned to a mission in the rear, "far from Moscow"; and Muza Filippovna, Beridze's secretary, a "flabby elderly woman wearing pince-nez attached to a cord" (*rykhlaia pozhilaia zhenshchina v pensne na shnurochke*). Muza Filippovna says to her boss:

> "There's no one to talk to. I was moved to tears when you agreed to take on an old woman like me as your secretary. Usually they pick young girls for secretaries, the younger and prettier the better."
>
> "I'm glad to have a Muscovite, a person of culture, for a secretary. I don't particularly care to have very young and gay girls working with me," Beridze said, flashing a look in the direction of Aleksei, who was listening to the conversation in silence.[5]

Beridze orders Muza to fulfill a certain task, and she leaves the room. What follows could be entitled "Between Men," or, more specifically, "Between Engineers":

> Aleksei sprang to his feet lightly, walked over to the window, and opened it wide. Wearing only trunks, he went through a few warm-up exercises, his muscles rippling under the suntanned skin. Beridze watched him with a smile.
>
> "It would be interesting to know when the change will set in and you'll abandon good habits like gymnastics for bad ones like smoking or a drink before dinner. I've noticed that a man is bound to acquire bad habits as he grows older."
>
> "I'll do my best to resist that law of nature," said Aleksei.
>
> His usually pallid face took on a warm glow, and a lock of fair hair fell over his brow. He breathed deeply and felt the blood coursing faster in his veins. Sitting down on a chair, he began to massage his left arm. From wrist to elbow it was seared by three wide scars.
>
> "How's the arm, Aleksei?"
>
> "Quite all right. Soon be as good as it ever was."
>
> They looked out of the window. The four-story brick building housing the offices of the construction job overlooked a sharp incline. Down below, the river, eternally alive, spread out its broad back, the ripples on

its surface playing in the rays of the newborn sun. On the opposite bank the broken silhouette of the hills loomed through the blue haze. The earth was garbed in browns and yellows and golden hues—a sign that the year was on the wane.

"Old Man Adun is magnificent!" Aleksei said with a note of awe in his voice. "You wouldn't be able to swim across that stream."

Somewhere in the distance a locomotive emitted a plaintive wail, reminding the engineers of their twenty-day ride across the endless fields, forests, and mountains of their country. They both sighed.

Aleksei shivered. He dressed quickly and ran out to wash.

"Let's stick together, shoulder to shoulder, or, as sportsmen like to say, run nose to nose," Beridze said when Aleksei returned. He saw the longing in his assistant's eyes and sought to cheer him.

Beridze outlined a plan of action.[6]

Is this a case of "homosocialist" desire? Azhaev's text undoubtedly contains phallic elements, from Muza's "pince-nez" (the castration of the Muse?) to Beridze and Aleksei's "running nose to nose," and, of course, the pipeline, viewed as the real hero of the novel by contemporary critics. The whole scene has aspects of sexual arousal and "little death," especially if one recalls the passages of the first (*Dal'nii Vostok*) version of the novel that were reworked for the Stalin Prize edition. "Beridze watched him with a smile" was initially "Beridze watched with a smile the abrupt movements of the young engineer's strong body" (*Beridze s ulybkoi sledil za rezkimi dvizheniiami sil'nogo tela molodogo inzhenera*); "He breathed deeply and felt the blood coursing faster in his veins" was "He breathed deeply, his chest rose, and he felt the blood warming up inside him, reaching the farthest capillaries" (*On gluboko dyshal, vzdymaia grud' i chuvstvuiia, kak nagrevalas' v nem krov', razbegaias' po samym dal'nim kapiliaram*); "They sighed" (*Oni vzdokhnuli*) replaces "They both sighed" (*Oni razom vzdokhnuli*); and, finally, "Aleksei shivered. He dressed quickly and ran out to wash" was simply "Aleksei began dressing" (*Aleksei nachal odevat'sia*).[7] The *Novyi mir* edition of the novel adds "disambiguating" glosses to the text, such as the passage about the "three wide scars" on Aleksei's arm, which adds a heroic, and therefore public, element to Aleksei's private body.

Far from Moscow, the engineers keep embracing, kissing, touching each other, as if to generate some human warmth in the hostile environment of nature:

Aleksei and Rogov shared the same sledge. They had contrived to ride together by a tacit agreement born of a mounting feeling of mutual sympathy.

"Aleksei, you can't imagine how glad I am to be going out to the strait,"
Rogov said, pressing slightly closer to Kovshov, lying beside him on the
sledge. . . .

He turned over and crushed Aleksei with the whole weight of his
body. . . .

"Wouldn't I like to!" Rogov said, clenching his fists.

A mighty strength seethed in him. He hugged Aleksei and began maul-
ing him until the latter cried for mercy.[8]

Sometimes the textual changes from the Far East to the New World edition can be explained by social(ist realist) etiquette, or simply by the intervention of a "good editor": "I understand you, my eagle" (*Ponimaiu tebia,
orel*), says Beridze to Aleksei in the *Dal'nii Vostok* version. In *Novyi mir*
the "eagle" is (literally) transformed into the more conventional "dove": "I
understand you, my little dove" (*Ponimaiu tebia, golubchik*), meaning "my
dear," or "little buddy."[9] During their journey from Moscow to the Far
East, Beridze and Kovshov—called Pervov in the first version—are
caught in a German air raid. A bomb explodes. In *Dal'nii Vostok*, Georgii
Davydovich (Beridze) falls on Aleksei. In the second version apparently it
was felt that this needed to be reversed, with Aleksei falling on Beridze.
Understandably, the junior engineer should protect the senior and not the
other way around:

Dal'nii Vostok:
The engineers had only enough time to embrace, and Georgii Davydovich, falling down during the explosion, crushed Aleksei, protecting the
latter with his body. When they picked themselves up, they were hardly
able to believe that they had escaped without injury. Pervov cried out,
frightened, when he saw blood on his comrade's face and hair.[10]

Novyi mir:
When the bomb exploded, Kovshov had fallen on top of the chief engineer, protecting the latter with his body. When they picked themselves
up, they were hardly able to believe that they had escaped without injury.
True, Beridze was frightened at first when he saw blood on his comrade's
face and hair.[11]

We know from Azhaev's biography that, like Mitia Promyslov, the hero
of *The Boxcar,* he was doomed to be "a Communist without a Party card
for the rest of his life." In *Far from Moscow,* the desire to be admitted to
the party is projected onto the chief engineer, Beridze, in a scene in which
love between engineers is reenacted on "the day and evening of November
seventh."[12]

> [Zalkind] pressed the chief engineer's hand in both of his, looked him in
> the eyes, and embraced him warmly. Then Batmanov came over and he
> too embraced Beridze, whispering: "High time, old man." Aleksei ap-
> proached behind the others. Beridze glanced at him and smiled. Aleksei's
> face, an open book as always, revealed at once his embarrassment and the
> joy he shared with his comrade. Beridze pulled the young man toward
> him and kissed him heartily on both cheeks [*Beridze pritianul ego k sebe.
> Oni rastselovalis'*].
>
> The day was coming to an end. Everyone hurried back to work. Zal-
> kind, dressed for the street, caught up with Aleksei in the corridor.[13]

Beridze's integration into the party, however, is only the consequence
(at the beginning of chapter 13) of another event on the morning of the
same day. Titled "The Morning of November Seventh," chapter 13 opens
with an act of "transference-love" at the highest symbolic level, the erotic
character of which can hardly be denied. After this event, the theoretical
victory of the new over the old (theoretical because it is realized only after
endless discussions in the offices of the construction project) gets its resolution in praxis: from that moment on, to construct the pipeline is nothing less than "to defend Moscow on the [left] bank of the river Adun."
Here is what happens on "the morning of November seventh":

> Stalin's voice came suddenly, taking everyone by surprise although they
> had been waiting for some time to hear him speak. Now they held their
> breath to listen.
>
> Stalin spoke calmly and unhurriedly, with a tremendous inner power.
> Some of his words, traveling over thousands of kilometers, were lost in
> space amid the hum and crackle of the ether. The people gathered in the
> club missed the beginning, and it was the general impression that the lo-
> cal relay station had been late in picking up the broadcast.
>
> "Missed it, the blockheads!" Grechkin hissed wrathfully, but lapsed
> into immediate silence in response to a vigorous prod in the back from
> Aleksei, who stood behind him.

"Blueprint" variant of "The Morning of November Seventh" (book 1, chapter 13) of *Far from Moscow*. In this earlier version it was chapter 11, titled "Workday—the Seventh of November" ("Stalin's voice came suddenly, taking everyone by surprise although they had been waiting for some time to hear him speak").

Kovshov, his face pale, his eyes glued to the loudspeaker, stood drinking in every sound, at times guessed at rather than heard. The entire conscious life of Aleksei's generation was inseparably linked with Stalin, his work, his books, his speeches. From Aleksei's very schooldays, beginning with the day when the words: "We vow to you, Comrade Lenin . . ." had been uttered, Stalin had become for Aleksei Kovshov and other young people of his age the sole mentor whose authority was invariably lucid and infallible. When the war had broken out and many of the strongest and stoutest hearts had faltered, thoughts had turned with hope to Stalin. And they heard his heartfelt words: "Comrades! Citizens! Brothers and Sisters! Men of our army and navy! My words are addressed to you, dear friends!"

. . . And now Stalin was on the tribune once more. At this moment Aleksei was oblivious to all but the sound of Stalin's voice. That voice infused him with faith and courage.

Stalin did not offer solace. He knew that it was not consolation the people wanted, they wanted the truth. And as always it was the truth the people heard from Stalin's lips: ". . . Far from having abated, this danger is greater than ever. The enemy . . . is threatening our glorious capital, Moscow. . . ."

He who had instilled in the nation the consciousness that man is the most precious capital on earth courageously informed the people that hundreds of thousands of Soviet men and women had died fighting for their country. A profound grief could be felt in his voice as the words came slowly forth.

Suddenly Zhenia began to weep. She wept unashamedly, sobbing and wailing like a child. A hot lump rose to Aleksei's throat, choking him. Batmanov, who was standing next to Zhenia, raised his hand and silently stroked her hair, and the gesture seemed to embrace all those gathered there, as if the tears of this merry, vivacious girl were expressive of the grief felt by all.

"Ours is a just cause—victory will be ours!"

For several minutes a veritable tempest of applause raged in the loudspeaker. And here too, far from Moscow, in the dead of night, the three hundred people assembled in the log cabin club on the banks of the Adun stormily applauded Stalin. . . .

As Aleksei was elbowing his way out of the crowd, he was stopped by Beridze, a pale, agitated Beridze with inflamed eyes.

"Let's go over to my place, Aleksei, I want to talk to you. . . ."

"I'm sorry, Georgii Davydovich, I can't. I must be alone for a while." [14]

Aleksei Kovshov refuses to talk to Grechkin or anyone else, and heads back home:

> He wanted to treasure that feeling of uplift that filled him. He entered his room and locked the door. The place was as chilly as usual: a white cloud of steam issued from his lips at every breath, and a velvety layer of hoarfrost clung to the ceiling and the outer wall.
>
> Aleksei undressed swiftly and got into bed and for a long time he tossed restlessly on the hard lumpy cot, with his sheepskin jacket thrown over the blanket for warmth.[15]

The scene is followed by a description of Aleksei's thoughts about the war and the importance of "defending Moscow on the banks of the Adun." Some voices can be heard in the corridor; Zhenia Kozlova knocks at his door, but he does not respond; and he weeps over the "absurd dream" of eating strawberry ice cream with Zina at the Moscow agricultural exhibition, mourning the time when they were "like happy children."

A comparison of these perhaps surprising passages with the blueprint variants of *Far from Moscow*, which are more or less reproduced in the *Dal'nii Vostok* version, offers some additional surprises: as far as "The Morning of November Seventh" is concerned, the eroticism is less overt in the early manuscript versions. Stalin's voice, which here expresses "calm" and "tremendous inner power" was originally—and quite realistically— only "dull, unhurried, calm" (*Vozhd' govoril glukhovatym spokoinym netoroplivym golosom*); instead of "instilling" the "consciousness that man is the most precious capital on earth," as here, Stalin "establishes almost a personality cult in the country" (of the same "precious capital") (*Vozhd', utverdivshii v svoei strane pochti kul't lichnosti, prekrasnuiu istinu o tom, chto samym tsennym kapitalom na svete iavliaetsia chelovek*). As for the embraces, scenes of "undressing," and the lonely "treasuring of that feeling of uplift that filled him," they are already present in the early versions of *Far from Moscow*, but their *effet de texte* is weaker, if it can be felt at all, mainly because they are informed by a context that lends no ambiguity to their casual character. When, for example, Zhenia Kozlova knocks at Aleksei's door, the latter "could hardly refrain from bursting out with loud laughter": apparently the urge to "treasure" what had so recently "infused" and "filled" Aleksei had abated here, whereas it had not in the canonical version.

Did transference-love increase with the rewriting of the novel? There might have been a reason for this. "Write a novella and come back," were the words of the Chekist to the young lad in Azhaev's unpublished novella, written in the Corrective Labor Camp of the Baikal-Amur Main Line. We know that the writer felt much emotion when he sent his manuscript to Konstantin Simonov. In other words, the young lad had come back, and the editor in chief of "The New World" was his new reader. Now, we must discover what Simonov's response was.

During the months of May and June 1948, *Far from Moscow* went into production again, but this time the collective of the editorial board of *Novyi mir,* with Simonov at its head, helped the author turn the novel into a Stalin Prizewinner. As Dolmatovskii recalls, the "iron Simonov put the concrete [made of cement] Azhaev to work" (*Zheleznyi Simonov zasadil betonnogo Azhaeva za rabotu*).[16] The editorial reports document in great detail the rewriting of *Far from Moscow:* about 300 pages had to be cut, and more than 200 had to be rewritten. Many remarks pertain to the "bureaucratic" style of the Far East version, the many clichés and linguistic inaccuracies. Simonov strongly disliked one of the subplots, "related to crime, spying, and sabotage," and he suggested that Azhaev "weaken" this line considerably. Obviously, any allusions to the real experiences on which the novel was based had to be suppressed.[17] But the most objectionable aspect of the early version happened to be the various love stories involving the hero of the novel and other characters, which brings us back to our theme.

According to Simonov, love in *Far from Moscow* lacked integration. "Literature" was intruding into "life":

> Here is man who writes absolutely mature pages and passages. This is written by a man who has seen what life is. And besides all this you find these passages, these letters, memories of Moscow, these passages about Zina, and everything related to that, and this is very bad. Then we have Tosia and Serezha. They quarrel like some heroes by Inber used to quarrel.[18] This is the way students used to argue in some other stories. This is "literature," a "literature" taken from somewhere else and mechanically brought into this novel. . . . I don't like his Zina at all. And I got angry at the fact that this man shows off [*chto etot chelovek chto-to izobrazhaet iz sebia*].[19]

Zina is Aleksei's wife. In the *Dal'nii Vostok* version of the novel she stays behind in Moscow, longing for the return of her husband. The editor in chief of *Novyi mir* imagined a new beginning and a new end for Azhaev's novel—and a different Zina for Aleksei. "About Zina, about the beginning of the novel" (*O Zine, o nachale romana*), one of the editorial

reports is headed: the first chapter, depicting Aleksei's heartbreaking farewell to Zina shortly after their wedding, would have to be dropped; Zina
would appear only in flashbacks, as a partisan and intelligence officer op-
erating behind the German lines. This would reinforce the theme of Zina
in the novel. "About an active ending" (*Ob aktivnoi kontsovke*) reads another heading in the report: "I think that the end should be like this, that
the airplane gains altitude and the station is reduced to the size of a matchbox . . . and here one can feel the immensity of the homeland and the immensity of the future" (*oshchushchenie kakoi-to gromadnosti strany i gromadnosti budushchego*).[20]

Azhaev followed Simonov's instructions almost literally. Here are the
last lines of the Stalin Prize novel:

[Zhenia] darted impulsively to Aleksei, wanting to embrace him, then
stopped with upraised arms, and gazed hungrily into his face through a
blinding mist of tears.

He drew her towards him simply, with a newborn sense of freedom,
and kissed her. Zhenia turned and ran away, waving her red kerchief.

. . . The plane gained altitude, and the big town, the squares and rectangles of its blocks, swiftly diminished in size. The mirrorlike sheen of the
Adun was left far behind. The dense tangle of the trees, merging into a
dark green mass, sailed past under the wings of the plane.

The feeling of inner freedom, which had possessed Aleksei, did not
pass [*Chuvstvo vnutrennei svobody, vladevshee Alekseem, ne prokhodilo*].[21]

Kovshov gazed out eagerly, and the scenes of the past year seemed to
flash by him. It had been a hard year, a very hard year. But it had not been
lived in vain. He had found here, far from his native Moscow, something
that had come to be as precious to him as life itself.

The taiga below was suddenly cut through by a lane with two silver
threads of railway tracks. A railway station, reduced to the size of a matchbox, flashed backwards. Aleksei remembered having flown over the construction line several days before, and the amazing scope of it had struck
him. Now he thought with a thrill—in comparison with the whole country our tremendous pipeline is also no bigger than a matchbox.

He almost physically sensed the immensity of his country and of
everything that was taking place in its boundless spaces. He experienced
such a sense of exultation that he could have sung with sheer joy. Never
before had he, Aleksei Kovshov, been so keenly, so palpably conscious,
aware of his place in the life of his great Homeland, in her titanic struggle
for the future.[22]

Azhaev's archive indicates that the writer had been considering other possibilities. It even includes a synopsis, dated 1946, of a fourth book, depicting the hero's return to the Far East after his climactic encounter with the engineer of engineers, Joseph Stalin.

The editorial report contains an impressive thirteen-point list of what must be eliminated, rewritten, or added, and here again, love is targeted. It should never divert the story from "life," and if it does, the writer must revise. Aleksei's story is "complicated" by Zhenia Kozlova, one of his colleagues on the construction site, who falls in love with him. And he resists, thinking of Zina. In its *Dal'nii Vostok* version the novel ends with the image of Aleksei's "wounded heart" as he bids farewell to Zhenia: "Before Aleksei's eyes the red kerchief disappeared on the endless horizon. All that he cherished, that he found here, far from his Moscow, was literally gathered in this sign of farewell, wounding his heart."[23] Simonov helped the writer to resolve this conflict:

> I am against the fact that he has some philosophy with Zhenia. I want him to be uncompromised. Aleksei will be entirely pure, principled, and will not make any compromises. . . . It is important to underline the motive of male dignity. Not the fact that he does not want to live with another woman and that he is a man without romantic nature, but the fact that he does not want to live with another woman for the precise reason that he is a man, and that his wife is fighting at the front lines, and not here, and that he, as a man, cannot allow himself such a mean thought under these circumstances . . . and Zhenia, when she understands this, will begin to love him more.[24]

"Make [Zhenia] ugly" (*Zdelaite ee nekrasivoi*), suggests Simonov. Azhaev answers: "I don't much like the idea of introducing ugly women" (*Ia ne ochen' liubliu vvodit' nekrasivykh zhenshchin*). Here is the textual resolution of the dispute: in the *Dal'nii Vostok* edition Aleksei "looks at [Zhenia's] high breasts, outlined by the soft fabric of her silk blouse." In the *Novyi mir* version Zhenia is still "wearing a light silk blouse," but Aleksei's admiring gaze is given to the (omniscient?) narrator, who then shifts the focus: Zhenia "fixes her hair with plump arms bare to the elbows raised to her head."[25]

Zina/Zhenia and Aleksei are not the only couples in the novel; there are some secondary love stories. The doctor Ol'ga Rodionova is tormented by the specter of her husband, Konstantin, who died in mysterious circumstances related to the sabotage plot line of the novel. According to Simonov, this too must change: "With whom is Ol'ga tied up, let's think about it, how to relate her to other people. Let's agree about the fact that a knot has to be added concerning the love between Ol'ga and Rogov, a couple of pages have to be written about this."[26] Ol'ga, who develops a "positive" relationship with the heroic commander of the eleventh column, Rogov, will further develop that relationship in the *Novyi mir* version of the novel. Also, the senior engineer, Beridze, not only is interested in Aleksei, but also gradually becomes involved with the Komsomol shock worker and mechanic of communication Tania Vasil'chenko, calling her "Little Red Ridinghood on the Adun" (a translation of *krasnaia shapochka na Adune*).[27] This story "sounds real" and has to be developed, argues Simonov. But Beridze's past relationship with a certain Masha has to go. Batmanov's private life must also be better motivated: initially his wife refuses to rejoin her husband after (and because of) their son's death. Simonov suggests another reason: she cannot rejoin Batmanov because she is trapped behind the German lines on the southern front. The editor in chief proposed embedding Zina's and Aleksei's separation between front and rear in a parallel—and equally tragic—story line that would serve the mentor theme: the young engineer, Aleksei, must follow his role model, Batmanov, not only in work but also in life.[28] The "concrete" Azhaev only partly complied with these suggestions. Krivitskii, another member of the editorial board of *Novyi mir,* proposed complicating the relationship between Zalkind (the novel's *partorg*) and his wife with a dispute and a divorce, but the proposal was ignored by both Simonov and the author. Obviously this complication would not have made any sense at all. Only Zalkind's first name and patronymic were changed, from Abram Izraelevich to Mikhail Borisovich. This Russification remained incomplete, however, because the combination is still perceived as "Jewish" (although to a lesser degree), and it conforms to the complex dialectics of the struggle against "rootless cosmopolitanism."

There was not much space for resistance by the writer, and we can even evaluate how much was left of Azhaev's "subjectivity": in the margin of Simonov's list one finds "pluses" and "minuses," and sometimes "plus-and-minuses" added by Azhaev himself. In the novel published in *Novyi mir,* the "pluses" prevailed. The author somehow weakened the triumph of "patriarchal heterosexuality" in later editions of the novel by reintroducing some elements of Zina and Aleksei's unintegrated love story. This happened when the "objective conditions of possibility" were realized, namely, after Stalin's death. As a result of Simonov's remarks "about Zina, about the beginning of the novel," the lonely hero of the Stalin Prize version (chapter 3) pulls out of his pocket a folded note, written by Zina, who, as we already know, is now actively working for the partisans behind the German lines:

> "I've gone for my exams. Think of me. Only don't worry too much—I'm sure I'll pass. Zina."
> How much it had meant to him, this brief note which Aleksei had chanced to find in the drawer of the desk after discharge from hospital! He could spend hours reading it over and over again.[29]

In later editions of the novel the slip of paper is no longer found in the drawer of the desk, but is given to Aleksei by Zina at the last minute, before they part. "These were words of incantation, a naive and heartbreaking expression of a love which did not have time to blossom and was already torn off": "Alesha, my darling Alesha, I want this letter to be always with you. You must never, never forget that I am in this world and that I love you. . . . Alesha, my dear husband, I believe in our happiness. Because it's just that we should be happy. And we will be happy, we will, we have to. If this war would only end." [30] In the Far East version the following words were added: "How good and how painful love is!" (*Kak khorosho i kak tiazhelo liubit'*!).[31]

Let us go back "there," to the river Adun. On 3 March 1942 Azhaev wrote in his diary:

> We accompanied half of the leadership [of the camp] on their way to Saratov. I accompanied three: the boss V. A., M——va, and F. It is always sad to see somebody off when you know that you will stay behind. The impression that I won't be able to leave this place. At the railway station, everybody is dismayed. I accompanied F. further. Signed a book, *Gorky on the Volga,* for her with the following words: "There, on the Volga River, don't forget that somebody else stayed behind on the Amur." . . . We sat down, drank red wine, and kept silent. We got out of the train and went for a walk. Serezha and A. I. bothered us. We managed to kiss secretly before her departure. I returned home and was seized by a feeling of sadness. Part of it was the fact that it was very important for me to go west, and I was left here. Part of it is also the fact that I am attached to V. A., even more that I thought. I lay on my bed and closed my eyes. And I felt

gloomy: memories are left of all this; consequently, they are all turned into literature.[32]

What Azhaev had in mind can be seen in an eight-page story titled "Na sed'moi den'" (On the Seventh Day), found in his archive.[33] From the content it is clear that the piece was written sometime between 1942 and 1945 and belonged to the cycle of novellas on the "dialectics of love" that Azhaev mentioned to his friend Zhagir on 20 April 1941. "These seven days in Moscow were a real feast for air force captain Golubov." In a letter to his unit, the captain reports—in addition to his irrepressible desire to go back to the fighting—his impressions: the cordiality of unknown people whom he visited on behalf of his comrades at the front, the continuous music, the salutes, the Moscow Metro, the theaters, the Golden Star medal received from the very hands of Mikhail Ivanovich Kalinin.[34] We see the hero visiting his friend's family. To his enraptured listeners, among them a silent young woman named Lida, he narrates the ordeal by which he and his crew made it back home through enemy lines after their plane was shot down by the Germans over Smolensk. Then the story takes a private turn and develops along the lines of a romance, with heroic ingredients and a solid dose of "graphomania." After a visit to the Bolshoi Theater, where he sees a performance of *Eugene Onegin* and, during intermission, treats a group of admiring female students to chocolate and fruit, Golubov meets Lida again. He had received a scrap of paper with a mysterious telephone number which turned out to be hers. They talk about their mutual feelings ("I have known you for a thousand years"); they go to the movies, "where lovers always kiss" (and they kiss); he accompanies her back home; she feels a great deal of shame (he "forbids her to insult the woman he loves most on earth"); she invites him to her place (voicing feelings of shame again), where he discovers what he had not even suspected, "that cooking was such an interesting pursuit." At two o'clock in the morning Golubov proposes to her: "I drink to our marriage on the day I come back from the war." But the story has a tragic and "moral" ending. Lida, in tears, shows him a photograph of her fiancé, a navy officer, whose chest is covered with medals. The picture is signed "Captain Lieutenant Mironov, Hero of the Soviet Union." Golubov does not condemn her but cannot stay: "I cannot be here, with you, when Mironov is there. The day will arrive when we will both come to see you." "On the Seventh Day" ends with the sound of Golubov's footsteps on the stairs, the closing of a door, then "complete silence and solitude."

This is indeed literature "taken from somewhere else," and we have already seen what happened to this literature once it entered the official space of the late 1940s Soviet literary establishment. One can only speculate whether this specific story could have entered any other literary space, for romance or popular literature clashed here with socialist realism, in other words, with "highbrow" literature for the masses. At times, such romantic ingredients of socialist realism could function as a "declaration of independence," a "way of securing privacy while at the same time providing companionship and conversation," analogous to the one we find in Janice Radway's readers of Harlequin romances.[35] But because its function was determined by an entirely different context, simultaneously creating a time or space of one's own and its denial, the socialist realist romance failed for reasons that certainly included, but also went far beyond, male patriarchy.

Disturbed by the objective forces of history that the novel truly depicted, *Far from Moscow* lost many traces of the author's "personal fellow feelings." When the time came for Azhaev to voice them again, and to "explain," *The Boxcar* suffered the same fate as Aleksei's "feeling of inner freedom" that had been purged in the post–*Novyi mir* editions of *Far from Moscow*.[36] When the objective forces of history finally allowed this freedom to be felt again, well after the author's death, the explanation came too late, "sounded wrong," and aroused "bad feelings." Nonetheless, the many authors and "good editors" of *Far from Moscow* and other novels of Stalin's time left traces of many personal relationships and affections and gave the collective reader of the late Stalin era his or her, or their, own very subjective role to play in the "pearl of creation." As we already saw in the sample of letters written to the author, these traces could even save one's life.

Bakhtin, as I mentioned earlier, believed that Chernyshevsky had invented the principle of polyphony in his unwritten novel. Azhaev's novel paradoxically realized this principle: it was a story within the story, a novel and not a novel, a collection and not a collection, written by him or her, or them, unknown, with the difference that it was dedicated not to "Mlle V. M. Ch." but to Stalin. Personal relationships became objects of (ex)-changeable property for the primary purpose of cementing the bonds between men, or, to avoid any form that might be read as what the theorist L. I. Timofeev described as "distorted, absurd, and so on," for the primary purpose of cementing the "fraternity of the people of the whole world."[37] But this was to the advantage of neither men nor women, nor to the advantage of literature, and certainly not to the advantage of subjectivity in general. As far as "transference-love" was concerned, we could paraphrase Freud in changing part of his message: to urge the patient to suppress, renounce, or sublimate his instincts the moment he has admitted his erotic transference is certainly not an analytic way of dealing with them, but it was definitely a way that made sense for those who were busy implementing, at any cost, the concepts of integrated love and male dignity.

It also made sense for some of the novel's readers. Alla Lubenskaia, a tenth-grade student who lived in Moscow, loved Tolstoy, and declared her intention of becoming a teacher of literature, wrote the following letter to the author of *Far from Moscow* in June 1949:

Comrade Azhaev!
A couple of days ago I read your novel *Far from Moscow* and I would like to make known to you, the creator, my impressions. In fact, I don't know whether the word "creator" is suitable in the given case. You collected, reworked, and put into form a true story about the great achievements of simple Soviet people. But let me first say a few words about me. I am a tenth-grade student here in Moscow, I am very fond of literature, I love children, and therefore I want to choose an occupation that will satisfy these two conditions. I want to become a teacher of literature. But this should not be a formal regurgitation of what I have learned, this should be creative work. I want to teach them to love our literature, our great and powerful, our truthful and free Russian language (Tolstoy). I want to teach them to understand it, this is the most important thing (and for this I have to understand myself). I have been told that I understand literature, but I am looking forward to having your entirely unbiased judgment as an author. I regard your book highly, and I could elaborate on this quite at length. But I think that you have been told about its merits a lot and many times. I would like to share with you what I did not like. I find the relationships between A[leksei] Kovshov and Topolev, and A[leksei] Kovshov and P[et'ka] Gudkin (at the end of the book) not very real and truthful. I understand the great significance of friendship, and, if you want, I will even admit that friendship between men is stronger than between women, that it is less egoistic, but male friendship distinguishes itself by the fact that it needs few words, that it avoids the outpouring of loving declarations and lyricism. This kind of love is rather coarse, but that's what makes it touching. I would qualify the relationship between Topolev and Aleksei as too sweet, even affected. Why use all these words:

dear [*milyi*], my dear [*dorogoi*]; why all these embraces, these triple kiss-
ings, what for? This makes these relationships inauthentic, even false,
it doesn't suit these strong men. Aleksei, this powerful, strong-willed,
and courageous man, has on several occasions "tears of emotion" in his
eyes. I hope you won't need other examples. These lyrical comments ac-
company these men all through the novel, almost from the beginning to
the end. Don't get me wrong, I won't say anything against Aleksei's tears
when he learns about Zina's death. On the contrary, this makes him closer
to us, more understandable, more charming, but you can't lump everything together.

The letter continues in the same vein: the future teacher of literature ac-
cuses Azhaev of not understanding the psychology of young boys, and she
quotes a scene where the young Pet'ka Gudkin "sneaks up to Aleksei, embraces him; then, following a short walk, again these same kisses and embraces, and other sweetnesses without end." Alla Lubenskaia writes that
this criticism will not do the writer any harm, but it will be useful for her,
so that she can "understand [her] own mistakes." A postscript asks the author if he can tell her about "the further destiny of Aleksei, and of all his
friends. . . . Because a great life awaits them and much work." [38]
    Although the doors were now open to a "great life," Azhaev could tell
his readers as little about the "further destiny" of his characters as he could
tell them about their past. There was no destiny. He had called on the Styx
to witness his promise, the river of the oath of the gods. But he had also
crossed the Lethe, the river of oblivion. Vasilii Azhaev had come back and
given the People's Commissariat of Internal Affairs (NKVD), now renamed
the Ministry of Internal Affairs (MVD), and its various organs their Stalin
Prize literary work—in coded form, of course. But if transference-love
had happened, the patient had been called upon to suppress, renounce, and
sublimate his instincts.

11

A THOUSAND AND ONE NIGHTS:
FAR FROM MOSCOW
AND ITS READERS

Dear editor!
We ask you to inform us about the real author of the book *Far from Moscow*. This book has attracted the attention of many readers in our sub-unit and there are disagreements as to the authors [*sic*] of this remarkable book.
It would be good if the newspaper could publish a short autobiography of the author of the book.

> Second Sergeant V. Razumov
> Second Sergeant E. Evtushenko
> Second Sergeant A. Rudenko
> —Letter to the editor (date and name
> of newspaper unknown)

The granite tombstone was placed over [Topolev's] grave. It was hidden by the wreaths of fresh flowers. The red ribbons of the wreath which Rodionova and Aleksei had placed on top fluttered in the breeze, and it looked as though red butterflies were beating their wings, lingering over the grave. . . .
Nikifor, the Nivkh, stopped Batmanov and told him that he had brought down the body of Kondrin.
"The birds have pecked him a little," Nikifor said apologetically. "But he's all there. What are we to do with him?"
"Bury him in the taiga. Flatten down the grave so that there should be no trace of it."

> —*Far from Moscow*, book 3, chapter 10

From the stenographic transcript of a readers' conference discussion of *Far from Moscow,* we learn about Azhaev's own emotion before his collective, a collective that "taught me how to live." The document is untitled and undated, but Azhaev, as always, organized the work of the future archivist ahead of time: a list headed "Readers' Conferences and Discussions about the Novel of V. Azhaev *Far from Moscow*" found in his archive indicates that the conference took place at the Dzerzhinskii Club of the MGB and MVD (the Ministry of the State Security and the Ministry of the Interior) on 3 February 1949.[1] Konstantin Simonov, opening the session, commented at length on the conditions under which the novel had been rewritten, and on the fact that the writer had shown a lot of "character" in his work with the editors of *Novyi mir,* a quality that he had undoubtedly acquired on the construction site depicted in *Far from Moscow.* Complying with the unavoidable ritual of criticism, Simonov mentioned one "serious shortcoming," which was, again, the treatment of love. Love, he said, was shown "with less depth than the relations between the characters in their work and in their friendships," and Simonov expected that in Azhaev's future writing "his wonderful heroes will not only be good and strong people, but they will feel with more intensity, they will love more profoundly, their love will be stronger."

One of the conference participants agreed with Simonov's remarks and went even further, saying that he "shared the pain" of an acquaintance who secretly confessed to him that she would have liked Zhenia's (Kozlova's) love for Aleksei to have been "realized." Other readers related the book to their own specialty: "I want to express to Azhaev our gratitude that he wrote a good and truthful book about the construction, which was the project of our Chekists"; "from this tribune one should speak about the book's educational aspect, about the fact that it inspired feelings of pride (applause)* in our Soviet man, who is building and who will continue to build, thereby advancing toward the majestic completion of communist construction, overcoming all difficulties on the road toward the shining

*Notation in the stenographic report.

future." Another reader conveyed the "great expectations" of his collective: "Some of the colleagues of our Main Administration were on that pipeline and thus had a particular interest in reading Comrade Azhaev's book." According to this reader, the author had succeeded in conveying their feelings at a time when, though stationed about 10,000 kilometers from the theater of military operations, they had worked as if they were actually on the front line. He expressed his hope that some of the other great construction projects carried out by the collective of construction workers of the Ministry of Internal Affairs would be depicted in future publications.

Critical voices could also be heard. One reader did not like the character K. at the end of the novel (the abbreviation evidently stands for Kondrin, the wrecker who is killed on the island of Taisin): "Everything was fine and suddenly he arrives. This is a wrecker of the 1930s, but he should have been shown differently, so that we could recognize him as a wrecker of the present day." Another reader also felt the need to keep abreast of the times when he quoted the words that Topolev (an old engineer who turns out to be progressive) addresses to the conservative engineer (and near-wrecker) Grubskii about the latter's lack of "Russianness." [2] We know that the readers' conference took place in 1949, the year of the struggle against "rootless cosmopolitanism." [3] "Comrades!" said yet another participant, "Many collectives from our Ministry have indeed worked far from Moscow, and therefore we greeted the novel of the same name very warmly." But he too criticized the author for his treatment of love: "The author has been a little cruel with Zhenia, who was nurturing good feelings toward Kovshov. It would have been more colorful if the author had united the destiny of these heroes." The same reader declared that "many of the characters existed in reality. . . . Some of them are people we know—Batmanov, Beridze. What a pity that Comrade Barabanov, represented by the name of Batmanov [in the novel], is absent. But Kovshov is here with us today." And he proposed that Kovshov come forward and talk "about himself and to what extent the author had been successful in depicting his heroes." "Kovshov," however, kept silent.

Asked several times about the main idea of the novel, Azhaev answered: "Our socialist system is remarkable for the fact that it helps each person find his place in life. This person should not have a passive attitude toward his fate. One needs to have a personal Five-Year Plan of development and growth." Responding to those readers who attempted to identify the characters in "life," Azhaev insisted that his novel was not a photograph of events, but reflected the "typical characteristics of the human being," of "our human being, educated by the Bolshevik Party." One of the MGB/ MVD readers commented on the geography of the novel: "The title *Far from Moscow* was not chosen by accident. The distance is geographic, but the reader does not feel any distance, in fact, he feels only the Soviet approach to reality. What happens is actually very close to Moscow." Before this reader could continue he "was interrupted" (*ne dali dogovorit'*). Whenever, in his response to readers, Azhaev addressed questions of the novel's geography or of the "real" identities of his characters, his sentences become vague and end in a series of ellipses: "In the construction site I changed the geographic names; as to representing people . . ." The typed document has been corrected by hand, the ellipsis inked out, and this sentence is linked to the one that begins the next paragraph: "I followed the method of selecting features typical of people I knew, among whom I was working. In this sense, it was important to show the characters rather than such or such a detail or feature. I am a writer, and I cannot say whether Batmanov is Barabanov, and whether Kovshov is—" The sentence ends with a triple correction: some initials followed by ellipses, a name that could be "Akopian," and another that looks like "Karapetian." On 7 February 1941 a person bearing the latter name had told his colleagues of the Camp of the Lower Amur a story about a fugitive and his "foolish struggle with nature." Confronted by his collective of readers, Azhaev obliterates the traces of real life at the very moment he utters them. But by now it was increasingly difficult for the writer to control his own montage, for the "whole country" was reading *Far from Moscow,* as we know from Azhaev's list of conferences.

According to this list, between 12 October and 31 December 1948, twenty-four "conferences and discussions" were organized, starting with the Soviet Writers' Union in Moscow and ending with a middle school in Gzhatsk (Novosibirsk Region). The next year brought many more. The author's typed list ends on 30 March 1949 with another sixty-five, about fourteen of which have been added by hand. Obviously Azhaev was unable to keep up. The list itself is worth reproducing here because it shows the very process by which the Soviet readership of the late 1940s was organized.

Readers' Conferences and Discussions about
V. Azhaev's Novel *Far from Moscow*

1. Soviet Writers' Union	12 October 1948
2. Builders of the Zaporozh'e Industrial Complex "Zaporozhstroi"	22 October 1948

3. Dostoevsky Library (Moscow) — 27 October 1948
4. Factory No. 30 (Moscow) — 1 November 1948
5. Central Aerohydrodynamics Institute (TsAGI) and A. N. Tupolev Construction Bureau (Moscow) — 3 November 1948
6. Turgenev Reading Room (Moscow) — 11 November 1948
7. Lenin Pedagogical Institute (Moscow) — 19 November 1948
8. Moscow State University — 25 November 1948
9. Pushkin Library (Moscow) — 26 November 1948
10. Pedagogical Institute in the city of Khabarovsk — 27 November 1948
11. Marx Library (Moscow) — 29 November 1948
12. All-Moscow readers' conference in the newspaper *Moskovskii Komsomolets* — 30 November 1948
13. Shevchenko Factory, city of Sverdlovsk — 2 December 1948
14. Konin Club, city of Egor'evsk — 7 December 1948
15. Shevchenko Library, city of Orsk — 11 December 1948
16. Collective farm club "Molod'" (Leningrad Region) — 17 December 1948
17. Central House of Engineers and Technicians (Moscow) — 17 December 1948
18. Lenin Regional Library, city of Gor'kii — 18 December 1948
19. Library of the Factory of Cold Ore, city of Lipetsk — 19 December 1948
20. Lenin Library (Moscow) — 20 December 1948
21. Stalin Factory (Moscow) — 22 December 1948
22. Officers' House, city of Alma-Ata — 22 December 1948
23. Pedagogical Institute, city of Syktyvkar (Komi ASSR) — 29 December 1948
24. Gzhatsk middle school, city of Gzhatsk — 31 December 1948
25. Central Hospital of war pilots — 4 January 1949
26. City Party Office, city of Sovetskaia Gavan' — 9 January 1949
27. Railway Library, city of Shcherbakov — 12 January 1949
28. Library No. 3, city of Samarkand — 15 January 1949
29. Pushkin school, city of Erevan — 5 January 1949
30. Municipal District Committee of the VLKSM, city of Baku — 21 January 1949
31. Mining-Metallurgical Institute, city of Alma-Ata — 25 January 1949
32. Kirov Pedagogical Institute, city of Kirov — 28 January 1949
33. City Committee of the VKP(b), city of Nal'chik — 29 January 1949
34. State public library, city of Stalinabad — 29 January 1949
35. Municipal library, city of Krasnoiarsk — 30 January 1949
36. All-City conference, city of Lipetsk — 30 January 1949
37. District library, city of Abakan — 1 February 1949

38.	MGB and MVD (Dzerzhinskii Club)	3 February 1949
39.	Moscow River Technical School	4 February 1949
40.	Regional library, city of Khabarovsk	8 February 1949
41.	Pedagogical Institute, city of Kemerovo	9 February 1949
42.	All-City conference, city of Voroshilov	11 February 1949
43.	All-City conference, city of Astrakhan	11 February 1949
44.	All-City conference, city of Alma-Ata	13 February 1949
45.	Municipal library, city of Michurinsk	13 February 1949
46.	Lenin Palace of Culture, city of Groznyi	13 February 1949
47.	Editorial-Publishing Institute and Technical School of the OGIZ (Moscow)	14 February 1949
48.	District library, city of Dmitrovo	18 February 1949
49.	State ball-bearing factory (Moscow)	21 February 1949
50.	Herzen Pedagogical Institute (Leningrad)	22 February 1949
51.	Municipal library, city of Murmansk	22 February 1949
52.	Central Club of the Workers of Art (TsDRI)	28 February 1949
53.	Factory "1905" (Moscow)	1 March 1949
54.	Library of the road construction workers, city of Omsk	2 March 1949
55.	Pedagogical Institute, city of Kuibyshev	3 March 1949
56.	Podol'sk factory, city of Podol'sk	4 March 1949
57.	Magnitogorsk factory (Magnitogorsk)	4 March 1949
58.	Palace of Pioneers (Leningrad)	5 March 1949
59.	Zaporozh'e, All-City conference	6 March 1949
60.	All-City conference, city of Saratov	6 March 1949
61.	Central library, city of Novosibirsk	8 March 1949
62.	Regional library, city of Cherkessk	8 March 1949
63.	Officer's House, city of Baku	9 March 1949
64.	Moscow Institute of Oil Industry	10 March 1949
65.	School No. 333 (Moscow)	12 March 1949
66.	Central Teacher's House	16 March 1949
67.	Factory "Bogatyr'" and library of the Sokol'niki district (Moscow)	18 March 1949
68.	Library of the Alabushevo settlement and Library Institute (Moscow Region)	18 March 1949
69.	City Committee of the VKP(b), city of Kashira (Moscow Region)	18 March 1949
70.	Factory "Hammer and Sickle" (Moscow)	19 March 1949

71. Vorovskii library, city of Ramenskoe   19 March 1949
72. Library of the Palace of Culture, city of Vyks   20 March 1949
73. Regional Committee of the VLKSM, city of
    Vladimir   20 March 1949
74. Potemkin Pedagogical Institute (Moscow)   21 March 1949
75. Administration of the UITLK MVD of the
    Moscow Region   22 March 1949
76. Committee of the District Party Organization
    of the VKP(b) and library of the Sovetskii district
    (Moscow)   24 March 1949
77. Ministry of Communication and Transportation   25 March 1949
78. The Red-Bannered Fleet of the Amur   25 March 1949
79. Zhukovskii War Academy (Moscow)   26 March 1949
80. Krasnogorsk Factory (Moscow suburb)   27 March 1949
81. Textile Institute (Moscow)   28 March 1949
82. The Rublevskii district conference
    (Moscow suburb)   28 March 1949
83. Readers' conference of the enterprises, institutions,
    and institutes of learning of the Krasnopresnenskii
    district (Moscow)   28 March 1949
84. Central House of railway workers (Moscow)   29 March 1949
85. Dormitory of Moscow State University   29 March 1949
86. Higher School of the Ministry of the State
    Security (MGB)   29 March 1949[4]

The conferences added to the list by hand took place from the end of March through mid-May 1949 at the Frunze Academy, a coke and gas factory, the Main Administration of the Northern Shipping Ways (Glavsevmorput'), and the regional library of the city of Birobidzhan (Jewish Autonomous Region); a "radio conference" was broadcast at 9:00 P.M. on 13 April 1949. It goes without saying that these meetings and conferences mushroomed throughout the country well beyond April 1949. They seem to have abated somewhat at the end of that year. The last two readers' conferences that I found documented in Azhaev's archive were organized in 1951 and 1953, the first in a regional bank in Gor'kii, the second by the mobile library of a factory.[5]

Some of the stenographic reports of these conferences were sent to the writer and preserved in his archive, which also contains materials beyond

Readers' Conference poster announcing a discussion of V. Azhaev's novel *Far from Moscow*, Committee of the Library of the District Party Organization of the All-Union Communist Party (Bolshevik) of the Sovetskii District (Moscow, 24 March 1949).

those on his list. It is clear that Azhaev could not be present in person at all these conferences, many of which were held simultaneously in different parts of the country. Most of the readers' statements reflect the ideology of the moment and offer few surprises, responding in accordance with a scenario planned well in advance. For example, conference 76 on Azhaev's list, which took place on 24 March 1949 in the Sovetskii district of Moscow, was organized according to a plan provided five weeks earlier, listing the following items:

1. Supply the library with the maximum possible quantity of copies of V. Azhaev's book *Far from Moscow*.
2. Make a poster in triplicate announcing the event.
3. Put together exemplary themes for the discussion of the novel.
4. Put together a recommended list, a folder of materials, critical articles from newspapers and journals.
5. Prepare no fewer than 15 readers for their appearance at the conference.
6. By 1 March elaborate the themes of discussion of each reader who will speak at the conference.
7. Organize a collection of readers' discussions about V. Azhaev's book *Far from Moscow* and prepare a bulletin devoted to it for publication.
8. Compose the text of the invitation and send out 300 invitations.
9. Invite to the readers' conference the author of the book, V. Azhaev.
10. Generalize [*obobshchit'*] the materials of the conference, collect from the conference participants their discussions, impressions, and desires.
11. Make up an album devoted to the readers' conference discussing V. Azhaev's novel *Far from Moscow*.[6]

A few months later the plan itself "went public" in an article titled "Chitatel'skie konferentsii" (Readers' Conferences), published in the July issue of *Novyi mir* and signed by N. Kovalev, "Party organizer of the Central Committee of the VKP(b) in the Stalin automobile factory" (in Moscow).[7] After a general introduction, the lengthy, inevitable quotation from Lenin's "Party Organization and Party Literature," the demonstration of the superiority of Soviet belles lettres over all others, of the free and democratic character of this literature, "read not by the 'top ten thousand' bored and suffering from obesity" but by "millions and tens of millions of laborers," the institution itself is presented through the example of the "Palace of Culture" of the Stalin automobile factory in Moscow, or simply ZIS, for

Azhaev speaks to readers at the Club of the Herzen Institute, Leningrad, 12 April 1949.

zavod imeni Stalina (Stalin factory). In the Small Hall and Lecture Room of the Palace, we learn, discussions had recently been held on a series of literary works, among others Azhaev's *Far from Moscow* and *Across the Map of the Homeland* by N. Mikhailov. Then follows a detailed description of the conditions under which the conference will take place, containing the same elements that we have already seen itemized in the plan of the Sovetskii district library, plus a few details that are worth mentioning:

> And now arrives the day of the readers' conference. The passionate readers of belles lettres (and there are a lot of them in our factory) don't stay too long in their shops and sections, but instead try to go home earlier in order to put on a better dress, to have another look at the book, reread the passages that they like most, prepare their remarks for the discussion. . . .
>
> The Small Hall or the Lecture Room is gradually filling up. It is called the Small Hall not because it is in fact small, but because in the Palace of Culture there is also the Great Hall, which holds more people. The Small Hall normally welcomes about five hundred participants to readers' conferences. The spacious Lecture Room, with its circle of benches, like a student lecture hall, contains about three to five hundred people. The participants of the conference will occupy all the benches and aisles.[8]

According to Kovalev, the readers' conferences "represent the last link of a long chain of tremendous work, provided by the Party organizations and the Party committee of the factory in the propaganda of ideas contained in the works of literature."[9] As a result, literature is explicitly deprived of any autonomy. Kovalev writes: "Our readers, in contrast to some backward critics, compare the books to life and not to some kind of literary genre. One can understand the worker Borisoglebskaia when she speaks angrily of these aesthetes who see in the heroes of V. Azhaev's novel not living people but only schemes." And he quotes her words: "These aesthetes don't know the living people, they are detached from them, but we know them well, we are ourselves similar to V. Azhaev's heroes, every day we meet Beridze and Kovshov in our factory."[10] None of this means that the literary work being discussed is devoid of flaws. On the contrary, the imperfections revealed, far from diminishing its artistic valor, allow the author to correct and perfect it. In sum, Stalinist literature and culture can be theorized as driven by the "dynamics of two tendencies: the affirmation of the excellence attained by Soviet works of art, and the recognition of the fragility of such achievements (it is always necessary to do better, to advance in the hierarchy, etc.)."[11]

The reader depicted by Kovalev is strikingly close to the "ideal" reader of the late Stalinist era, about whom Evgeny Dobrenko writes: "Born in the pages of the press," this reader is a "pure product of State power"; she or he is its "horizon of expectations." But should we leave—as the author suggests—the "material dimensions" of this ideal reader "to sociology or cultural anthropology" and focus only on "certain proper historical and cultural aspects of the phenomenon" (*nekotorye sobstvenno istoriko-kul'turnye aspekty iavleniia*)? [12] It seems to me that the "ideal" itself is always the product of material dimensions because there is no such thing as history and culture proper, unless it is itself the product of idealization. Fortunately, Dobrenko goes beyond the "pages of the press" and infers from various data, such as statistics on readers' preferences and check-out counts from provincial libraries, some very concrete and material dimensions showing that the "ideal," or "state," reader did not always read the same books, that, for example, readers in the countryside and on the periphery read authors different from those read in the city or at the center.

The stenographic reports found in Azhaev's archive, along with other, similar materials, are of exceptional interest because they represent a stage prior to the "pages of the press." Not unlike the writer's own ellipses and corrections, or the shifting positions of the pipeline and the river Adun, they show the space of encounter between the material realization and its ideal. Suffice it to compare an excerpt reproduced by Kovalev in his *Novyi mir* article on a speech given by Comrade Muromtsev, foreman of the Motor No. 2 division of the Stalin factory, during a discussion of Azhaev's *Far from Moscow* on 22 April 1949, with the stenographic report of the same event found in Azhaev's archive but not included in his list. The translation attempts to reproduce the discursive specificities of both versions.

Novyi mir:
We are the people of peaceful work, we don't want war. Now a gigantic struggle goes on between two social systems: the world of socialism and the world of capitalism. And here one world demands that man lives well, happy, secure, not exploiting and not being subject to exploitation, and the other world is built on hatred against man, on the negation of man.

I read A. Fadeev's speech at the congress of the advocates of peace in Paris. A. Fadeev quoted excerpts from the book of the American commentator William Vogt. [13]

Stenographic report:
We are the people of peaceful work, we are people of the construction,

we don't want war. We know that the future is for us. We are not afraid that we'll have too many people, we don't have to exterminate them. Now a gigantic struggle goes on between two social systems. And here you have a world that demands that man lives well, so that there won't be exploitation of one man by the other. The other world, today was published the speech by Com. Fadeev at the Congress for peace, where he says graphically about this other world, which is opposed to our peaceful construction site, against what is done in the capitalist world.

He quotes an excerpt from the works of William Vokht.[14]

Going beyond copy editing an oral text for publication, the editors of *Novyi mir* literally "make sense" of the at times incoherent sentences of Comrade Muromtsev's speech. Before reaching the "pages of the press," the flow of his discourse is truly polyphonic, with verbal islands of the "Big Other" alternating with words and phrases from his own world, a world that focuses on the construction site. All this undergoes a thorough transformation (almost in Chomsky's terms) into standard sentences, with additions (and some deletions) that elevate the still formless material of the foreman's performance into the well-formed ideal of state language and thought. The operation strikingly recalls some analogous phenomena that make up the very stuff of Soviet literary history. What I have in mind are the changes undergone by such texts as Fedor Gladkov's production novel *Cement,* from the original of the 1920s to its socialist realist canonized version of the 1930s and 1940s: oral speech (*skaz*) and other stylistic and thematic devices of Russian modernist writing were systematically tranformed into the type of discourse so well exemplified by Comrade Muromtsev's "literary" embodiment in *Novyi mir.*[15]

The fact that the "line" of the day was reflected in these readers' discussions as in a mirror, with many citations of Lenin, Stalin, Zhdanov, and Gorky, did not prevent its audience from "reading in," as we saw with Muromtsev's authentic speech, their real-life concerns, using their own formulations, their own language and style, in accordance with their position in the social field, their geographic or class origin, their gender, and other parameters.

Here are a few more examples from Azhaev's archive. As the stenographic report of the readers' conference of 12 October 1948 (the first on Azhaev's list) shows, one could be altogether "in tune" and still be a "backward critic." Fedor Levin, who had earlier participated in the discussion of 15 April 1947 organized by the Committee of the Soviet Writers' Union on Russian Literature of the Regions and Districts of the RSFSR (see Chapter 9), decided to abandon the polemical style of his earlier criticism. Now, according to him, Azhaev's novel belonged to the "great series" of classics, which included Gladkov's *Cement,* Valentin Kataev's *Time, Forward!* and Iurii Krymov's *Tanker Derbent.* At the same time, Levin could not resist challenging the author to continue to work on his "literary and professional know-how." For example, "instead of declaring that Batmanov suffers (when he learns about the death of his son), the author should have shown the suffering." Levin urged the author not to feel "dizzy" at the novel's huge success, but to go on working.[16]

Other interventions explicitly addressed the issue of popular literature. "Azhaev is good every time he writes about the production process," said another reader. "But when he treats such problems as love and the personal feelings of the heroes, he falls to the level of very low quality belles lettres."[17] Aleksei Kovshov's conduct in love "sounds hypocritical," stated the critic Anatolii Tarasenkov, who also touched on the problem of rewriting history by pointing out some of the novel's "historical inaccuracies": the fact that the characters use personal radios, which were confiscated during the very first days of the war, and that Stalin is characterized as "commander in chief" (*verkhovnyi glavnokomanduiushchii*), a title he assumed "only later." All this shows that Azhaev "violated the artistic truth of the image."[18] Other readers, such as Comrade Akshinskii, who came from the Far East and was an "auditor of the Higher Party School attached to the Central Committee," expressed institutional and regional concerns. Akshinskii regretted that Azhaev had failed to attach enough importance to the role of the party and to "the transformations by which the Nivkh, Nanai, and other small peoples of the North joined the great Soviet family."[19] For the writer Aleksandr Chakovskii, on the contrary, the publication of *Far from Moscow* represented the "triumph of the communist worldview" and "served as an example for the Stakhanovite movement."[20]

The response of the Stakhanovites to Azhaev's novel can be deduced from the stenographic report of a readers' conference organized among the "Builders of the Zaporozh'e Industrial Complex" [*Zaporozhstroi*] (22 October 1948; item 2 on Azhaev's list).[21] Like the account of the Dzerzhinskii Club, the typed transcript reveals the intervention of a pen (or pencil) which, this time, belonged not to the author but to the person who, as we shall see, prepared the readers' interventions (and the author's response) for publication in the newspaper of the construction site. Some passages or words (such as names of local bosses) are crossed out; others are underlined or queried in the margin. The transcript also contains critical comments and editorial remarks such as "to be kept," "to be corrected, but very slightly" (*nado popravit', no ochen' miagko*), "and what about the conclusion?" and so on. Finally, each page is numbered and initialed by the typist, whose name is spelled out at the end of each reader's text. Some pages are missing, including the first six (out of fifty-eight).

Most of the readers praise the novel and point out only minor "inaccuracies." But Ivan Vikent'evich Sobolevskii, the party organizer of Zaporozhstroi, has a lot to say against Azhaev's novel.[22] He is the alter ego not only of Kovalev, the *partorg* of the Stalin automobile factory who made it to the most central "pages of the press" with his article on readers' conferences in *Novyi mir,* but also of Zalkind, the party organizer in *Far from Moscow.* Comparing the two construction sites—his own and the one depicted in the novel—Sobolevskii wonders about the conditions that led to the catastrophic situation depicted at the beginning of the book, when almost everybody wants to leave the shores of the river Adun, discouraged by the inefficiency of the (former) leadership, which had brought the project almost to a standstill. He raises questions about Azhaev's party leaders—where they were at that time and why the party organizer Zalkind allowed the situation to degenerate. At the Zaporozh'e construction site, says Sobolevskii, it was enough for the party leaders and the builders to intervene, and most problems were solved. Sobolevskii gives very concrete examples from 1946, when Zaporozhstroi missed its first government deadlines. After a successful struggle headed by the party organization, both the director of the construction, Nazarenko, and the main engineer, Komissarov (both names are crossed out by the editorial pen), were "dismissed with great noise" (*sniaty s treskom*), including the "recovery of unauthorized expenditures [*s nachetom*] and reprimands." They had been more interested in their personal affairs than in the construction: Nazarenko "had brought back a radio from Germany and was busy building his own house." As for Komissarov, he "liked to drink." Therefore, argues Sobolevskii, those who were responsible for slowing down the construction in *Far from Moscow* (Merzliakov, the head of the last section on the mainland, for example) "should have been depicted as saboteurs, counterrevolutionaries, or as members of some underground organization."

Following Comrade Zhdanov's directives on the need to organize "socialist competition," the Stakhanovites of Zaporozhstroi made the construction a success. The characters in Azhaev's novel, however, failed to follow these principles. Although the book depicts the enthusiasm of the leaders, it neglects the participation of the workers themselves. Sobolevskii frankly dislikes the mechanic of communication Tania Vasil'chenko ("little Red Ridinghood on the Adun"). He demonstrates that "there are no such people in reality": she takes too many liberties with the leaders; she even uses *ty* (the second-person singular) and other familiarities in addressing the *partorg* and other leaders. We also see her in the editorial office of the newspaper of the construction site, where she starts to rummage through the papers. In real life she would have been thrown out of the office immediately. Commenting on the negative character Kondrin, Sobolevskii notes some disturbing inconsistencies: at the end of the novel Zalkind discloses Kondrin's identity—he was the son of a kulak. "For whom did he work before?" asks Sobolevskii. "Where did he come from? . . . How can it be that he is first a dangerous wrecker, but then turns out to be a pitiful coward? . . . The novel takes place in the Far East, i.e., in the border zone. It would have been correct to link Kondrin's activities to the very real presence of Japanese spies. All this would have served to educate the reader to be more vigilant."

In these comments Sobolevskii effectively reconstructs the subplot of the novel "related to crime, spying, and sabotage," a subplot that the "iron Simonov" and the "concete Azhaev" had eliminated, or at least "weakened," during their work on the novel a year before. Sobolevskii admits that "it would be unjust to say that the novel is not interesting," for the problems "are well posed, and in practical terms correct." But instead of showing the builders themselves, he says, Azhaev showed only the leadership: "We have to attract to our construction effort the carpenter, the bricklayer, the plasterer, the electric welder, the gas welder, so that they will see their heroes in the novel and will imitate them. When they showed *Chapaev* in the movie theaters, the next day the militia had to disperse the population, who started to riot: some were playing Chapaev, others the machine-gunner, the fights spilled over into one street after another . . . (laughter)."[23] Sobolevskii concludes by encouraging Azhaev to correct his novel and to add "more fighters, more Matrosovs."[24]

Some participants agreed with Sobolevskii that there were too many leaders in Azhaev's novel and not enough real builders. "Where are the carpenters, the concrete workers, the fitters, the boiler-makers, etc.?" asked one participant. "Azhaev knows the construction only superficially."[25] Others disagreed, some quite strongly: "One should not forget the fact that the construction in the novel took place during the war, that the heroes of 1941 did not build like those of 1947."[26] "Azhaev showed the collective and the initiative of the masses correctly," said Comrade Usyskina, referring to the dispute over the "left variant." She also rose to the defense of Tania Vasil'chenko and explained her "liberties" by recalling the fact that Zalkind and her father "had been partisans in the same detachment [during the civil war]."[27] What Usyskina is "reading in" here, referring to a passage from the novel, is one of the important myths of the Stalin period: that ties created by the Revolution are stronger than kinship, and thus Zalkind is "more than a father" to Tania Vasil'chenko. Mark Ivanovich Nedushko, "former head of Stal'montazh" who was also a welding specialist, noted that "the whole pipeline seems to have been built by one welder, Umara Magomet." And he shared with the participants his own experiences: "In order to build thirty-four kilometers of pipeline in Leningrad, eighty welders were needed, and for the Astrakhan–Saratov pipeline four hundred." He asked the visitors from Moscow and from *Literaturnaia gazeta* "to take a hard look at our construction, which is a great source for great novels."[28]

The conference ended with Azhaev's response. He explained how difficult it had been to write his first novel and said that "it is easier to write a chronicle than to give the generalized plan that I imagined." He would take the stenographic report with him and return to it "more than once." His last words, before expressing his gratitude to the builders of Zaporozhstroi, were addressed to the party organizer:

> I could engage in a polemic, in particular with Comrade Sobolevskii. I was awaiting his speech with great interest, I had been told in Moscow a lot of interesting things about him, but, to be honest, I have to say that I was disappointed by his speech; it seemed to me to be below Comrade Sobolevskii's potential; perhaps he did not have the time. He summoned me to correct my book, but this is not an easy thing to do; this should be done on the basis of very serious and qualified criticism, addressed to the novel.[29]

An editorial comment in the margin reads, "This here is not so good" (*vot eto uzhe nekhorosho*).

Far from Moscow had aquired a dynamic of its own. From another list found in Azhaev's archive, we discover that the author attempted to integrate the novel's increasing plurality in his montage of life. A handwritten document, headed "Criticism and Bibliography on Vas. Azhaev's Novel *Far from Moscow,*" lists reader responses from an "authoritative" and "representative" array of sources published between August and December 1948.[30] Articles on Azhaev's novel appeared in the central press, in *Literaturnaia gazeta,* which published several editorials on the novel as well as articles by such "big names" as N. Atarov, V. Ermilov, A. Makarov, P. Pavlenko, and V. Smirnova, as well as in *Komsomol'skaia Pravda, Kul'tura i zhizn', Moskovskii komsomolets, Smena, Trud,* and *Vecherniaia Moskva.* The Soviet periphery was represented by *Tikhookeanskaia zvezda* (with an article by N. Rogal', who, as we recall, had helped Azhaev to "resolve the question of publication of the novel [in *Dal'nii Vostok*] through Glavlit"), *Molodoi bol'shevik* (Petrozavodsk), *Krasnoiarskii Rabochii, Sovetskaia Belarussia, Kommunist Tadzhikistana,* numerous local *Pravda*s (*Amurskaia, Leningradskaia, Grodnenskaia, Orlovskaia, Poliarnaia, Tambovskaia, Ul'ianovskaia*), and many others. We also learn that the readers' conference described in the preceding paragraphs actually occurred by "decision of the Party committee" of Zaporozhstroi. Azhaev's list mentions an article published on 2 October 1948 in *Stroitel'* (The Builder), the newspaper of the Zaporozh'e construction. The stenographic transcript of the conference was published a week after it took place "as an editorial on the second page" of the same newspaper.[31] The interventions of the editorial pen mentioned earlier give us an idea of the final product. To what extent this product conformed to the text for the ideal reader could not be established; I did not find it in Azhaev's archive.

We have seen that the author of *Far from Moscow* did not always appreciate the critiques of his readers. He also disagreed with some opinions that were expressed in the major pages of the press. In a letter of 10 April 1949 to Vladimir Ermilov, editor in chief of *Literaturnaia gazeta,*[32] Azhaev vigorously complained about an article by M. Shkerin published that same month in the journal *Oktiabr'.* It was titled "On One of the Main Heroes: Apropos of Some Written and Unwritten Novels."[33] According to Azhaev, this article had minimized the work he had done with the editorial staff of *Novyi mir* on *Far from Moscow* since its original publication in *Dal'nii Vostok:* "During this work, I cut 300 pages (about 30 percent) of the text and wrote about 240 pages anew" (*Ia sokratil 10 avtorskikh listov* [*ili pochti 30 protsentov*] *teksta i do 8 listov napisal zanovo*).[34] Azhaev felt that Shkerin's article was "yet another attack by *Oktiabr'* against the journal *Novyi mir*" and requested that his letter—a copy of which was sent to the Secretariat of the Soviet Writers' Union—be published in *Literaturnaia gazeta.* One month later the Secretariat answered with a short "excerpt of a decision" acknowledging Shkerin's declaration "that he had no intention of minimizing the work of the journal *Novyi mir* with the book of V. N. Azhaev."[35]

Azhaev's intervention must, of course, be understood in the double context of a previous polemic between the two journals and the contemporary campaign against "rootless cosmopolitanism," during which almost everybody was trying to outbid everyone else. In early 1948 Shkerin had published a series of articles in *Oktiabr'* criticizing Il'ia Ehrenburg's novel *Buria* (The Storm), which had appeared in *Novyi mir* the year before. *Novyi mir* counterattacked with various articles and published in October and November 1948 a critique by D. Danin of Mikhail Bubennov's *Belaia bereza* (White Birch Tree), praised by Shkerin in the May 1948 issue of *Oktiabr'* as the "most important work of the year 1947." In the January 1949 issue of *Oktiabr'*, Shkerin responded by accusing Danin of being a "consummate aesthete and cosmopolitan." As far as Azhaev was concerned, personal reasons may have increased his solidarity with "his" journal: according to Irina Leonidovna Liubimova-Azhaeva, the author of *Far from Moscow* had previously submitted his manuscript to Fedor Panferov, the editor in chief of *Oktiabr'*, but the manuscript had been "lost."[36] In any case, Shkerin's minimization challenged Azhaev's montage of life. Because a "great deal" was invested in this work, and because "on the human level" Azhaev wanted "very very much for this novel to please," the author paid great attention to the "plurality of spaces" that it engendered. The fact that this plurality included the reproduction and dissemination of *Far from Moscow* is confirmed by the following letter, written on 8 April 1949 to the director of Mezhdunarodnaia Kniga, the agency for publishing works abroad:

> After having been informed by you that my book *Far from Moscow* was designated for publication in a series of foreign countries, I feel the need to let you know beforehand that one should recommend for translation into foreign languages the definitive revision of the text of my novel published in the separate edition of Sovetskii Pisatel', not the previous version published in the journal *Novyi mir*.
>
> After its publication in the aforementioned journal, the book underwent a substantial revision by me. I include the text of the novel and I ask that the publication of the book for sale abroad follow this text (and only this text!).
>
> I ask you also to notify about this matter other organizations con-

nected with you which are engaged in publishing books by Soviet writers abroad (Sovinformbiuro, VOKS, etc.).[37]

The author's recurrent "definitive revisions of the text," however, went against the tide of readers' expectations. A student officer of the Tomsk Artillery School in Siberia wrote to the editorial staff of *Novyi mir* in June 1950: "It requires a lot of guessing and interpreting of the words of the novel's heroes, namely, those of the engineer Beridze, voicing his recommendations to the workers about the achievement of the construction, to guess that the construction will actually be achieved. What happened here is what happened in *A Thousand and One Nights*, where the tale was interrupted at the most interesting moment and one had to wait for the next night."[38]

"We liked the book very much, but we are not quite satisfied with the end of your novel. We are interested in the further destiny of the heroes," wrote a female reader from the village of Novo-Vasil'evka, Zaporozh'e Administrative Region, Ukrainian Soviet Socialist Republic.[39] "We send you our miners' brotherly greetings," reads another letter, which came from Zapoliar'e, more precisely from the city of Vorkuta, Komi Autonomous Soviet Socialist Republic.[40] The author of the letter, "born in 1895," asked Azhaev to send him a copy of *Far from Moscow* "because it is impossible to purchase the book here. . . . How good it would be to sit in the evening with the children all gathered, and to read the book aloud. But I can't find it anywhere."[41] A letter of 20 June 1949 by the same author thanked Azhaev for having sent him a personal copy of the book and invited him to his house: he would welcome him "like [his] own son."[42] And here is the opinion of a reader from Leningrad: "What a wonderful book you have written, Vasilii Nikolaevich! . . . I am told that your heroes are too ideal. But the new people of the new order should be like this." She added in a postscript that the director of the factory where her husband worked suggested that all the heads of departments read *Far from Moscow* "without fail" (*v obiazatel'nom poriadke*).[43]

Azhaev's archive contains many such letters, although the author's widow notes that "whole boxes" were thrown away. Some letters are very private, whereas others can be categorized as official or business correspondence. A young author asked the Stalin Prize laureate for help in getting his first novella published; a translator from East Germany requested the author's intervention in his struggle with the editors of the Berlin publishing house Kultur und Fortschritt, who took too many liberties in correcting his translation.[44] A letter on the letterhead of the Chinese People's Literary Publishing House inquired whether the author would like to revise his novel for a new edition in the People's Republic.[45] L. Olitskii, who translated *Far from Moscow* into Yiddish, wrote to Azhaev to inform him that his translation had not only appeared at Yidish-bukh in Warsaw but also been reprinted in the Parisian newspaper *Noye Presse* and by the Buenos Aires publishing house Haymland.[46] A Pskov theater director asked for Azhaev's permission and advice on adapting *Far from Moscow* for performance on the local stage, since this would be his "first large-scale staging for the theater."[47] A student of the Philological Faculty of the T. G. Shevchenko State University in Kiev wrote to the author about his projected dissertation, tentatively titled "The Solution to the Problem of Socialist Labor as Aesthetic Category in V. N. Azhaev's Novel *Far from Moscow*."[48]

Because these letters to the author belong to a specific tradition, a ritual falling somewhere between the public sphere and intimacy, they display more openness than the organized conferences and discussions and show an increased investment by the readers in Azhaev's "pearl of creation." Many of these letters came from deep within Russia and many were written on simple notebook paper or pages torn from accounting or other official books. Their writers were mainly students, soldiers, workers, novice or would-be authors, members of local editorial boards. Evidently very few came from collective farmers or other inhabitants of the countryside. Often these letters were produced at a school desk or in a workers' club as a result of a discussion, on assignment by a teacher, or at the suggestion of the director of a reading room or of the party organizer. They retell the plot, repeat the "correct" commentary, and congratulate the author on his Stalin Prize. At times, whole essays and notebooks of interpretation were attached, and some letters were written in verse:

Ia uzhe stara, mne trudno v vozraste
                                        takom
Nachat' pisat' na knigi otzyvy
                                        stikhom
I prozoi ia pisat' tolkovo ne umeiu
Skazhu slov neskol'ko o Vashei knige,
                                        kak sumeiu!
Vo-pervykh, khochetsia mne Vam skazat',
chto esli b tak, kak Vy, mogli pisateli pisat'
Chitatel' mog-by dumat'—Vy ne sochiniali
Vy prosto tochka v tochku—zhizn'
                                        pereskazali. . . .[49]

I'm old already, and find it hard at such
                                a time
To start writing book reviews
                                in rhyme
And because to write in prose I am equally incapable
I'll say as few words about your book
                                as I am able!

First of all, I'll make quite clear:
That if all writers wrote like you
Readers would think—no story here
But life itself all told,
                                all true. . . .

Other letters were more personal: they urged the author to rewrite part of the novel, to increase or change the moral qualities of a hero, or to emphasize the role of diverse professions and social categories, including women. Some writers were less anonymous or more professional than others; some even take us back to Komsomol'sk and Camp Freedom. A former colleague from Komsomol'sk invited the author to join the builders who had started a new section of the pipeline in January 1949, stating that it would be "very useful" for the writer to familiarize himself with the continuation of this work after eight years "under the conditions of peaceful and creative labor" (*v usloviakh mirnogo sozidatel'nogo truda*).[50] At the end of July 1949, a former prisoner sought Azhaev's help. Section 39 of the Instruction on Passports gave him no right to reside in Komsomol'sk-on-the-Amur, his permit was set to expire on 1 August, and he needed 2,500 rubles to leave the Far East with his children, "if only to [get to] Irkutsk." He promised to pay back the money.[51] And in September of the same year, a physician wrote from Podol'sk that she had recognized herself—and even a report she had composed—in the pages of his novel:

Podol'sk 9.27.49

Com. Azhaev! I read your book *Far from Moscow* with twofold great pleasure. I danced, sang, and laughed, in seeing the regrouping of facts used by you in the depiction of your heroes. In Tan'ia Vasil'chenko, I recognized myself. Thanks to the author, that he mentioned my work on this Project. Tan'ia's whole line of conduct is the line of conduct of the sports physician. Obviously, the report that I sent to the head of the sanitary

ХАБАРОВСК ОТДЕЛЕНИЕ

МСвязи СОЮЗ СОВЕТСКИХ ПИСАТЕЛЕЙ

ад ВАСИЛИЮ НИКОЛАЕВИЧУ

АЖАЕВУ

К-маркса 15

5 этаж

=УСТЬЕ ОМЧУГА ДАЛЬСТРОЯ 2 61 2 0444=

=МЫ ИЗ ДАЛЕКОГО УСТЬ ОМЧУГА ДАЛЬСТРОЯ ПРОВЕДЯ
КОНФЕРЕНЦИЮ ЧИТАТЕЛЕЙ ПО ВАШЕМУ РОМАНУ
,,ДАЛЕКО ОТ МОСКВЫ ,, ШЛЕМ ВАМ ГОРЯЧИЙ ПРИВЕТ И
БОЛЬШУЮ БЛАГОДАРНОСТЬ ЗА ВЫСОКО ИДЕЙНУЮ И
ПАТРИОТИЧЕСКУЮ КНИГУ ЗПТ ВОСПИТЫВАЮЩУЮ СОВЕТСКИХ
ЛЮДЕЙ В ДУХЕ КОММУНИЗМА И ЖЕЛАЕМ ВАМ ЕЩЕ БОЛЬШИХ
ТВОРЧЕСКИХ УСПЕХОВ ЗПТ ПОМОГАЮЩИХ СОВЕТСКИМ ЛЮДЯМ

УСПЕШНО СТРОИТЬ КОММУНИЗМ ТЧК

=180 ПОДПИСЕЙ ЧИТАТЕЛЕЙ++

Telegram signed by "180 readers" from Ust' Omchug of the Dal'stroi Complex to V. Azhaev in Khabarovsk, thanking him for having written a book that helps the Soviet people to build communism.

department of the Camp of the Lower Amur got into your hands, and served as the canvas after which you stitch the heroes of the novel.

The regrouping of the facts is unavoidable. You did a great job. I thirst to meet you. What a pity that I did not notice you at that time, or forgot about you. Please write to me. In September you were expected in the Writers' Union, but then your arrival was somehow postponed, so I decided to write to you.

My work address: city of Podol'sk, D. S. O. Stadium "Machine Construction," Sports Physician Il'inskaia Taisia Leonid[ovna].

Home: village of Pokrov, house 60, Strel'kovyi s. o., Podol'sk District, Moscow Region.

Come and see me when you are in Moscow. After you arrive at the Podol'sk station, give a call to the motor pool and they'll give you a light vehicle—I live about five km from town. We'll talk personally about all the heroes of the novel, they all existed, you only put some makeup on them—some got a lot, others only a little.

With com. [radely] greetings, physican Il'inskaia[52]

Another series of letters came from an old acquaintance, P. Zhagir, Azhaev's colleague at the Camp of the Lower Amur and coauthor of "An Alien Calendar." Between 1950 and 1953, Zhagir several times asked Azhaev for help, and his old friend complied, as one can infer from these letters. In a letter of November 1950, sent from Alma-Ata, Zhagir told the author of *Far from Moscow* about his "new life." Zhagir had now decided to return to literature; he was writing for some local newspapers, but this was not enough to support himself. Despite the fact that their last meeting "was not very gratifying" because of "the huge difference in status, and other matters," Zhagir asked Azhaev to assist him in finding a job "in some Moscow-based publishing houses," as a "special correspondent for Kazakhstan," for example. Zhagir was still writing and had published three essays after visiting various collective farms, but people had not yet gotten used to him "as an author." And, above all, he still needed a permanent job. He would like to publish something in the Moscow journals, but "would not take a single step without [Azhaev's] advice."[53] From a letter of 1 August 1951, we learn that Vasilii Nikolaevich had replied. More than a year later a letter from Zhagir informed Azhaev that a collection of his reports would be published by the Alma-Ata Publishing House, news that filled him with "unlimited joy and gratitude."[54] His next letters were sent from Stalingrad, where Zhagir had found a "permanent job." In one of these letters he asked Azhaev to intervene in order to "push through" the collection, still in limbo at the Alma-Ata publisher. Azhaev noted in the margin, "Inquiry to the publishing house [*Zapros v izdatel'stvo*], 16 April 1953."[55]

Some of the letters received by Azhaev go farther back in time: a group of former schoolmates congratulated their colleague "Vasia" (diminutive for Vasilii) on his Stalin Prize.[56] A former colleague from BRIZ (the Bureau of Rationalization and Invention) hoped that the writer would still be inspired by his previous activity and offered his services and expertise.[57] Azhaev's supreme distinction had refreshed the memory of many old friends and acquaintances. It also created new ones. A letter from the communist writer Jack Lindsay to his "dear friend," written in the early 1950s and forwarded to Azhaev by the Foreign Committee of the Soviet Writers' Union, informs us that the British author was then "writing a novel together with the dockers," and that he was attempting to "introduce socialist realism in our literary tradition" and to learn Russian.[58] Among the letters I also found a list of questions to be asked by the French novelist Pierre Daix, editor of the newspaper *Ce Soir,* in an interview that took place—as a brief note by Azhaev indicates—on 22 August 1950. Daix was interested in, among other things, "how Azhaev had become a writer," "what he had written before *Far from Moscow,*" "how the idea of the book had occurred to him, and how the writer had worked on it."[59]

Reader responses came from the satellite countries and beyond, well into the 1950s: the archive contains letters from Bulgaria, Hungary, Romania, East Germany, Poland, North Korea, France, Holland, and even from the United States. Sovinformbiuro, VOKS, and above all the journal *Soviet Literature,* of which Azhaev became editor in chief in 1960, did their job well. "Today I read for the fifth time the translation of your book *Far from Moscow,*" wrote a reader from Czechoslovakia on 3 January 1957. He informed the author that his novel was among the most valuable books in his personal collection "of six hundred volumes" and asked him to "write something else on this theme" and to send the addresses of some of his friends, depicted in the novel, so that he could start to correspond with them, enhance his knowledge of the life of these people together with his command of Russian, and exchange stamps.[60]

" 'When a word comes from the heart, it falls into the heart,' says an Arab proverb." We find this quote in a letter sent to the author in 1949 by a student at the Institute of Oriental Studies, Leningrad University. The letter continues:

> From the first pages, the book captivates the reader by its simplicity and its proximity to life, almost palpable through the reality of its images. In introducing the reader to his hero, the author arouses the joyous feeling of satisfaction and dignity which appears whenever one happens to meet a very decent person. All the heroes of the novel are real people (I don't have in mind those freaks of the Soviet family, such as Grubskii, Khmara, Rodionov). The image of Batmanov is so charming that it is difficult to believe that it is the product of the writer's imagination. . . . As to Tania Vasil'chenko's courage, her strength, her spontaneity, her conviction—all this does more than delight us, we want to be like her, resemble her a little bit.[61]

But not all of Azhaev's readers were charmed. Here is a letter sent from a somewhat cryptic location: Usta station, Gor'kii Railway, village 2 Chernoe, Bureau of Timber Exploitation of the Factory "Krasnoe Sormovo," a place that is, as the letter writer says, "not far from Moscow":

> The deeds, the motives of the heroes are well justified, they correspond to reality, one believes, all this is true. True.
> But this pains the ear:
>   Adun, Rubezhansk, Novinsk. . . .
>   Especially as there is: Boiko-Pavlov, Nevel'skoi (very good!).
>   "A great writer" called Sakhalin simply: Sakhalin. Chekhov's *Sakhalin Island*. Why classify it as a secret, what for?[62]

The novel by Vasilii Azhaev, this Scheherezade of the somber postwar years, has since been forgotten. But at the time of its publication, *Far from Moscow* fascinated its readers, sometimes even bewitching them, prompting a miraculous recovery or provoking a confession. Recall the letter from a female worker who told the author that her doctors had agreed to postpone a critical operation in order to grant her her last wish—to finish reading *Far from Moscow*—and she survived. An officer of the army, based in the capital, wrote: "We don't know each other, but I use the word 'comrade' to address you because we, the Soviet people, live under the sun of the Stalin Constitution, which makes us comrades."[63] In another letter, this one from "far away" in the Udmurtsk Autonomous Soviet Socialist Republic, the writer informed "Comrade Azhaev" of the friendship that he had felt for books and their authors since his childhood. But the real grounds for his message were more serious:

> The measures taken by our government have never been alien to me and I never doubted their validity. But then I found myself unexpectedly over-board from the life of our state [*no vot neozhidanno sluchilos' tak, chto ia ochutilsia za bortom zhizni nashego gosudarstva*]. I had committed crimes against the state in the past, I had been a convict, I was released before the end of my sentence because of good conduct, but after this I have not be-come better for all that and despite my immense desire to be an honest fighter for communism, I have become a black sheep which cannot find a way out of the haunted forest. . . . Why is it impossible for me to distin-guish good from evil? I am not able to sort things out. Everything is so confused that I was led to feel happy when I was notified that I would be put under arrest. Is there no other path for me to find a place in life? As strange as this sounds, I think that I am evil to the point that there is no other place for me than imprisonment.[64]

According to the author of this letter, *Far from Moscow* shows that its creator knows "what fills the human soul" and how to "sort things out." He would like to tell him everything, from the beginning of life to the present moment. There is no doubt that Azhaev's reader from the Udmurtsk Autonomous Soviet Socialist Republic perceived the possibility of transference-love as it was expressed in the "strictly objective" line of *Far from Moscow*. But this was only one of many possible readings. Other readers responded to the "subjective" line of the novel, to the romance of "F. and V.":

> Dear comrade! My beloved writer!
> I urge you ardently to respond to my great personal grief.
> Your opinion, your good word could play an enormous role in my life. The questions I address to you are complex. But it seems to me that their solution is possible. And this is so indispensable! I and my husband have lived apart for five years. There is only one reason why: my husband, who respects me deeply as a human being, cannot love me. He lives a lonely life, a painful one, like mine, enduring this irreconcilable misun-derstanding between the two of us.

Through all these years I deeply loved and suffered, realizing my inability to strengthen our family. But I believed that a strong, devoted love would gain me victory and would compel the heart of my beloved to wake up. Because we are equal in everything and first of all in labor! We have a wonderful daughter! But as of now, this has not happened.

1. Tell me, is our reunion possible, if only because of the love of the wife?

2. Can our daughter play a decisive role in the solution of this problem?

3. Can a Soviet person [*chelovek*] educate his feeling of love toward the other, in realizing the necessity of it?

4. What would be the conduct of an authentic Soviet person?

I believe that you will not remain indifferent to the fate of three simple Soviet human beings. Your answer can open our eyes a great deal, it can unite our family.

How happy we would be! For this there are so many possibilities, except one.

I very, very much ask you to answer.

Sincerely

Anna Gavrilova[65]

From a short note written on this and many other letters, we know that an "answer was sent." But while Azhaev still attempted to integrate his readers into the montage of life, the whole country had already started to watch *Far from Moscow* on the screen. And with this new phase of "mechanical reproduction," transference continued to be suppressed.

12

THE SCREEN

Com. Il'ichev:	What was left out from what we saw?
Com. Stolper:	The operations on the strait were left out.
Com. Dubrovina:	This will be in the film?
Com. Stolper:	Yes.
Com. Il'ichev:	What kind of remarks will there be? Make the film in this spirit.
From the floor.	Yes.
Com. Il'ichev:	This will be a good film.
Com. Dubrovina:	A good film, a real film.
Com. Zaslavskii:	A strong film.
Com. Dubrovina:	Ivanov plays Pankov well.
Com. Zaslavskii:	In the movie the storm is dragged out.
Com. Stolper:	Everything will be much shorter.
Com. Surkov:	The shooting is good.
Com. Zaslavskii:	The actors are good. All like one man.
Com. Il'ichev:	The girl gives out a little. Dobronravov should have played Topolev? This actor too acts pretty well. But he has red eyes.
Com. Surkov:	He is a tired man, he is old.
Com. Il'ichev:	During the meeting he stares with red eyes.
Com. Surkov:	He is a bit overintellectualized.
Com. Il'ichev:	Okhlopkov is good.
Com. Dubrovina:	I like him less than all the others.
Com. Surkov:	With the boy, it's a good scene, when they are sitting on the sofa.
Com. Zaslavskii:	This is a great scene. One can feel Okhlopkov's intelligence, his strong will.

Com. Il'ichev:	He is an intellectual, a smart leader. This is very good. Sverdlin is good. The scene with the telephone is good, after the criticism.
Com. Stolper:	Liberman's dialogues must be cut somewhat.
Com. Il'ichev:	Otherwise he will be the most laughable figure.
Com. Dubrovina:	This will be a good film. This is an achievement.
Com. Il'ichev:	We wish the comrades good luck.
Com. Stolper:	Thank you.
Com. Il'ichev:	With this I consider our meeting closed.

> —Minutes of the session of the Artistic Council of the Ministry of Cinematography of the USSR: viewing and discussion of the film *Far from Moscow* (27 June 1950)

I saw *Far from Moscow* on the screen, but I will tell you honestly that the film left no particular impression on me. One would think that such a work could not be stuffed into the frame of a film. On the other hand, this film is useful and good for the periphery, so that the weaker forces can get acquainted with it and be encouraged to read the book and absorb all the beauty that it provides.

> —Letter from Mariia Sergeevna Krukovskaia, Moscow (12 January 1951)

Far *from Moscow* engendered several sequels, including various theatrical performances and an operatic adaptation by I. Dzerzhinskii (1955). But the most important one was a film bearing the same title, directed by Aleksandr Stolper and based on a script by Mikhail Papava, itself inspired by Azhaev's novel. Released in 1950, the film was awarded a Stalin Prize (first class) in 1951.

In an article that appeared in a 1973 collection of essays dealing with the difficult question of the relationship between literature and cinema, the Russian film historian Maiia Turovskaia expressed her views on the problem of "screening the classics." [1] She wrote that some critics consider such an endeavor doomed to fail (the film diminishes the text, transforming literature into a product for mass consumption—in other words, "this has nothing to do with Tolstoy"). For others, a "good" cinematic version requires the invention of a specific "algorithm," a kind of grammar that transforms written narrative into film. According to Turovskaia, this is a false distinction. Rather than "translating" literary prose into cinematic language, the film uses its proper resources and the talent of the director to tell its own story. A good film of literary origin is therefore one that "struggles against the model," that "disrupts the process of perception"; or, to use the good old formalist term, it is one that "defamiliarizes." Turovskaia concludes that films inspired by secondary, qualitatively inferior works have a greater chance of becoming convincing products for the simple reason that they do not have to waste energy liberating themselves from the verbal structure of the model. Turovskaia gives an example of a "translation" that, despite its box office success, failed in trying to follow the model too closely: Samson Samsonov's film *Poprygun' ia* (The Grasshopper, 1955), adapted from Chekhov, reintroduces with all the power of its technique the materiality that the great author "spent all his life trying to dematerialize." [2]

The Soviet cinema of the late 1940s and early 1950s experienced a dramatic decline in production, a shortage that was inversely proportional to the volume prescribed by the "plan." From a stenographic transcript of a meeting of the Committee on Cinema of the Section of Scriptwriters on 9 January 1948, we learn that the Ministry of Cinematography had ordered the production of "more than fifty films of high quality, illustrating our era and, above all, the activities of our heroic people." [3] These projections turned out to be far ahead of reality: the Soviet "propaganda state" produced seventeen films in 1949, twelve in 1950, and hit an all-time low of nine films in 1951. A large percentage of Soviet postwar feature films were filmed theatrical performances, so one has to subtract them to obtain an overall count of genuine films. [4]

One of the rare genuine films of 1950 was *Far from Moscow*. How many people saw it is difficult to say, but it never attained the popularity of its literary model. Azhaev's archive contains very few letters mentioning the film, and those that do are rather negative or indifferent. The same is true of the press, which paid little attention to the Stolper-Papava version of *Far from Moscow*, beyond the ritual acknowledgment of its Stalin Prize. As it turns out, not only did the film have "nothing to do with" Azhaev, but

The head of the construction site, Batmanov (N. Okhlopkov), criticizes the supply chief, Liberman (V. Vladislavskii), for failure to carry out his orders. (Still from *Far from Moscow,* Mosfil'm, 1950.)

Workers carry the engineer Topolev (A. Khanov) on their shoulders after the successful explosion of charges, laid in a line across the Nevel'skii Strait in order to open a trench for the pipeline. This technical procedure had actually been conceived by Topolev. (Still from *Far from Moscow,* Mosfil'm, 1950.)

it also failed to be a better product than the "secondary, qualitatively inferior work" that had inspired it. Lacking distance from its model, it made visible—that is, it "materialized"—what lay on the surface of the novel, in turn obscuring what lay behind. For today's viewer, despite the fact that the film cuts the length of the story to about one hundred minutes and has some beautiful outdoor shots of taiga, a frozen river, and a lot of snow, it increases "conflictlessness" by reducing the plot to a succession of lengthy dialogues between the main characters which alternate with "epic" construction episodes. The film also provides a literal example of "varnishing" of reality: the use of color furthers the flattening of the narrative, depriving it of the documentary aesthetic it could have attained if the film had been shot in black and white.[5] Moreover, the film ensured that viewers of the early 1950s would have no chance of recovering any of the story's original transparency: it closed off access to the novel's "deep structure," which comprised the thousand and one disparate, contradictory, displaced, or sublimated utterances of the collective reader, who had recognized in this text not only more than life as it was but also some of the writer's own transference and other aspects of subjectivity.

If the film was judged useful and good for the periphery, this was also its status within the hierarchy of Soviet artistic values. In accordance with the often described primacy of literature over the other arts in Stalinist culture, of prose over poetry and other "lesser" forms, the novel's film version had to compete against the general model of the "mastery of life," as expressed by the "masters of the word," to quote the title of Mstislavskii's 1940 article. We recall from Azhaev's diary of 1941 that this article was literally the writer's bedside text: in addition to discussing it with his boss, he was reading it at night.

The definitive article on the film *Far from Moscow* appeared in January 1951 in the journal *Iskusstvo kino,* the organ of the Ministry of Cinematography of the USSR. The official critical discourse reproduces, in its own way, the mastery of the word over the other arts. The hierarchy is as follows, from top to bottom: literary model, script, art production, acting, work of the camera operators. The author of the article, Kira Paramonova, first elaborates on the success of the novel, which "organically" integrated "national/popular spirit" (*narodnost'*) with "Party-mindedness" (*partiinost'*)—two key concepts of socialist realism—by showing that the lives of the nation, of the people, and of the party realize themselves in collective work. The article also takes into account the inherent difficulty of transposing to the screen such a long and complexly structured work. On this front, says the author, Soviet filmmakers achieve victories but also

suffer defeats: "The road is far from being paved to the end." Although
scriptwriters often choose to rewrite the original completely, this practice
"often lays bare the scriptwriter's weakness and gives bad results." Instead,
"the correct approach [is] to find a dramatic solution to the [literary]
source, and this is precisely what Mikhail Papava has done." Rather than
depicting individuals and their particular destiny, "the experienced and
thoughtful scriptwriter . . . has foregrounded the collective of pipeline
builders."[6]

Paramanova underlines the "creative complementarity of the screen-
play and the art production." Even if the film version betrays a certain
schematism, Papava has found a solution that is true and interesting overall, and this solution has been interpreted and enriched with subtlety
by Stolper's direction. The film's "authors" have succeeded in realizing the
atmosphere of free socialist labor on the screen. They have not limited
themselves to representing but have succeeded in expressing what is creative, what is new, and the fact that it brings happiness. For Paramonova,
Stolper was able to repeat the originality of his direction in the film *A Story
about a Real Man*—that is, "the bringing out of the collective."[7] The critic
insists on the simplicity of the expressive possibilities used. Without re-
sorting to "spectacular" resources, Papava has been able to reproduce Soviet life in its most real and typical manifestations.

For Paramonova, the actors whom Stolper has chosen accord perfectly
with the novel's characters; they are "true to life." Her highest praise goes
to Nikolai Okhlopkov, who plays the key role of Batmanov, head of the
construction site, "experienced organizer and political leader." Recalling
the role Batmanov played in real life, we understand Paramonova's approval, and why this character is present in almost all the scenes of the
film. Other characters, carefully chosen from the novel's long cast, receive
an adequate interpretation. Some of them, however, do not meet Paramonova's expectations. The portrait of Zalkind, the party organizer, for
example, leaves much to be desired: "The talented and skilled artist L[ev]
Sverdlin failed to render the living characteristics of the wide-ranging
Party leader." His speeches and replies to other people are too "monotonous and declarative. . . . A charming smile and some meaningful glances,
this is all that the actor has found to compose his character."[8] The archaeology of the texts that are the source of the film has shown us that the
character Zalkind had experienced literary problems of representation well
before he had reached the screen.

For the work of the camera operators A. Shelenkov and Chen Yulan—
work of the lowest grade in the cultural hierarchy—Paramonova has only

praise. They, like the screenwriter, were careful not to "distinguish" themselves: their work "does not stick out" (*ne vypiraet*). Rather than insisting on complicated technical solutions, they chose to follow a more difficult course: they shot each scene as simply as possible in order to express the greatest authenticity, the very chronicle of life, the document. Paramanova ends with some general remarks: the film offers a number of "superficial solutions"; the scriptwriter, Papava, and the director, Stolper, are blamed for a certain "dryness" and lack of depth in the depiction of their characters' internal states. But overall, the film shows that its creators are headed for a bright future. Paramonova concludes by quoting the supreme literary reference, a classic among the classics: "The great Gorky wrote: 'Our books are expected by the people, and the people are waiting for books that are strictly realistic, that are made to shine and glow by the fire of the pathos of labor and heroism, of which all our Soviet life is filled.'"[9] "How close these words are to the art of film!" adds Paramonova. "Our films too, are expected by the people. The people too are waiting for films that are made to shine and glow by the fire of the pathos of labor and heroism, of which all our Soviet life is filled. The noble duty of our filmmakers is to give the country such films!"[10]

A file of documents, deposited in the Russian State Archives for Art and Literature, shows that the cinematic version of *Far from Moscow* had been prepared at the highest levels.[11] On 21 June 1949, the Artistic Council of the Ministry of Cinematography held a discussion on Mikhail Papava's script in the presence of some of the supreme dignitaries of Soviet culture. Chaired by L. F. Il'ichev, editor of *Izvestiia* and head of the division of propaganda of the Central Committee, the council was composed of, among others, Vladimir Ermilov (editor in chief of *Literaturnaia gazeta* and chief literary theoretician of the Zhdanov era); the novelist Leonid Leonov (delegate to the Supreme Soviet, member of the presidium of the Soviet Writers' Union, and at that time busy writing his *Russian Forest*);[12] the poet Aleksei Surkov (who was about to receive his second Stalin Prize and become one of the secretaries of the presidium of the Soviet Writers' Union); David Zaslavskii (a notoriously visible publicist of the period, one of the champions of the struggle against "rootless cosmopolitanism," despite the fact that he was Jewish); and the minister of cinematography, Ivan G. Bol'shakov. Because the document does not indicate first names, other participants are more difficult to identify.

Azhaev gave his opinion of the script, since he would "not be able to participate in the discussion of the Artistic Council," in a letter addressed to Il'ichev on 4 July 1949. The author confirmed that Papava and Stolper had conducted their work in "close contact" with him, that they had done a much better job than those who had prepared various recent theatrical stagings, which he had judged "very inferior," and that they had agreed with all of his remarks and made the necessary changes. Azhaev expressed his "special satisfaction" that both had agreed to end the film with a scene in the Kremlin, and he asked the Artistic Council to ratify the script.[13] The fourth part of *Far from Moscow*, which the author had sketched out in 1946 but which never became part of the published novel, was therefore to be realized in the movie version.

Azhaev's letter is followed by the stenographic transcript of the meeting, during which Papava's script was submitted to thorough criticism. According to the Artistic Council, the role of the party and "the importance of the construction project for the whole country" were insufficiently described: instead of focusing on meetings of the construction site's leaders, the script should give more space to the people. Various participants commented on the "personal line" of the story (the triangle of Aleksei Kovshov, Zhenia, and Zina), as well as the "bureaucratic" language of the dialogues and some problems of detail and style. Leonov, for example, who also thought that the leaders overshadowed the people, insisted on the "symphonic meaning" of the pipeline and proposed that it should be "composed as a totality, with the frost, the snowstorm, the lack of roads, etc." With its abundance of dialogue and its division of the plot into equal parts, the script was "lacking in passion, in everything that constitutes the music of the work."[14] Ermilov, on the contrary, argued that the simplicity of its plot was one of the attractions of Azhaev's novel, which was "straight like that pipeline" (*pramolineen, kak tot nefteprovod*): "The reader always knew just which stage the construction had achieved." Indeed, Ermilov had some problems with the "personal line" because it "obscured the progress of the construction." He also strongly disliked the language of the script, but his criticisms "actually could be attributed to the novel on which the script was based."[15] The end of the script also attracted the attention of council members, especially the passages devoted to Aleksei Kovshov's visit to the Kremlin and Beria's statement to Stalin: "The young engineer Kovshov has come with me. Batmanov and Beridze could not leave the construction."[16] The participants agreed with the view expressed by Surkov, which boiled down to the following statement: "That's not how one goes to see Stalin" (*k Stalinu tak ne ezdiat*).[17]

A second meeting, held in October 1949, dealt with the production script (*rezhisserskii stsenarii*). As its concluding document reports, most of the expectations voiced during the session of 21 June 1949 were met. In order to reinforce the party's leading role, for example, some scenes had been rewritten, and the "meaning of the construction for the whole country" had been emphasized by the addition of a new episode—a rally in the oil fields of Konchelan. "To make the plot more believable," some changes had been introduced in the "Kovshov–Zina–Zhenia personal line." The lengths of certain scenes had been severely cut and the dialogues edited.[18]

The same file of the Russian State Archives for Art and Literature contains several letters that reveal the efforts of Stolper and Papava to "bring the film nearer to Azhaev's novel," as well as the response of various authorities, such as the director of Mosfil'm, Kuznetsov, and the head of the script and stage producton department, V. Dulgerov.[19] Other documents follow: an "excerpt from the protocol of the session of the Artistic Council of the Ministry of Cinematography of the USSR" of 27 July 1950, which recommended that production work on *Far from Moscow* be continued "after consideration of the opinions voiced by various members of the council,"[20] and, finally and most important, an "excerpt from the protocol of the session of the Artistic Council of the Ministry of Cinematography of the USSR" of 9 November 1950, during which the film was recommended for public release.[21] This time Azhaev was present.[22]

Films burn more easily than manuscripts. In the movie version of *Far from Moscow,* at least the one that is now available, the scene in which Aleksei Kovshov meets Beria and Stalin in the Kremlin is missing. The film ends as Batmanov and Zalkind talk about the project that awaits them after the completion of the present task, and with a quote from Gorky. Whether the Kremlin scene was abandoned during some later meetings and discussions or was cut during "de-Stalinization" (or after Beria's execution) could not be verified. What remained, however, shows that "real" geography was reestablished when the novel was turned into a film, the activity of fiction engendering once again "a plurality of spaces in the totality of one project." During one of the last scenes of the movie, we see on the wall of Batmanov's office a large topographic map showing the route of the pipeline from Novinsk to Konchelan. Everything corresponds to the version of *Far from Moscow* published in *Novyi mir,* except one detail: the "reality" *of the novel* is reflected in a mirror. At the spot where the river and the pipeline diverge, the river Adun sweeps on majestically to the left, while the route of the pipeline swings northward to the right. It is safe to assume that this time the utopic schema had nothing to do with Azhaev. A screen had intervened between the writer and the montage of his own life.

13

---•◦◦❀◦◦•---

BORDERLINE III: THE DEATH OF
THE CHEKIST

The other books in the pile were belles-lettres, but reading them made Khorobrov sick. One was a new hit, *Far from Us*, which at this moment was being widely read on the outside. But after reading a little of it Khorobrov felt nausea. The book was a meat pie without the meat, an egg with its insides sucked out, a stuffed bird. It talked about a construction project which had actually been carried out by zeks, and about camps, but nowhere were the camps named, nor did it say that the workers were zeks, that they received prison rations and were jailed in punishment cells; instead, they were changed into Komsomols who were well dressed, well shod, and full of enthusiasm. And there the experienced reader sensed that the author himself knew, saw, and touched the truth, that he might even have been a security officer in a camp, but that he was lying with cold, glassy eyes.

—Aleksandr Solzhenitsyn, *The First Circle*

We already know what followed: still qualifying as a "young author" in 1948, Azhaev became a "classic of Soviet literature." He chaired, among others, the Committee for Work with Novice Writers (*Komissiia po rabote s nachinaiushchimi pisateliami*); was a member of the prose section of the Soviet Writers' Union, then a member of the union's board; received—together with Evgenii Dolmatovskii and Vera Ketlinskaia—an apartment in

V. Azhaev, "a classic of Soviet literature," in 1952.

the new block of the Writers' House at 17 Lavrushinskii Lane (opposite the Tret'iakov Gallery);[1] participated in numerous committees, discussions, and "creative conferences" of the union; and was in 1960 appointed editor in chief of the journal "for export" *Soviet Literature,* a post he occupied until his death in 1968. Already in February 1949, for example, we see him chairing the "morning session of the creative conference of writers of the Far East" and discussing, among other things, the revised collection of reports "V doline Burei" (In the Valley of the Bureia) by his former acquaintance from Komsomol'sk, Rustam Agishev. Azhaev suggested that his colleague "observe life better, as Iuliia Shestakova had done with the Udege," quoted examples of his own novel's descriptions of the work of the welders,

and advised the author to go back on site so that he could seek further inspiration and better study the miners of the Bureia, which would allow
him "to show more boldness in the depiction of people."[2]

Several dissertations were written on *Far from Moscow,* and many reviews and articles. The novel itself continued to be reprinted, until the era of
perestroika, in enormous print runs, including many provincial and "re-
publican" editions and translations in more than twenty languages. Here
are a few figures for the largest "central" publications: 150,000 in 1949
(Sovetskii Pisatel'); 150,000 in 1957 (Goslitizdat); 100,000 in 1966 (Izvestiia); 150,000 in 1967 (Molodaia Gvardiia—this was already the thirty-
second edition); 100,000 in 1974 ("Karelia," Petrozavodsk); 100,000 in
1975 (Lenizdat); 100,000 in 1978 (Sovetskii Pisatel'); and, more recently,
an all-time record of 300,000 in 1985 (Sovremennik). In 1989 *Far from
Moscow* was issued, perhaps for the last time, by Moskovskii Rabochii,
with a print run of "only" 50,000 copies. The volume also included a
slightly abbreviated version of Azhaev's posthumous novel, *The Boxcar.*

As his old friend and teacher Domatovskii wrote in his memoirs, Azhaev
"put on the main shelf of Soviet literature a single book."[3] He never finished
his novel *Vechnaia merzlota* (Permafrost), but bought up the whole print
run before its release and destroyed it after a negative critique in *Pravda.*[4]
His other reports and stories, including the novella "Predislovie k zhizni"
(A Foreword to Life), published in 1961, passed without much notice.[5] Except for its title, "A Foreword to Life" had nothing in common with the
story published within the "limits of the camp" in 1935, although it was related to the beginning, to a time before the events depicted in *The Boxcar.*
But, as we have seen, time and space were progressively canceled, the accounts of memory merged with the questions of the present, and narrative
itself was dispossessed. There remained Azhaev's archive and the opinion
of his contemporaries. Those who knew the writer personally remember
him as an exceptionally good and sincere person, eager to help and to
serve.[6] Those who knew him only as the author of *Far from Moscow* and
who were writing and reading the *other* literature probably agreed with
these verses, written by Boris Pasternak in 1956:

> It's unbefitting to be famous
> And say fame elevates our souls;
> It's unbefitting to trouble over
> Your notes and manuscripts and rolls.

The way of art is self-surrender,
Not born of praise or great success.
How shameful when your name's a byword;
Your labor—vain and meaningless!

Oh, live! Not as pretenders live—
In emptiness, with many fears,
But give your heart to vast horizons
And hear the call of future years.

Leave out the faceless present, leave
Whole chapters out! Deliberate
The matter nearest to creation—
The themes of freedom, life, and fate.

Then pass into your deep seclusion,
A man alone and unespied,
As vanishes in evening mist
And sudden dark the countryside.

Another, step by step, will follow
After, and enter your retreat,
But you yourself must not prefer
Your victories to your defeat.

You must never violate your purpose
One jot, one atom, to survive.
But be alive—this only matters,
Alive, to the end of ends alive![7]

There is not much to find beyond celebration or condemnation in the critical heritage of *Far from Moscow,* except perhaps a literary response, written in "internal emigration" between 1949 and 1955 and first published abroad in 1972 by Lidiia Chukovskaia.[8] *Spusk pod vodu* (Going Under) tells the story of Nina Sergeevna, a woman working on a translation during February and March 1949 in a so-called writers' retreat, not far from Moscow. There she gets to know Bilibin, a writer who is working on a novel set in Siberia. From time to time Nina Sergeevna is "going under," toward her inner self, or rather toward her husband, Alesha (diminutive of

Aleksei), who was sentenced to "ten years without the right to correspondence." One night the radio reports on the struggle against "rootless cosmopolitans." Some guests immediately leave the house. The rumor goes around that people who had once been deported are being arrested only because of that earlier sentence. A poet who writes war poems in Yiddish is arrested. Nina Sergeevna learns from Bilibin—who also has been "there"—that "ten years without the right to correspondence" means execution. Bilibin is now the only link between her and her dead husband. She wants to know what "there" was like, and Bilibin tells her. Toward the end of the story, Bilibin has completed his novel and gives it Nina Sergeevna to read. And this is her response:

> "You're a coward," I said. "No, you're something worse. You're a false witness." He started to get up. "You're a liar. . . . Good-bye. Why did you not have the dignity to keep silent? Just not say anything. Surely out of respect for the people you buried you could have found some other way of earning a crust of bread. Without resorting to your forest and your mine and that child, and your friend's stutter?" He went out. . . . I once counted how many paces it was from his door to mine. It was nineteen. But now it had become nineteen miles, not one less, nineteen centuries.[9]

Bilibin had reworked his labor camp experience into a euphoric production novel. The dissident critic Grigorii Svirskii concludes: "Lydia Chukovskaya rose to do battle for the Word. The Word had deceived millions and is still a terrible weapon, possibly even more terrible than the atomic bomb or nerve gas. She attacks not only the hangmen, but also those of their victims who have become their accomplices. They are no different from the hangmen, and she hates them just as fiercely, and has even more contempt for them than she has for the hangmen."[10] Svirskii does not quote Nina Sergeevna's thoughts, which we find a few pages later, at the end of Chukovskaia's book. She silently asks Bilibin to forgive her: "'Forgive me!' I wanted to say. 'I didn't have the right to judge you; least of all I, for no dogs ever threw themselves on me and I've never seen the wooden tag on the leg of a dead man. . . . Forgive me! You wouldn't wish to go back there: to felling trees, to the mines. Go back for a second time! The story you wrote is your weak shield, your unreliable wall.'"[11]

Are we not in the presence of a new code, from *Azhaev* to *Bilibin* and a common central character *Alesha*? As it turns out, Azhaev and Svirskii knew each other. I found in Azhaev's archive a dedication by Svirskii,

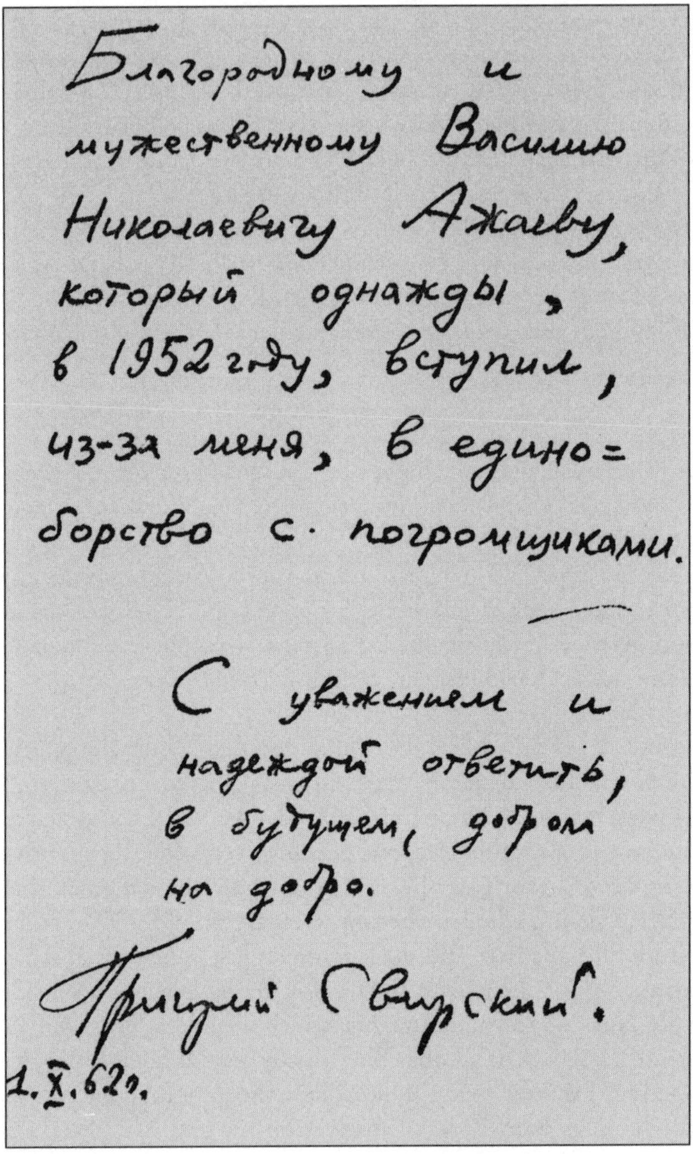

Благородному и
мужественному Василию
Николаевичу Ажаеву,
который однажды,
в 1952 году, вступил,
из-за меня, в едино=
борство с погромщиками.

С уважением и
надеждой ответить,
в будущем, добром
на добро.

Григорий Свирский.

1.X.62 г.

A dedication for V. Azhaev by G. Svirskii, 1 October 1962.

dated 1 October 1962: "To the noble and courageous Vasilii Nikolaevich Azhaev, who once in 1952, because of me, joined the common battle against those who took part in the pogrom. With respect and the hope of returning good for good."

About the same time, Azhaev was finishing *The Boxcar*. In a small notebook titled "Memory of the Heart," containing early variants of the novel, sketches, and thoughts, he noted:

> Recently I had been thinking a lot about V. A. Barabanov. I heard that he was not on the job anymore, that he worked at the reception desk of *Izvestiia*. Did someone suppose this to be an appropriate position for such as him? About two years ago [his wife] Aleksandra Ivanovna died. How is he now?

V. Azhaev, the Kremlin, Moscow, April 1968; "the last photo."

> I will soon finish my novel and I will take the novel and go to see him, that's what I thought. And now, suddenly, a blow to my heart: Barabanov has died. He was riding on a bus, on his way to draw his pension: he fell, and that was the end.

> The funeral. One of the eleven clubs of the Ministry of Preservation of Public Order.[12] Here lies my former commander and friend. Music. On a cushion, the Golden Star and the orders. They placed my fresh flowers on his chest.[13]

Among the former colleagues who were present to convey Commander Barabanov on his last journey, Azhaev mentions Chkheidze, Figel'shtein, Evstigneev, Mel'nikov, and others. As far as literature was concerned, the young lad had come back, but it was too late: the Chekist had gone. And there was, indeed, no other life.

EPILOGUE

HOW LIFE FINISHES
WRITING THE BOOK

"It riles one to think that in the year 2005 some writer will come to what is now the construction site and will dig into the 'fossilized muck,' rummage in the archives and question the oldest inhabitants. Our contemporary writers simply can't tear themselves away from Rubezhansk, they prefer to sit there in the library and write another book about Nevel'skoi."
—*Far from Moscow*, book 2, chapter 1

At the close of the fifth day Beridze and Karpov reached the big taiga river, the Oi. Here Rogov was building a wooden bridge. Several kilometers of ready-made road led up to this bridge. The work was nearing completion. Rogov, nevertheless, was dissatisfied and grumpy.
—*Far from Moscow*, book 3, chapter 7

Nothing was left of the memorial desk placed near Cape Lazarevo in the early 1950s in honor of "Batmanov," who had "ordered the explosion" ten years before. But we looked for it, as we looked for "Topolev's" grave during our visit of 19 and 20 August 1995. Somebody had seen the tomb of some engineer on one of the surrounding hills some years ago. Was it really the 1942 pipeline that plunged into the Nevel'skii Strait toward Pogibi on Sakhalin, or was this the second or third line? Nobody could tell us. Azhaev's archive contains the manuscript of an article that, as the writer's pen indicates, appeared in *Sovetskaia Rossiia* on 3 January 1964. Titled "Once Again Far from Moscow: How Life Finishes Writing the Book," the article reports on the construction of the second pipeline, duplicating the first one, some twenty years after Project No. 15 was completed.[1] It also anticipates the building of a gas main, finished in 1987. The day we visited Cape Lazarevo, new pipes were being laid to replace older ones that had become obsolete.

We had reached Tsimmermanovka-on-the-Amur by hydroplane, after a one-night stopover in Komsomol'sk, where Marina Aleksandrovna Kuz'mina had joined us. Viktor Ivanovich Remizovskii, a retired geologist, now living in Khabarovsk, who had spent many years in Magadan and Sakhalin, had reread *Far from Moscow* especially for this trip. In other words, "Batmanov" and his comrades were with us, constantly. We left Tsimmermanovka around four in the afternoon on 17 August, heading to De-Kastri, across the taiga. Thanks to Marina Aleksandrovna's connections, the GAZ-69 (a Soviet version of the jeep) and its driver, Oleg Valentinovich Inozemtsev, were both rented from the Tsimmermanovka Oil Main Section of Sakhalinmorneftegaz, now a joint-stock company.

Belov, Bondarenko, and Badiul had reached De-Kastri after five days. It took us only a couple of hours. We did not take a bath in the river Iai, but we crossed it, with some difficulty. Like the engineers of *Far from Moscow*, we filled our notebooks with fresh notes, and also like them, we embellished our topographical maps with new lines of corrections, using a camera, of course. The engineers had the sun's company on the second day, too, and on the third and fourth. And so had we, during the first part of our expedition on our way to the "world's end," despite the bad forecast. It rained the entire day as we drove back from Lazarev to Sofiisk, and the track was transformed into a sea of mud. Between De-Kastri and the settlement of Vidanova, several miles after Blockhouse No. 15, the old tubes of 1941–42 had been dug out and replaced with new ones. For almost the entire journey we followed the line, with a short excursion to Tabo Bay on the Tatar Strait, where we hoped to find an Ul'ch fishers' settlement, but everything was deserted.[2] Most of the time we drove on a log road, and that is how I discovered the meaning of the word *lezhnevka*. Like Azhaev's engineers, we dropped in at all the villages—actually there were just a few of them—and questioned the inhabitants closely about the past. Only a few were old enough to remember Project No. 15.

Among those who still lived on the line, Aleksandr Kirillovich Serebriannikov had probably been a guard at the Camp of the Lower Amur.

Replacement of a section of the 1941–42 pipeline, near Blockhouse No. 15, De-Kastri region, August 1995. (Photograph by Thomas Lahusen.)

When questioned about *Far from Moscow,* he wept: he "had read twenty pages and couldn't read further." He had seen the film. The pipeline, he said, "had been built on bones." Georgii Iosifovich Irganov had served as a soldier between 1941 and 1945 in the Volochaisk regiment, stationed in De-Kastri. In the garden of his cottage we discovered the silvery bust of Marshal Voroshilov, almost disappearing in the high grass and the weeds.[3] Irganov had never read the book, but had seen the film. He thus belonged to those "weaker forces of the periphery" that got to know Azhaev's story through the Papava-Stolper version. But, as he said, "the tractors, the bull-dozers, nothing of this ever existed, only shovels and bare hands." He remembered how the prisoners were chased from one place to another, poorly fed and poorly clothed. The soldiers too, he added, were poorly clothed, and they also died of hunger. Sometimes they were able to tap the pipeline, which was not buried very deep in the ground, and often there were breaches. Then they distilled the oil—like *samogon**—to make their own fuel, a dangerous operation.

*Home-distilled vodka.

Il'ia Danilovich Kurda and Vladimir Petrovich Losevskii had been "privileged" prisoners with "unrestricted circulation": they had worked as communication mechanics in 1941–42, and, like Tania Vasil'chenko in *Far from Moscow,* had rigged up a temporary telephone line stretching from tree to tree through the taiga.[4] We asked them whether they remembered Zinaida Petrovna Pogodaeva, a communication mechanic who had received a medal for labor prowess on 30 October 1942, and they did.[5] But Zinaida Petrovna, as they recalled, was blond, whereas Tat'iana Petrovna Vasil'chenko—"Little Red Ridinghood on the Adun"—was dark-haired. Kurda had read the novel "twenty times" and had also seen the film. "It was all a lie. There was no truth in there." He remembered how the pipeline was laid through the Nevel'skii Strait in two months' time: "A man every two meters, no dynamite, no explosions, people using their own hands to dig into the ice." Twelve colonies worked on the pipeline construction, about one thousand people in each. Losevskii, who was convicted "for stealing a few ears of grain" (*sidel za koloski*),[6] worked on Project No. 15 and other projects from 1939 or 1940 until the end of the war. He had read the book and seen the film. Then he remained in Lazarev with his wife, Nadezhda Kirillovna, until the present. Both Kurda and Losevskii remembered the "bosses" Barabanov and Chkheidze, the former as an "exceptional leader," the latter (repeatedly) as a "good man" and "very competent engineer." Chkheidze stayed in Lazarev with his children and his wife, who had come back from Georgia. Other names were also mentioned, some of them associated with ferocity and death. A few passages of Azhaev's notebooks started to make better sense.

Tat'iana Innokent'evna Nadykto, whom we visited in her "summer kichen," a tiny Sofiisk cottage beside the house now inhabited by her children, recalled the hungry prisoners from the nearby camp, shot by the guards for having stolen potatoes. "We used ration cards at that time," she said, as if there was a need to explain. Tat'iana Innokent'evna had worked all her life in the Sofiiskoe post office, through which passed the letters and parcels mailed to the prisoners. A shipping clerk arrived by car to receive or send out the mail: both the clerk and his driver were prisoners themselves. Later, when the pipeline offices were transferred to Tsimmermanovka, the inmates, the free laborers, those who were assigned to remain after their release, the administration, and all the others left, and the settlement regained its peace. Tat'iana Innokent'evna had seen the film *Far from Moscow* and later started to read the novel, but she could not finish it: it contained "too many lies."

"So this is the world's end!" Sovetskaia ulitsa (Soviet Street) and the Nevel'skii Strait, Lazarev, August 1995. (Photograph by Thomas Lahusen.)

Two days later we spoke to Filipp Antonovich Andreev, the former prisoner of Cape Chernyi, and to Iakov Efimovich Rubinchik, who is still trying to get rehabilitated. We met in our room at the Hotel Amur in Komsomol'sk, built by Japanese prisoners of war after 1945. Filipp Antonovich gave further details of his ordeal of the 1940s. It was also he who claimed that the "journalist Zhagirnovskii" (P. Zhagir?), a former prisoner, not Azhaev, had written *Far from Moscow*.[7] Both remembered Vasilii Mikhailovich Gorskii, one of the section commanders of Project No. 15, a fierce and frightening man who treated both prisoners and free laborers badly and "slept after lunch until 6 or 7 P.M., keeping the men at work until two in the morning." I remembered Azhaev's notebook entry of 18 March 1941: "Gorskii: the workers supply the *zeks* with vodka."

After we returned from Komsomol'sk, Viktor Ivanovich and I spoke on Khabarovsk radio about our expedition and the "montage of life." The broadcast was aired later in September, and a few listeners called to express their positive and less positive reactions. One of them even gave us a complement of information: he had worked as a guard during the second phase of Project No. 15 in the early 1950s, when the pipeline was extended from Sofiiskoe to Komsomol'sk. He recalled that people who had participated in the building of the first section came to talk about the history of the construction. One of the visitors, whose name was Belov, declared that

The river Amur, August 1995. (Photograph by Thomas Lahusen.)

Azhaev had portrayed him as Rogov. In *Far from Moscow,* Batmanov liked Rogov. He was a fellow "who could move mountains," so Batmanov "gave him the most difficult section on the line and a free hand."[8]

On the morning of 2 September 1995, I boarded flight 202 of Alaska Air. The plane gained altitude, and the big town, the squares and rectangles of its blocks, swiftly diminished in size. And soon the mirrorlike sheen of the Adun was left far behind.

APPENDIX

DECREE
of the Supreme Soviet of the USSR
ON AWARDS TO CONSTRUCTION WORKERS
OF SPECIAL PROJECTS

*For outstanding fulfillment of the Government's mission
in respect to the construction of special projects,
the following are to be awarded:*

Order of Lenin
1. **Mukhamediarov** Shafy Gula, instructor of welding operations.
2. **Okaemov** Ivan Vasil'evich, head of Project No. 201.
3. **Rubin** Ivan Ivanovich, group mechanic of dredging caravan.
4. **Chkheidze** Grigorii Davydovich, chief engineer of Project No. 15.

Red Banner of Labor
1. **Bondarenko** Gavriil Nikiforovich, head of division.
2. **Bukatov** Ivan Maksimovich, senior dredger master of suction dredge.
3. **Buianov** Leonid Sergeevich, deputy head of GULZhDS.
4. Commissar of State Security 2d Rank **Goglidze** Sergei Arsent'evich.
5. **Domanov** Pavel Vasil'evich, superintendent of division welding operations.

Source: *Tikhookeanskaia zvezda,* 3 November 1942, p. 1.

6. **Karapetian** Aleksandr Gerasimovich, head of production and technical department, head of operations.
7. **Karpov** Vladimir Mikhailovich, engineer of NKVD of USSR.
8. **Korganov** Sergei Georgievich, chief engineer of Project No. 201.
9. **Kravchenko** Ivan Ivanovich, foreman of lathe operator group of ship-repair shops.
10. **Kuchera** Viktor Ivanovich, head of political department of Project No. 15.
11. **Makhov** Anatolii Ivanovich, head of division operations.
12. **Mashnitskii** Anatolii Nikolaevich, engineer, commander of suction dredge.
13. **Meierson** Vladimir Pavlovich, head of department of planning and prospecting.
14. **Marev** Ivan Spiridonovich, head of dredging caravan.
15. **Orentlikherman** Genrikh Moiseevich, head of Project No. 15.
16. **Spiridonov** Aleksei Mikhailovich, secretary of *obkom* of VKP(b).
17. **Tonkonogov** Vasilii Rufovich, electrical welder.
18. **Shatalin** Grigorii Ivanovich, secretary of *kraikom* of the VKP(b).
19. **Shenivskii** Grigorii Ivanovich, head of department of motor transport, head of urgent-task unit of division.

Badge of Honor
1. **Andreev** Afanasii Nikolaevich, senior operational commissioner of division.
2. **Akimov** Fedor Fedorovich, deputy head of Project No. 15.
3. **Badiul** Grigorii Afanas'evich, commissar of militarized guard.
4. **Belov** Koz'ma Koz'mich, head of construction bureaus of NKVD of USSR.
5. **Belov** Nikolai Maksimovich, head of division.
6. **Burdaeva** Valentina Ivanovna, assistant director of political department for Komsomol and head of section.
7. **Burman** Mikhail Iakovlevich, field commander of construction.
8. **Galantsev** Vladimir Dmitrievich, head of department of general supply.
9. **Grachev** Ivan Ivanovich, secretary of *gorkom* of VKP(b).
10. **Gorskii** Vasilii Mikhailovich, deputy head of division and head of section.

11. **Dorfman** Mark Markovich, senior mechanic of suction dredge.
12. **Zamiatin** Aleksandr Mikhailovich, electrical welder of division.
13. **Zimenko** Kornei Onufrievich, senior superintendent of division.
14. **Ivkin**, Petr Antonovich, field commander of construction.
15. **Kozlenko** Stepan Iakovlevich, commander of suction dredge.
16. **Kononenko** Anatolii Ivanovich, senior engineer of GULZhDS production department.
17. **Krivtsov** Roman Nikitich, head of cultural-educational unit and secretary of Party organization.
18. **Kroshko** Anatolii Nikolaevich, head of assembly shop of Project No. 15.
19. **Kubyshkin** Vasilii Aleksandrovich, senior engineer of GULZhDS production department.
20. **Lebedev** Anatolii Sergeevich, head of communication department.
21. **Lebedev** Ivan Ivanovich, commander of suction dredge No. 1.
22. **Liapugin** Georgii Alekseevich, head of political department of construction.
23. **Minichenko** Feofan Matveevich, secretary of *obkom* of VKP(b).
24. **Moiseenko** Nikolai Aleksandrovich, division commander.
25. **Napalkov** Vasilii Stepanovich, deputy chief engineer and head of production department.
26. **Polozhii** Nina Petrovna, lathe operator of ship-repair shops.
27. **Popov** Mitrofan Nikolaevich, deputy head of Glavpromstroi.
28. **Raevskii** Pavel Matveevich, engineer of GULZhDS.
29. **Riabov** Nikolai Dmitrievich, head of electromechanical department and head of division.
30. **Sentilev** Ivan Petrovich, senior operational commissioner of division.
31. **Sokolov** Nikolai Fedorovich, head of operational division.
32. **Solov'ev** Ivan Aleksandrovich, deputy head of department of projection and survey.
33. **Tumarkin** Aleksandr Savel'evich, head of GULZhDS assembly division.
34. **Chekhonin** Aleksei Andreevich, head of terminal section.

35. **Shel'man** Avgust Adol'fovich, head of division.
36. **Ianovskii** Isaak Semenovich, deputy head of construction.

Medal "for Labor Prowess"

1. **Bogachev** Nikolai Pavlovich, senior engineer and head of blasting operations.
2. **Bogdanov** Vladimir Ivanovich, head of 3d dredging caravan.
3. **Bogush** Pavel Pavlovich, head of division motor transport unit.
4. **Bolotin** Georgii Aleksandrovich, technician, head of topographic survey detachment of prospecting party.
5. **Burmakin** Nikolai Semenovich, senior operator of suction dredge.
6. **Byrin** Vladimir Il'ich, head of division group.
7. **Bystrov** Andrei Mikhailovich, head of division general supply unit.
8. **Vainshtein** Vladimir Moiseevich, deputy head of construction department of general supply.
9. **Viktorov** Mikhail Filippovich, platoon political instructor.
10. **Voinov** Pavel Ivanovich, senior electrician of suction dredge.
11. **Vorob'ev** Ivan Afanas'evich, division welding foreman.
12. **Garnar** Polikarp Nikitovich, senior operator of suction dredge.
13. **Danilenko** Fedor Sidorovich, head of division group.
14. **Denisov** Nikolai Grigor'evich, mechanic of pressure testing.
15. **D'iakov** Vasilii Petrovich, electrical welder.
16. **Zhukov** Sergei Vladimirovich, suction dredge operator.
17. **Zigmond** Boris Semenovich, commander of detachment of militarized guard.
18. **Zinov'ev** Nikolai Andreevich, head engineer of topographic survey detachment of river prospecting party.
19. **Kabatskii** Konstantin Mitrofanovich, electrical welding instructor.
20. **Kats** Mark Isaevich, group leader of control inspection.
21. **Kilemenchuk** Fedor Afanas'evich, EPRON diver.
22. **Kirillov** Georgii Grigor'evich, head of pressure testing operations.
23. **Kozhevnikov** Iurii Nikolaevich, leader of welding group.
24. **Korovin** Viktor Gavrilovich, senior topographer.
25. **Kochin** Mikhail Alekseevich, commissar of detachment and secretary of Party organization.

26. **Krasnov** Nikolai Ivanovich, brigade leader of alignment workers.
27. **Krupennikov** Vasilii Anisimovich, head of control and planning department.
28. **Kubanov** Dmitrii Ivanovich, assembly mechanic.
29. **Lunin** Petr Timofeevich, gas welder.
30. **Makukh** Grigorii Vasil'evich, electrical welder.
31. **Molodozhenov** Ivan Andreevich, mechanic of pressure testing operations.
32. **Molchanov** Ivan Eremeevich, electrical welder.
33. **Pakhomov** Konstantin Nikolaevich, engineer of assembly works.
34. **Perekrestov** Nikolai Aleksandrovich, mechanic.
35. **Petrash** Nikolai Vasil'evich, superintendent of assembly works.
36. **Povorozniuk** Ivan Timofeevich, senior deputy steamship captain.
37. **Pogazhil'skii** Vladimir Stepanovich, senior operational commissioner.
38. **Pogodaeva** Zinaida Petrovna, communication mechanic.
39. **Rapoport** Aleksandr Naumovich, deputy head of construction department of technical supply.
40. **Rozenko** Aleksandrius, gas welder.
41. **Sedovskii** Mikhail Ivanovich, commissar of independent division of militarized guard.
42. **Sevast'ianov** Ivan Ivanovich, electrical welder.
43. **Slepnev** Pavel Vasil'evich, head of electromechanic unit.
44. **Tokar'** Izia Grigor'evich, head of cultural-educational department.
45. **Frolov** Sergei Petrovich, senior dredger master.
46. **Sheliutin** Nikolai Ivanovich, commander of suction dredge.
47. **Shkaev** Ivan Petrovich, senior mechanic of self-propelled barge.
48. **Shtraikher**, Meer Iosifovich, engineer of assembly works.
49. **Shutov** Vasilii Nikolaevich, head of planning department.
50. **Iurchenko** Grigorii Timofeevich, metalworker of ship-repair shops.

Medal "for Labor Distinction"

1. **Agafonov** Nikolai Ivanovich, division commander.
2. **Belikov** Mikhail Petrovich, head of division of projection and survey department.

3. **Beskhmel'nitskii** Nikolai Kirillovich, foreman of boiler operations.
4. **Bitiutskov** Mikhail Ivanovich, head of unit.
5. **Borisov** Vasilii Alekseevich, foreman of welding operations.
6. **Bulyshev** Petr Aleksandrovich, senior topographer.
7. **Buriak** Fedor Semenovich, deputy head of motor transport unit.
8. **Valov** Boris Lavrent'evich, tractor driver.
9. **Varres** Oskar Petrovich, department head.
10. **Vechkanov** Mikhail Fedorovich, deputy head of operations.
11. **Gatsenko** Viktor Grigor'evich, head of communication unit.
12. **Goroshko** Lidia Ivanovna, construction physician.
13. **Derevianko** Timofei Gavrilovich, head of colony.
14. **Ershov** Petr Antonovich, electrical welder.
15. **Esin** Lavrentii Pavlovich, rifleman of militarized guard.
16. **Zhagirnovskii** Petr Efimovich, director of garment factory.
17. **Zeletsko** Ivan Abramovich, electrical welder.
18. **Zel'tser** Isaak Iosifovich, head of ship-repair shops.
19. **Zliuchii** Ivan Ivanovich, head of transport department.
20. **Kirillov** Nikolai Pavlovich, senior foreman of electrical welding.
21. **Kozhevnikov** Iakov Vasil'evich, electrical engineer of suction dredge.
22. **Koz'min** Konstantin Andreevich, head of technical supply department.
23. **Kondrashov** Semen Artem'evich, mechanic.
24. **Konevskii** Sigizmund L'vovich, senior engineer of line operations.
25. **Lysenko** Isidor Timofeevich, deputy head of bureau.
26. **Makaida** Feoktist Emel'ianovich, head of boiler and welding shop.
27. **Molchanov** Vasilii Isaevich, foreman of welding operations.
28. **Monakhtin** Vasilii Ivanovich, foreman of ship-repair group of metalworkers.
29. **Mostovoi** Vasilii Fedorovich, electrical welder.
30. **Muchaev** Usman Izmailovich, gas welder.
31. **Netrebin** Petr Il'ich, head of motor vehicle pool.
32. **Nikolaev** Nikolai Petrovich, deputy head of section.
33. **Novikov** Nikolai Vasil'evich, manager of mechanical shops.
34. **Novokhatnii** Grigorii Maksimovich, head of cartage unit.

35. **Ponomarev** Boris Vasil'evich, head accountant of construction.
36. **Reznichenko**, Aleksandr Mikhailovich, leader of insulation group.
37. **Reutov** Aleksandr Egorovich, senior superintendent of communication.
38. **Rogov** Konstantin Mikhailovich, head of general supply department.
39. **Sokolenko** Samuil Ivanovich, gas welder.
40. **Sotov** Nikita Ivanovich, group leader.
41. **Starnovkin** Nikolai Georgievich, head of sanitary unit.
42. **Tishchenko** Viktor Iosifovich, engineer-head of field operations.
43. **Falin** Aleksandr Vladimirovich, head of motor transport unit.
44. **Tsiva** Ivan Mikhailovich, head of general supply unit.
45. **Shevtsov** Aleksandr Fedorovich, electrical welder.
46. **Shestakov** Ivan Nikiforovich, head of production and technical unit.
47. **Shubin** Semen Alekseevich, senior dredger master of suction dredge.

Chairman of the Presidium of the Supreme Soviet of the USSR
M. KALININ
Secretary of the Presidium of the Supreme Soviet of the USSR
A. GORKIN

Moscow, Kremlin
30 October 1942

NOTES

Introduction

[1] Marc Slonim, *Soviet Russian Literature: Writers and Problems, 1917–1977*, 2d ed. (New York: Oxford University Press, 1977), p. 319.

[2] Thomas Lahusen, "Das Geheimnis des Adun: Rekonstruktion einer Geschichte," *Wiener Slawistischer Almanach* 24 (1990): 115–126; idem, "The Mystery of the River Adun: Reconstruction of a Story," in *Late Soviet Culture: From Perestroika to Novostroika,* ed. Thomas Lahusen, with Gene Kuperman (Durham: Duke University Press, 1993), pp. 139–154.

[3] Abram Tertz, *On Socialist Realism* (New York: Pantheon, 1960); Katerina Clark, *The Soviet Novel: History as Ritual* (1981; rpt. Chicago: University of Chicago Press, 1985); Hans Günther, *Die Verstaatlichung der Literatur: Entstehung und Funktionsweise des sozialistisch-realistischen Kanons in der sowjetischen Literatur der 30er Jahre* (Stuttgart: J. B. Metzler, 1984); Régine Robin, *Socialist Realism: An Impossible Aesthetic,* trans. Catherine Porter (Stanford: Stanford University Press, 1992); Boris Groys, *The Total Art of Stalinism: Avant-Garde, Aesthetic Dictatorship, and Beyond,* trans. Charles Rougle (Princeton: Princeton University Press, 1992).

[4] Fredric Jameson, *The Seeds of Time* (New York: Columbia University Press, 1994), p. 74.

I. Project No. 15

[1] "Akt sdachi i priema tovarno-nefteprovodnoi kontory 'Dal'neftekombinata' ot 28 iiulia 1944 g., napravlennogo v Kraikom VKP(b) Khabarovskogo kraia." GAKhK, f. P-35, op. 1, d. 1694, ll. 104–116, 119–122.

[2] Sofiiskoe has become Sofiisk (Sofiisk-na-Amure), according to Zinaida Grigor'evna Nadeniuk, secretary of the village council. Interview, 21 August 1995.

[3] The tubes were unloaded in 1940. Sources from the Information Center of the Administration of Internal Affairs of the Khabarovsk Region (ITs UVD Khabarovskogo kraia), file "Stroika No. 15": f. 54, op. 1., l. 3. Excerpts compiled by Marina Kuz'mina, journalist from Komsomol'sk-on-the-Amur. Kuz'mina participated in an expedition that I organized in August 1995 along the pipeline from Komsomol'sk to Cape Lazarevo. See Epilogue.

⁴"Postanovlenie SNK i TsK VKP(b) No. 457–156 ot 5. 4. 1940g. na narkomneft' spetsstroiupravlenie No. 15 Okha–Tsimmermanovka. Prikaz No. 416a Narkomata toplivoi promyshlennosti ot 29 iiunia 1940 g." ITs UVD Khabarovskogo kraia. Sources provided by M. Kuz'mina.

⁵GARF, f. 9414, op. 1, d. 853, ll. 7–12; cited in O. P. Elantseva, *Obrechennaia doroga: BAM, 1932–1941* (The Doomed Track: BAM, 1932–1941) (Vladivostok: Izdatel'stvo Dal'nevostochnogo Universiteta, 1994), pp. 109–110. The labor camp system of the Far East had the following structure: a certain number of camps and colonies, together with their various divisions, departments, and sections, as well as their human and material resources, were components of the Primor'e and Khabarovsk Administration of the Correctional Labor Camps of the GULAG; others were part of separate administrations, such as the Main Administration of Railway Construction Camps of the NKVD. This system was subject to frequent revisions, depending on the ever-increasing economic requirements from above. See G. A. Tkacheva, "Osuzhden kazhdyi tretii . . . : Prinuditel'nyi trud na Dal'nem Vostoke Rossii v gody voiny" (Every Third Person Was Sentenced . . . : Forced Labor in the Russian Far East during the War Years), *Rossiia i ATR* (Vladivostok), no. 1 (1995): 74; as well as E. N. Chernolutskaia, "Prinuditel'nye migratsii na sovetskom Dal'nem Vostoke v stalinskii period" (Forced Migrations in the Soviet Far East during the Stalin Period), *Vestnik DVO RAN* 6 (1995): 71–79.

⁶A. Suturin, "Amurlag," in *Koliuchaia pravda: Dokumental'nye rasskazy, ocherki i vospominaniia o sud'bakh dal'nevostochnikov v 30-40-e gody* (Barbed-Wire Truth: Documentary Stories, Reports, and Memoirs on the Fate of the Far Easterners during the 1930s and 1940s) (Khabarovsk: Khabarovskoe knizhnoe izdatel'stvo, 1990), pp. 94–95.

⁷GAKhK, f. 35, op. 1, fd. 1050, l. 2; d. 1306, l. 2; cited in Tkacheva, "Osuzhden kazhdyi tretii," pp. 75, 82.

⁸These explanations were suggested to me by Jonathan A. Bone, who also suggested that the idea for Project No. 15 probably came from a collaboration between the Workers' and Peasants' Red Army (RKKA) and the Defense Sector of the State Planning Commission (Gosplan) and went administratively through the Defense Committee of the Sovnarkom.

⁹From Aleksei Stakhanov, a Soviet miner who mined 102 tons of coal (fourteen times the quota) in a single shift on 30 August 1935.

¹⁰Wolfgang Kasack, *Dictionary of Russian Literature since 1917*, trans. Maria Carlson and Jane T. Hedges (New York: Columbia University Press, 1988), pp. 31–32.

¹¹V. Ermilov, "Poeziia nashei deistvitel'nosti" (The Poetry of Our Reality), in *Novye uspekhi sovetskoi literatury* (The New Successes of Soviet Literature) (Moscow, 1949), cited in E. Dobrenko, "Ne po slovam, no po delam ego" (Not by His Words, but by His Deeds), in *Izbavlenie ot mirazhei: Sotsrealizm segodnia* (Ridding Ourselves of Mirages: Socialist Realism Today), ed. E. A. Dobrenko (Moscow: Sovetskii Pisatel', 1990), p. 313.

¹²Abram Tertz, *On Socialist Realism*, intro. Czeslaw Milosz (New York: Pantheon Books, 1960), p. 53.

¹³Vera S. Dunham, *In Stalin's Time: Middleclass Values in Soviet Fiction*, enl. ed. (Durham: Duke University Press, 1990), p. 13.

¹⁴Peter L. Berger and Thomas Luckmann, *The Social Construction of Reality: A Treatise in the Sociology of Knowledge* (1966; rpt. London: Allen Lane, 1971), p. 121.

¹⁵Vasili Azhayev, *Far from Moscow: A Novel in Three Parts*, trans. R. Prokofieva (Moscow: Foreign Languages Publishing House, 1950), bk. 1, p. 79; translation modified.

[16] Ibid., p. 80.

[17] Vasilii Azhaev, "Vagon," *Druzhba narodov*, nos. 6 (1988): 162–183; 7 (1988): 139–174; 8 (1988): 102–174.

[18] For a history of the BAM through the 1950s, see O. P. Elantseva, "BAM: Maloizvestnye stranitsy istorii 30-kh gg." (The BAM: Unknown Pages of the History of the 1930s), *Izvestiia TsK KPSS*, no. 8 (1991): 144–147; "BAM: Pervoe desiatiletie" (The BAM: The First Decade), *Otechestvennaia istoriia*, no. 6 (1994): 89–103; "Kto i kak stroil BAM v 30-e gody" (Who Built the BAM and How in the 1930s), *Otechestvennye arkhivy*, no. 5 (1992): 71–81; *Obrechennaia doroga*; and *Stroitel'stvo No. 500 NKVD SSSR: Zheleznaia doroga Komsomol'sk-Sovetskaia Gavan' (1930–40-e gody)* (Project No. 500 of the NKVD of the USSR: The Railway Komsomol'sk-Sovetskaia Gavan' [1930s and 1940s]) (Vladivostok: Izdatel'stvo Dal'nevostochnogo Universiteta, 1995). One of Elantseva's publications is specifically devoted to the "poets of the Camp of the BAM" in Svobodnyi. See O. P. Elantseva, *Poety i poeziia BAMLAGa: Obzor dokumentov i materialov k spetskursu "Velikie stroiki stalinskoi epokhi"* (The Poets and Poetry of the BAMLAG: Survey of Documents and Materials for the Special Course "The Great Constructions of the Stalin Era") (Vladivostok: Izdatel'stvo Dal'nevostochnogo Universiteta, 1994). Elantseva does not mention Azhaev.

[19] V. A. Barabanov commanded the Camp of the Lower Amur from January 1940 until the spring or summer of 1942. "Prikaz No. 370 NKVD SSSR ot 04.01.40 ob obrazovanii Nizhne-Amurskogo ITL NKVD SSSR za schet sliianiia Vostochnogo, Iugo-Vostochnogo i Nizhne-Amurskogo zheleznodorozhnykh lagerei. Upravlenie v Komsomol'ske. Nachal'nik Upravleniia—V. A. Barabanov." M. Kuz'mina, *Chernyi kamen' na krasnoi zemle* (Black Stone on Red Earth) (Komsomol'sk-na-Amure: Gorodskoi Komitet "Memorial," 1992), p. 70; M. Kuz'mina, "Grazhdanin Lekpom" (Citizen Medic), *Dal'nevostochnyi Komsomolets*, 3 October 1989, p. 3.

[20] Evgenii Dolmatovskii, *Bylo: Zapiski poeta* (The Past: Notes of a Poet) (Moscow: Sovetskii Pisatel', 1982), pp. 439–440. For some information on Dolmatovskii's activities in the Far East, including the organization of various literary associations in Khabarovsk, Komsomol'sk, Voroshilovsk [Ussuriisk], Vladivostok, and the Poset' frontier zone (on the Korean border), see L. Ia. Ivashchenko, *Istoricheskie aspekty sozdaniia i razvitiia mnogonatsional'noi khudozhestvennoi literatury na Dal'nem Vostoke Rossii, 1917–seredina 1980-kh godov: Ocherki* (Historical Aspects of the Formation and Development of the Multi-National Literature in the Russian Far East, 1917–mid-1980s: Essays) (Vladivostok: Dal'nauka, 1995), p. 70.

[21] V. Azhaev, "Piat' let zhizni: Rasskaz" (Five Years of Life: A Story), *Smena*, no. 8 (1934): 10–11.

[22] M. Kuz'mina, *Eto nashei istorii stroki: Putevoditel' po istoricheskim i pamiatnym mestam goroda* (These Are the Lines of Our History: Guide to the Historical and Memorial Places of the City) (Komsomol'sk-na-Amure, 1992), p. 50.

[23] A resolution of the Sovnarkom of 6 May 1942 decided that the pipeline should end in Sofiiskoe instead of Tsimmermanovka. It also fixed the deadline for completion in September 1942. "Postanovlenie SNK SSSR No. 637.327SS ot 6.5.1942g." Material provided by Kuz'mina from the same file 35 of the Khabarovsk archives, to which I had no direct access. For a general picture of the restructuring undergone by the administration of the labor camp system during the war, see the report by V. G. Nasedkin of August 1944: "Doklad nachal'nika GULAGa NKVD SSR V. G. Nasedkina. Avgust 1944 g." (Report of the head

of the GULAG of the NKVD of the USSR V. G. Nasedkin, August 1944), *Istoricheskii Arkhiv* 3 (1994): 60–86. I am grateful to Moshe Lewin for calling my attention to this source.

[24] This report was given to V. Azhaev by the NKVD at his own request in 1945. "UITLK UNKVD po Khabarovskomu Kraiiu, tov. Azhaevu. Nachal'nik biuro po delam izobretatel'stva NKVD SSSR (Strat'ev)." Private archive of V. Azhaev (AA). UITLK stands for Upravlenie ispravitel'no-trudovykh lagerei i kolonii (Administration of Corrective Labor Camps and Colonies).

[25] The Komsomol'sk–Sofiiskoe section was not completed until the late 1940s and early 1950s. See n. 33.

[26] A. Kirichenko, "Rassekrechennye sekrety, ili O stroitel'stve nefteprovoda 'Okha-Komsomol'sk'" (Declassified Secrets, or, On the Construction of the Pipeline "Okha-Komsomol'sk"), *Priamurskie vedomosti*, 4 July 1993, p. 2; 5 July 1993, p. 3. Jonathan A. Bone has suggested to me that these men are probably described more accurately as *tyloopolchentsy;* that is, persons of draft age considered unreliable.

[27] G. A. Tkacheva, "Osuzhden kazhdyi tretii," 75–76, 82, citing GAKhK, f. P-35, op. 1, d. 1306, ll. 91, 92.

[28] See Yuri Slezkine, *Arctic Mirrors: Russia and the Small Peoples of the North* (Ithaca: Cornell University Press, 1994), pp. 1–7.

[29] The files for the mainland unit through which the Okha–Komsomol'sk pipeline passed are deposited in the Russian State Military Archives (RGVA) (Moscow), f. 33913, "Upravlenie De-Kastrinskogo ukrep. raiona 1933–1940." Information provided by Jonathan A. Bone.

[30] G. A. Tkacheva, "Osuzhden kazhdyi tretii," 76, 82, citing GAKhK, f. P-35, op. 1, d. 1306, l. 3.

[31] Ibid., p. 76, citing ITs UVD Khabarovskogo kraiia, f. 26, op. 1. d. 16, ll. 72, 76, 78.

[32] Included in this report is Project No. 500, which succeeded Project No. 15 in the Lower Amur Camp system in 1943. Doklad nachal'nika GULAGa NKVD SSR V. G. Nasedkina, 68. Various recently discovered documents show that the conditions in the eastern sections of the Camp of the Lower Amur were already so horrendous in 1940 that they triggered an intervention of the party committee of the Sovetskii district (Sovetskaia Gavan'). See O. P. Elantseva, "BAM: Pervoe desiatiletie" (BAM: The First Decade), *Otechestvennaia istoriia*, no. 6 (1994): 89–103.

[33] Archival material from Kuz'mina. This second phase of the pipeline construction was eventually interrupted (*zakonservirovan*) until the late 1940s, when the last section of the Sofiiskoe–Komsomol'sk pipeline was completed. It was ordered on 31 March 1948, together with the formation of the Lower Amur Correctional Labor Camp of the Ministry of the Interior of the USSR (Order of the MVD SSSR No. 05593). The Sofiiskoe–Komsomol'sk section was not completed until August 1952. The construction of the pipeline was interrupted in 1943 because at that time the Camp of the Lower Amur was charged with strategically "more important" projects, such as the construction of the Komsomol'sk–Sovetskaia Gavan' railway, officially named Stroitel'stvo No. 500 NKVD SSSR. For the history of Project No. 500, see Elantseva, *Stroitel'stvo No. 500 NKVD SSSR,* and V. F. Zuev and P. L. Fefilov, *Serdtse ostanovilos' na perevale* (The Heart Stopped Beating on the Pass) (Moscow: Finizdat, 1995).

[34] This "code" was suggested to me by Richard Hellie.

[35] Letter to Azhaev, 7 November 1949 (name of sender illegible), AA.

[36] Letter to Azhaev signed Prokhorova, Kurovskii kombinat (Kurov Industrial Complex), n.d., AA.

[37] Berger and Luckmann, *Social Construction of Reality,* pp. 118–119, 120.

[38] SSSR Khabarovskii Kraevoi Komitet Radioinformatsii, 14 III 1952 g. Mikhail B—— (remainder of name illegible), AA.

[39] E. Riabchikov, "Postup' bogatyrei" (Deed of the Heroes), *Ogonek,* 8 April 1951, pp. 2–4.

[40] A. Kirichenko, "Rassekrechennye sekrety," *Priamurskie vedomosti,* 5 July 1993, p. 3.

[41] V. Zuev, "K 100-letiiu DVZhD: Sozidateli Komsomol'skoi magistrali" (For the Centennial of the Far Eastern Railway: The Builders of the Komsomol'sk Main Line), *Dal'nevostochnaia magistral',* 24 August 1995, p. 2.

[42] The Far Eastern writer Iuliia Shestakova espouses this origin of the name. Interview conducted 15 July 1994.

[43] Vas. Azhaev, "Syn: Rasskaz" (The Son: A Story), *Na rubezhe. Zhurnal khudozhestvennoi literatury i publitsistiki. Organ dal'nevostochnogo pravleniia soiuza sovetskikh pisatelei* (July–August 1937): 60–74. On the circumstances of this publication and other issues of the Far Eastern purges, see Chapter 6.

[44] The shock worker movement was one of the forms of socialist competition. The title of shock worker was awarded to workers who made outstanding contributions to productivity. The movement, at its height during the First Five-Year Plan (1929–1932), was replaced by the Stakhanovite movement around 1935. See n. 9 above.

[45] Yury Trifonov, *The Exchange and Other Stories* (Ann Arbor: Ardis, 1991), p. 147.

[46] Iurii Trifonov, "Drugaia zhizn'" (Another Life), *Novyi mir,* no. 8 (1975): 87–99.

2. Utopics

[1] Frank E. Manuel and Fritzie P. Manuel, *Utopian Thought in the Western World* (Cambridge: Belknap Press/Harvard University Press, 1979), p. 15.

[2] Vasili Azhayev, *Far from Moscow,* trans. R. Prokofieva (Moscow: Foreign Languages Publishing House, 1950), bk. 3, pp. 465–466.

[3] L. I. Timofeev, *Teoriia literatury: Osnovy nauki o literature* (Theory of Literature: Foundations of Literary Science) (Moscow: Uchpedgiz, 1945), p. 28.

[4] Azhayev, *Far from Moscow,* bk. 1, p. 8.

[5] Louis Marin, *Utopics: The Semiological Play of Textual Spaces,* trans. Robert A. Vollrath (Atlantic Highlands, N.J.: Humanities Press International, 1990), pp. 11–12.

[6] N. N. Mikhailov, *Nad kartoi rodiny* (Moscow: Molodaia Gvardiia, 1947).

[7] Stalin Prizes were awarded for achievements in the arts and sciences beginning in 1939. The Stalin Prize for literature was first awarded in 1941.

[8] N. N. Mikhailov, *Nad kartoi rodiny,* 2d rev. ed. (Moscow: Molodaia Gvardiia, 1949).

[9] Ibid. (1947), p. 54.

[10] Ibid. (1949), pp. 66–67.

[11] N. Mikhailov, *Prostory i bogatstva nashei rodiny* (Moscow: OGIZ, 1946).

[12] *Nasha velikaia rodina* (Moscow: Politizdat, 1953).

[13] N. Mikhailov, *Moia Rossiia,* bk. 1, *Rossiiskie prostory* (Russian Spaces) (Moscow: Sovetskaia Rossiia, 1964).

[14] These are chapters in N. N. Mikhailov, *Po stopam ispolina* (Moscow: Politizdat, 1967).

[15] Azhayev, *Far from Moscow*, bk. 3, pp. 119-120.

[16] See Viktor Remizovskii, "'Za otsutstviem sostava prestupleniia . . .': Sud'by pervykh organizatorov neftianoi promyshlennosti na Dal'nem Vostoke" ("For Lack of Corpus Delicti . . .": The Fate of the First Organizers of the Oil-Extracting Industry in the Far East), *Dal'nevostochnyi uchenyi* 36 (1993): 7; 37 (1993): 7.

[17] Edith Hamilton, *Mythology: Timeless Tales of Gods and Heroes* (New York: Penguin, 1979), p. 39.

[18] Ibid.

[19] Azhayev, *Far from Moscow*, bk. 3, p. 215; translation modified.

[20] Marin, *Utopics*, pp. 87-89.

3. The Beginning

[1] Konstantin Simonov, "Takim ostalsia v pamiati," in Vasilii Azhaev, *Daleko ot Moskvy* (Petrozavodsk: Kareliia, 1974), pp. 678-679.

[2] According to his widow, Azhaev, who had completed *The Boxcar* before *One Day in the Life of Ivan Denisovich* was published, submitted his novel to Vsevolod Kochetov for publication in the journal *Oktiabr'*. Kochetov first asked him to shorten the work and then decided to "postpone" it. Interview with Irina Liubimova-Azhaeva, 10 November 1991.

[3] V. Azhaev, "Vagon: Roman" (The Boxcar: A Novel), *Druzhba narodov*, no. 6 (1988): 168.

[4] In reality, Azhaev married Irina Leonidovna Liubimova after *Far from Moscow* was published. They had met in 1948 in the editorial office of *Literaturnaia gazeta*, where Irina Leonidovna was working at the time. During an interview on 10 November 1991, she declared that she had been "charmed by his smile and his beautiful hands." After Azhaev told her his story, she was "inspired by something like a motherly feeling, not yet love."

[5] Azhaev, "Vagon," *Druzhba narodov*, no. 6 (1988): 164-165; no. 7 (1988): 139.

[6] Cathy Caruth, "Recapturing the Past: Introduction," in *Trauma: Explorations in Memory*, ed. Caruth (Baltimore: Johns Hopkins University Press, 1995), p. 153. I am grateful to Julia Hell for making me aware of this text.

[7] Ibid., pp. 154-155.

[8] People who were banished from Moscow or Leningrad were forbidden to live anywhere within a 100-kilometer radius of the city, so they settled in locations at the 101st kilometer point. According to Jacques Rossi, this system was replaced by exile to remote regions after the mid-1930s. Jacques Rossi, *The Gulag Handbook: An Encyclopedic Dictionary of Soviet Penitentiary Institutions and Terms Related to the Forced Labor Camps*, trans. William A. Burhans (New York: Paragon House, 1989), p. 434.

[9] Vasili Azhayev, *Far from Moscow*, trans. R. Prokofieva (Moscow: Foreign Languages Publishing House, 1950), bk. 1, p. 75; translation modified.

[10] Azhaev, "Vagon," *Druzhba narodov*, no. 8 (1988): 164.

[11] Ibid., p. 138.

[12] Ibid., p. 170.

[13] Dominique Maingenau, *Initiation aux méthodes de l'analyse du discours* (Paris: Ha-

chette, 1976), p. 102. The reference is to Émile Benveniste's seminal article "L'homme dans la langue," in *Problèmes de linguistique générale* (Paris: Gallimard, 1966), 1:225-266.
[14] Azhaev, "Vagon," *Druzhba narodov*, no. 8 (1988): 174.

4. Camp Freedom

[1] "NKVD. Upravlenie Baikalo-Amurskogo isprav.-trud. lageria. Otdelenie 8. 16 marta 1937. DVK. g. Svobodnyi. Spravka. Dana gr. Azhaevu Vasiliiu Nikolaevichu. God rozhd. 1912," AA.

[2] "Kharakteristika. Azhaeva Vasiliia Nikolaevicha Nachal'nika TsBRIZ'a UZhDS GULAG'a NKVD na DV. Bakin, Glavnyi inzhener UZhDS GULAG NKVD na DV. 30.XII.1939 g," AA.

[3] Ia. Kharon, *Zlye pesni Giioma diu Ventre: Prozaicheskii kommentarii k poeticheskoi biografii* (The Wicked Songs of Guillaume du Ventre: Prosaic Comments of a Poetic Biography) (Moscow: Kniga, 1989), pp. 80-81.

[4] "Kharakteristika. Tov. Azhaeva Vasiliia Nikolaevicha, starshego Inspektora pri Nachal'nike Upravleniia Nizhne-Amurskogo lageriia NKVD. Barabanov, Verno: Nach [illeg.] Chashnik," AA.

[5] See O. P. Elantseva, "Kto i kak stroil BAM v 30-e gody" (Who Built the BAM and How in the 1930s), *Otechestvennye arkhivy*, no. 5 (1992): 77-79; S. A. Paichadze, "Izdatel'skaia deiatel'nost' i ispol'zovanie literatury uchrezhdeniami OGPU-NKVD v zone stroitel'stva BAM (1933-1937 gg.)" (The Publishing Activities and Utilization of Literature by the Establishments of the OGPU-NKVD in the BAM Construction Zone [1933-1937]), in *Izdanie i rasprostranenie knigi v Sibiri i na Dal'nem Vostoke: Sbornik nauchnykh trudov* (The Publication and Dissemination of the Book in Siberia and the Far East: Collection of Scholary Essays) (Novosibirsk: GPNTB SO RAN, 1993), pp. 127-152. Paichadze mentions Azhaev's publishing activity in the BAM. For a history of the system of camp publications in the Soviet Union from 1918 to the 1950s, its scope, its geographical and social distribution, censorship regulations, and so on, see A. Iu. Gorchev, "Ne podlezhit rasprostraneniiu . . . ," *Sovetskaia bibliografiia*, no. 5 (1991): 56-79; no. 6 (1991): 63-83; and no. 1 (1992): 99-111 (this last issue is devoted to the "Press of the Establishment for Children of the OGPU and NKVD"). Gorchev mentions the creation, in January 1936, of the "fourth department" of the GULAG, responsible for camp publications throughout the country. One of the duties of the fourth department was to control the distribution process, restricted by categories: prisoners, free laborers, the militarized guard, and so on, and even the inmates of the special forced labor colonies for children, as well as prisoners of war. The names of those to whom the materials were distributed had to be communicated to the fourth department. In addition, all GULAG camp publications were submitted to the censoring authority of Glavlit. *Sovetskaia bibliografiia*, no. 6 (1991): 64-72.

[6] The view that "reeducation" was simply another means of increasing production (whereas in the 1920s correctional labor had stood for moral improvement) is developed in David J. Dallin and Boris I. Nicolaevsky's classic, *Forced Labor in Soviet Russia* (New Haven: Yale University Press, 1947), p. 235.

[7] Edwin Bacon's recent book devotes several pages to this problem. See Edwin Bacon, *The Gulag at War* (New York: New York University Press, 1994), pp. 47-53.

[8] A. Medvedev, "Montazh zhizni," *Putearmeets (Literaturno-khudozhestvennyi zhurnal BAMLAGa NKVD)* 4 (December 1935): 15–16, AA.

[9] In an "official" list of Azhaev's works, submitted in 1948 to the Far Eastern branch of the Soviet Writers' Union in Khabarovsk, which then became attached to his file, these works bear the note "*otdel'noe izdanie*" (separate publication). "Bibliografiia napechatan-nykh rabot V. N. Azhaeva, sostavlena 8 sentiabria 1948 g." GAKhK, f. 1738, op. 1, d. 109, l. 7.

[10] *Putearmeets* 3 (October 1935), AA.

[11] V. Azhaev and P. Zhagir, "Chuzhoi kalendar': Komediia v 1 deistvii," *Repertuarnyi biulleten' sektora pechati kul'turno-vospitatel'nogo otdela* 6 (May 1935): 12–20, AA.

[12] V. Azhaev, "Kak Umara Magomet poterial svoiu shapku" (How Umara Magomet Lost His Hat); "Otlozhennoe sobranie" (The Interrupted Meeting); "Bol'shoe spasibo" (A Great Thank You), all in *Prostye rasskazy o podvigakh,* Biblioteka "stroitelia Bama," ser. 7 (Svobodnyi: Izdatel'stvo KVO BAMLAGa NKVD, 1935), pp. 5–8, 23–26, 43–47, AA.

[13] Aleksandr I. Solzhenitsyn, *The Gulag Archipelago, 1918–1956: An Experiment in Literary Investigation,* vols. 3–4, trans. Thomas P. Whitney (New York: Harper & Row, 1975), pp. 75–80, 138–141; B. Shiriaev, "Neugasimaia lampada," *Nash sovremennik,* no. 6 (1991): 124–127; O. P. Elantseva, *Obrechennaia doroga: BAM, 1932–1941* (The Doomed Track: The BAM in 1932–1941) (Vladivostok: Izdatel'stvo Dal'nevostochnogo Universiteta, 1994), pp. 118–119. Elantseva refutes many of Solzhenitsyn's accounts of the life of Naftalii Frenkel' in light of the documents that she was able to find in the archives.

[14] See the (in)famous publication on Belomor Canal put together by a "brigade" of Soviet writers, headed by Maxim Gorky, *Belomorsko-Baltiiskii Kanal imeni Stalina: Istoriia stroitel'stva* (The Stalin White Sea–Baltic Canal: The History of Construction), ed. M. Gor'kii, L. L. Averbakh, and S. G. Firin (Moscow: Gosudarstvennoe Izdatel'stvo "Istoriia Fabrik i Zavodov," 1934).

[15] Elantseva, *Obrechennaia doroga,* p. 121.

[16] Jacques Rossi, *The Gulag Handbook: An Encyclopedia Dictionary of Soviet Penitentiary Institutions and Terms Related to the Forced Labor Camps,* trans. William A. Burhans (New York: Paragon House, 1989), p. 178.

[17] RTsKhIDNI, f. 17, op. 4, d. 928, ll. 5, 9, cited in Elantseva, *Obrechennaia doroga,* p. 122. The promotion was confirmed by the Council of the People's Commissariats of the USSR on 17 August 1933.

[18] V. S. Korobkov, *Falangovaia sistema na rabote* (Svobodnyi: Izdanie finotdela stroi-tel'stva bama NKVD, 1935), AA. Here are further publisher's notes on this unique document: Ne podlezhit rasprostraneniiu za predelami lageria. Otv. red.: B. N. Kuznetsov. Fotografii fotobiuro BAMLAGa NKVD. Khudozh.-tech. oformlenie, klishe i pechat' tipo-litografii BAMLAGa NKVD. Tir. 1500. Zak. No. 7945. PK 266. Gor. Svobodnyi, DVK. Despite its specific pathos, Korobkov's book gives an extremely detailed and technical description of the system of the phalanx, including schemes, reproductions, and an internal bibliography. One of its models was the Stalin White Sea–Baltic Canal. In Gor'kii et al., *Belomorsko-Baltiiskii Kanal,* we find phalanxes defined as "production units of from 200 to 500 shock workers" (p. 406). Phalanxes were low in the hierarchical structure of labor camp construction sites; relatively few in number, mobile, and independently managed, they were used for specific work within a larger project and were often directed by women. Because of its relatively small size, the phalanx allowed increased control over the prisoners and their work output. Each prisoner's work was evaluated on a scale of three: "shock

work–like" (po-udarnomu), "non–shock work–like" (ne po-udarnomu), and credit denied for the entire working day. The phalanx system and its gendered division of labor had
been introduced at the initiative of the head of BAM construction (and the BAMLAG),
N. A. Frenkel'. See Elantseva, *Obrechennaia doroga,* pp. 112–114; *Stroitel'stvo No. 500
NKVD SSSR: Zheleznaia doroga Komsomol'sk–Sovetskaia Gavan' (1930–40-e gody)* (Project No. 500 of the NKVD of the USSR: The Komsomol'sk–Sovetskaia Gavan' Railway
[The 1930s and 1940s]) (Vladivostok: Izdatel'stvo Dal'nevostochnogo Universiteta, 1995),
p. 43. For the general system of accounting in the camps of the Gulag and its economic impact, see A. S. Narinskii, "Uchet na stroikakh GULAGa" (Accounting on the Constructions of the GULAG), *Bukhgal'terskii uchet,* no. 11 (1992): 6–8. According to Narinskii,
many of the important labor camp construction sites were headed by "highly qualified specialists." This type of leader, Narinskii writes, was depicted by Azhaev in his novel *Far from
Moscow* under the name Batmanov, whose prototype was the real-life "head of the Far
Eastern construction site of the GULAG," Barabanov (p. 6).

   [19] *Putearmeets* 3 (October 1935): 1, AA. Concerning this title, assignments at the Baikal-
Amur Corrective Labor Camp varied considerably during the 1930s. Organized by a decree
of the OGPU on 10 November 1932, the BAMLAG was assigned the construction of a railway from the station at Takhtamygda to the village of Permskoe on the Lower Amur (later
known as Komsomol'sk-on-the-Amur). But by the spring of 1933, the BAMLAG was also
responsible for constructing a second track along the Trans-Siberian Transit Railway. At
the end of 1933 the production force of the BAMLAG was almost entirely concentrated on
this second track. See Elantseva, *Obrechennaia doroga,* p. 102.

   [20] Azhaev contributed two essays: "Zhena geroia" (The Wife of a Hero) and "Dva
dokumenta o cheloveke" (Two Documents on a Human Being). The latter told the "real
story" of Evgeniia Vinogradova (discussed later in this chapter). The issue also contains a
portrait of the "Stakhanovite Valeriia Vasil'chenko," who, besides lending her name, may
well have been the inspiration for the Komsomol shock worker and mechanic of communication Tania Vasil'chenko in *Far from Moscow.* See *Putearmeets* 7 (March 1937): 18–19,
24, 28, AA.

   [21] V. Azhaev, *Predislovie k zhizni: Povest'* (A Foreword to Life: A Novella), Biblioteka
"stroitelia Bama, ser. 8 (Svobodnyi: Izdatel'stvo KVO BAMLAGa NKVD, 1935), pp. 3–24,
AA. Coincidence or not, Evgeniia Vinogradova had two famous Stakhanovite name-
sakes—Mariia and Evdokiia. See Mariia Vinogradova, *Riadom s legendoi* (Beside the Legend) (Moscow: Profizdat, 1981).

   [22] A. S. Makarenko's *Pedagogicheskaia poema* (The Pedagogical Poem) is usually translated in English as *The Road to Life.*

   [23] For a general overview of the specialized camp publications for childen, see A. Gorchev, "Ne podlezhit rasprostraneniiu . . . ," *Sovetskaia bibliografiia,* no. 1 (1992): 99–111.

   [24] Azhaev, *Predislovie k zhizni,* p. 24.

   [25] V. Azhaev, "Slet prodolzhaetsia na zavode" (The Rally Goes on in the Factory);
idem, "Organ Polikarpova" (Polikarpov's Organ), *Putearmeets* 5 (August 1936): 2–5,
26–27, AA.

   [26] In the volume *Stakhanovtsy vtorych putei: Rasskazy stakhanovtsev o sebe* (The
Stakhanovites of the Second Tracks: Stories by Stakhanovites about Themselves), Biblioteka
"stroitelia Bama," ser. 16 (Svobodnyi: Izdatel'stvo KVO BAMLAGa NKVD, Sektor Pechati
BAMLAGa NKVD, 1936), the name of Azhaev appears only as editor, with L. Lisenko.

The volume contains a handwritten dedication by Lisenko, celebrating their "common Far Eastern work on the books that appear in the heroic BAM."

27 Vas. Azhaev, "Serdechnaia rech' sverstnika" (The Cordial Speech of the Contemporary), *Putearmeets* 6 (February 1937): 23–26, AA, with a photograph of the young author. P. 24 represents a "portrait in oil" by one N. Salomatin of "the Deputy of the People's Commissar of Internal Affairs of the USSR, Commissar of the State Security of the Third Rank Com. M. D. Berman." The issue is introduced by a portrait of Sergo Ordzhonikidze in a black frame and a text mourning the "painful loss." The text is signed by a list of personalities including I. Stalin, V. Molotov, L. Kaganovich, K. Voroshilov, A. Mikoian, M. Kalinin, A. Zhdanov, A. Andreev, M. Shkiriatov, and eleven others whose names are crossed out. Grigorii Konstantinovich (Sergo) Ordzhonikidze was a member of the Central Committee since 1921 and of the Politburo from 1930 to 1937. From 1932 to his death he was the People's Commissar of Heavy Industry. Sergo's death was allegedly caused by heart failure, but in reality he committed suicide after a violent dispute with Stalin, according to recent sources, over the arrest of some of his close colleagues, including his brother.

28 *Putearmeets* 6 (February 1937): 39–41.

29 Ibid., pp. 41–42.

30 See Slavoj Žižek, *The Sublime Object of Ideology* (1984; rpt. London: Verso, 1994), pp. 105–110. For Žižek, the way Iosif Vissarionovich Dzhugashvili's nickname, Stalin, functioned in Soviet culture is a case of such "symbolic identification." He writes: "In the case of Iosif Vissarionovich, it would be entirely erroneous to conclude . . . that 'Stalin' (Russian for '[made] of steel') alludes to some steely, inexorable characteristic of Stalin himself: what is really inexorable and steely are the laws of the historical progress, the iron necessity of the disintegration of capitalism and of the passage to socialism in the name of which Stalin, this empirical individual, is acting—the perspective from which he is observing himself and judging his activity. We could say, then, that 'Stalin' is the ideal point from which 'Iosif Vissarionovich,' this empirical individual, this person of flesh and blood, is observing himself so that he appears likeable" (p. 108).

31 Perhaps in Lacan's understanding, reinterpreted by Žižek, "the Lacanian formula for this object is of course *objet petit a,* this point of Real in the very heart of the subject which cannot be symbolized, which is produced as a residue, a remnant, a leftover of every signifying operation, a hard core embodying horrifying *jouissance,* enjoyment, and as such an object which simultaneously attracts and repels us—which *divides* our desire and thus provokes shame." Ibid., p. 180.

32 V. Azhaev, "Materialy k povesti o chekistakh," pp. 1–29, AA; hereafter cited as "Materialy k povesti o chekistakh (I)."

33 Ibid., p. 4

34 Rakhmetov is one of the characters in Nikolai Chernyshevsky's famous novel *What Is to Be Done? From Stories about the New People* (1863). He embodies radical ideology through asceticism, even to the point of sleeping on a bed of nails. Greatly esteemed by V. I. Lenin (who borrowed its title for one of his own publications), *What Is to Be Done?* was on the reading list of Russian classics throughout the Soviet period.

35 *Politgramotu,* literally, "political grammar."

36 "Materialy k povesti o chekistakh (I)," p. 9.

37 Ibid., pp. 10–13.

38 According to Ol'ga Elantseva, the camp documents completely cease to use the term "phalanx" after December 1936 and use instead the term "colony" (*kolonna*), perhaps to

avoid the fascist analogy. This also seems to indicate that Azhaev's "materials for the novella on the Chekists" were written after this date. Elantseva, *Obrechennaia doroga*, p. 112.

[39] V. Azhaev, "Materialy k povesti o chekistakh," pp. 1–20, AA; hereafter cited as "Materialy k povesti o chekistakh (II)."

[40] Vasili Azhayev, *Far from Moscow*, trans. R. Prokofieva (Moscow: Foreign Languages Publishing House, 1950), bk. 3, pp. 345–346.

[41] The Russian distinguishes the *pisatel'* (writer) from the *literator* (man of letters). The second term reflects the increasing bureaucratization and "democratization" of the profession during Soviet times, which culminated in the admission of many nonwriters to the Soviet Writers' Union. See, for example, John Garrard and Carol Garrard, *Inside the Soviet Writers' Union* (New York: Free Press, 1990), p. 114.

[42] "Materialy k povesti o chekistakh (II)," pp. 9–11.

[43] *Putearmeets* 6 (February 1937): 31–32.

5. Personal Files

[1] Valentin Kataev, *Vremia, vpered!* (1932), a novel about a shock worker brigade's record-breaking struggle in Magnitogorsk during the era of the First Five-Year Plan.

[2] "Lichnaia kartochka chlena Soiuza Pisatelei SSSR Azhaeva V. N., zapolnena 10 marta 1947 g." GAKhK, f. 1738, op. 1, d. 109, l. 15.

[3] "Lichnaia kartochka chlena SSP SSSR Azhaeva V. N. zapolnena 23 iunia 1947 g." GAKhK, f. 1738, op. 1, d. 109, ll. 4, 20.

[4] "Uchetnaia kartochka Azhaeva V. N., zapolnena 21 ianvaria 1940 g." GAKhK, f. 1738, op. 1, d. 109, l. 16.

[5] The autobiography states 1940, which is certainly an error. Another file (n.d., probably 1943) states, "10.V.43 St. Inspektor pri Nachal'nike TsITL i K NKVD po Khab. kraiiu (g. Khabarovsk)," AA.

[6] "Avtobiografiia Azhaeva V. N., napisana 22 apreliia 1946." GAKhK, f. 1738, op. 1, d. 109, l. 14.

6. Borderline I

[1] "Protokol razshirennogo zasedaniia DV Pravleniia SSP ot 26 noiabria 1936 g. No. 16." GAKhK, f. 1738, op. 1, d. 2, ll. 1–7.

[2] "Tikho v Pravlenii Soiuza Pisatelei" (Everything Is Quiet on the Board of the Writers' Union), *Tikhookeanskii komsomolets* (Organ Dal'kraikoma VLKSM, Khabarovsk), 22 November 1936, p. 2. The front page of the newspaper was devoted to the "trial of the counterrevolutionary Trotskyite wreckers' group in the Kemerovo mine."

[3] John J. Stephan, *The Russian Far East: A History* (Stanford: Stanford University Press, 1994), pp. 209–224.

[4] Tin'-Shan' (also identified in archival documents as "Tan'-shan'") was editor of the Chinese-language weekly *Gongren zhi lu* (*Rabochii put'* [The Workers' Path]). *Gongren zhi lu* was "liquidated" in July 1938. See "Spisok gazet na 1.1.1938 goda. Khabarovskii krai (byvshii Dal'nevostochnyi krai)," GAKhK, f. 719, op.6, d.2, l. 65.

[5] Lavrentii Iosifovich Lavrent'ev [Kartvelishvili] (1890–1938), First Secretary of Dal'kraikom from 1933 to 1937. See Stephan, *Russian Far East*, p. 324.

⁶The first issue of *Na rubezhe* had been criticized by Aleksandr Fadeev in *Pravda* on 24 March 1934 precisely for its omission of the poets of the BAM. See ibid., p. 196.

⁷Sergei Petrovich Fedotov was one of the prominent writers of the BAMLAG between 1934 and 1937. Almost every issue of *Putearmeets* and similar publications contained his work. See, for example, *Putearmeitsy: Stikhi i pesni lagkorov* (The Soldiers of the Tracks: Poems and Songs of Camp Correspondents) (Svobodnyi: Sektor pechati KVO BAMLAGa NKVD, 1935); *Putearmeets* 3 and 4 (1935), 5 (1936), 6 and 7 (1937). The sixth issue contains his portrait and a brief biography, from which we learn that Fedotov was twenty-eight years old in 1937, that he was released on 28 May 1934, and that, like Azhaev, he "remained on the construction site." At the time when this biographical note was published, he was "inspector of the Culture and Education Department (KVO)." The note mentions that *Joy* was performed not only in the Theater of the KVO in the BAMLAG, but also in the Far Eastern Theater in Khabarovsk and the Workers' Artistic Theater in Moscow; see *Putearmeets* 6 (1937): 19. On the tragic and exemplary life of Sergei Petrovich Fedotov, from his arrest in the late 1920s (for counterrevolutionary agitation), a second conviction in 1933, for which he was sentenced to the Belomor Canal construction site and then to the BAMLAG in Svobodnyi, where he was released ahead of schedule, his literary-educational work in the BAMLAG KVO, to his disappearance in 1937, see O. P. Elantseva, *Poety i poeziia BAMLAGa: Obzor dokumentov i materialov k spetskursu "Velikie stroiki stalinskoi epokhi"* (The Poets and the Poetry of the BAMLAG: Survey of Documents and Materials for the Special Course "The Great Constructions of the Stalin Era") (Vladivostok: Izdatel'stvo Dal'nevostochnogo Universiteta, 1994), pp. 12–15. Elantseva shows that Fedotov's career in the KVO of the BAMLAG was closely related to that of Anatolii Aleksandrovich Bel'skii, head of the Culture and Education Department from 1933 to 1937. When Bel'skii was arrested in the spring of 1937 (he was shot on 2 December 1937), Fedotov was fired. Despite his desire to be given "whatever work," the camp authorities refused. According to some rumors, Fedotov was eventually killed by common criminals.

⁸Protokol razshirennogo zasedaniia DV Pravleniia SSP ot 26 noiabria 1936 g., pp. 1–3.

⁹Sergei Georgievich Lazo (1894–1920), hero of the Vladivostok uprising of January 1920; arrested by the Japanese on 4–5 April, then killed by the Whites on 28 May 1920.

¹⁰Protokol razshirennogo zasedaniia DV Pravleniia SSP ot 26 noiabria 1936 g., pp. 3–6.

¹¹Ibid., pp. 6–7.

¹²"Protokol zasedaniia DV Pravleniia SSP ot 10 marta 1937 g. No. 4." GAKhK, f. 1738, op. 1, d. 2, ll. 8–9. See also Stephan, *Russian Far East,* pp. 195–196. Shabanov was still listed as a member of the editorial board of *Na rubezhe* in the journal's third issue of 1936 (together with M. Alekseev, A. Gai, D. Nikonov, A. Fadeev [responsible editor], and A. Estrin). The first issue of 1937 no longer lists him.

¹³Protokol zasedaniia DV Pravleniia SSP ot 10 marta 1937 g., ll. 8–9. The novella was published in 1934. I. Shabanov, "Lakirovka," *Na rubezhe* 2 (1934): 18–33; 3 (1934): 50–57.

¹⁴"Protokol zasedaniia DV Pravleniia SSP ot 19 aprelia 1937 g." GAKhK, f. 1738, op. 1, d. 2, ll. 10–11.

¹⁵"Protokol vneocherednogo zasedaniia DV Pravleniia SSP, sovmestno s chlenami SSP i litaktivom g. Khabarovska ot 23 aprelia 1937 g." GAKhK, f. 1738, op. 1, d. 2, ll. 18–21.

¹⁶Reference to the Central Committee's Resolution of 23 April 1932, "O perestroike literaturno-khudozhestvennykh organizatsii" (On the Restructuring of Literary-Artistic Organizations). The resolution, which liquidated all existing literary associations, is gener-

ally considered the starting point of Stalinist "totalitarian" literary politics, implemented two years later by the creation of the Writers' Union and the introduction of the socialist realist dogma.

[17] The plenum decided to exclude from the party ranks N. Bukharin and A. Rykov, who had been arrested on 27 February.

[18] "Protokol vneocherednogo zasedaniia DV Pravleniia SSP, sovmestno s chlenami SSP i litaktivom g. Khabarovska ot 23 aprelia 1937 g.," ll. 18-21, 1.

[19] Ibid., p. 2.

[20] The following year, the Soviet people were able to study this history with the aid of a highly "authorized" textbook, The *History of the All-Union Communist Party: Short Course*, published 1 October 1938, which determined for years to come the Stalinist dogma and sanctioned the rewriting "by Stalin" of the country's history. On the history of the *Short Course*, see Robert C. Tucker, *Stalin in Power: The Revolution from Above, 1928-1941* (New York: Norton, 1990), pp. 530-550.

[21] Recently released documents in the archives of the Khabarovsk Administrative Region illustrate the increased concern of the Soviet authorities during the years 1927-1938 about the education of the Chinese and Korean population of the region, as well as of the "nations of the North." They pertain to party and propaganda work; relations between the authorities and Chinese citizens and organizations such as trade unions, theaters, and schools; the campaign to wipe out illiteracy and semiliteracy (*ne- i malogramotnost'*) among the Chinese; the work of the Committee on the Creation of a Chinese New Alphabet (romanized); and so on. These documents—the study of which awaits its historian—seem to show how the gradual integration of the Asian population of the Far East was paralleled by its unavoidable purge and relocation, finally realized in 1937 and 1938. "Perechen' dokumentov po teme 'Kitaitsy na Dal'nem Vostoke. 1895-1989 gg.'" (List of Documents on the Theme of the Chinese in the Far East: 1895-1989) (Khabarovsk: GAKhK, 1995).

[22] Emi Siao (Xiao Aimei), Chinese writer and translator, participant in the May Fourth Movement in 1919, who had studied in Moscow in the early 1920s and emigrated to the USSR around 1927, remaining until 1939. In 1940 he went home to join the Chinese revolution in the liberated territories, and published various of his own works and translations until he was silenced during the Cultural Revolution. He died in the 1980s.

[23] "Protokol zasedaniia DV Pravleniia SSP ot 28 Aprelia 1937 g. No. 7, s prilozheniiami." GAKhK, f. 1738, op. 1, d. 2, ll. 22-35.

[24] Before 1935 Voroshilovsk was called Nikol'sk-Ussuriisk. In 1957 it regained half of its previous name and is now known as Ussuriisk.

[25] Neither the Jewish Autonomous Region nor other parts or "national" groups of the Far East had its own separate branch of the Soviet Writers' Union. Khabarovsk was therefore responsible for the whole Far East. Only in 1949 and 1960 were such privileges conferred on Primor'e and Magadan, respectively. See L. Ia. Ivashchenko, *Istoricheskie aspekty sozdaniia i razvitiia mnogonatsional'noi khudozhestvennoi literatury na Dal'nem Vostoke Rossii, 1917-seredina 1980-kh godov: Ocherki* (Historical Aspects of the Formation and Development of the Multi-National Literature in the Russian Far East, 1917 to mid-1980s: Essays) (Vladivostok: Dal'nauka, 1995), p. 125.

[26] Titov's arrest evidently prevented him from providing this assistance. Leshak's name does not appear in any bibliography of which I am aware. See R. K. Agishev, *Sovetskii Dal'nii Vostok v khudozhestvennoi literature: Bibliograficheskii ukazatel'* (The Soviet Far

East in Literature: A Bibliographical Guide), 2d rev. enl. ed. (Khabarovsk: Khabarovskaia Kraevaia Biblioteka, 1957); L. Ia. Ivashchenko, *Khudozhestvennaia literatura o Dal'nem Vostoke: Bibliograficheskii ukazatel'* (Literature about the Far East: A Bibliographical Guide), 2 vols. (Vladivostok: RIO Primuprpoligrafizdata, 1990–91).

[27] "Protokol zasedaniia DV Pravleniia SSP ot 28 Aprelia 1937 g. No. 7. Prilozhenie k protokolu No. 7 ot 28/IV-37 g." GAKhK, f. 1738, op. 1, d. 2, ll. 30–35.

[28] *Na rubezhe* 4 (July–August 1937).

[29] "Protokol zasedaniia DV pravleniia Soiuza sovetskikh pisatelei ot 4 iiulia 1937 g. No. 10." GAKhK, f. 1738, op. 1, d.2, ll. 38–42.

[30] A "Speech of V. M. Molotov on the Solemn Meeting in the Bolshoi Theater on 6 November 1937" opens the issue, followed by a series of "Documents about the History of the Civil War in the Far East," presenting the "correct" version of what had been planned. Literary writing is represented by names we have already encountered: P. Komarov, V. Afanasiev, S. Bytovoi, and others.

[31] Ivashchenko, *Istoricheskie aspekty*, p. 69.

[32] Stephan, *Russian Far East*, p. 221. A. Suturin, *Delo kraevogo masshtaba: O zhertvakh stalinskogo bezzakoniia na Dal'nem Vostoke* (A File on the Scale of the Region: On the Victims of Stalinist Lawlessness in the Far East) (Khabarovsk: Khabarovskoe knizhnoe izdatel'stvo, 1991), p. 183.

[33] Stephan, *Russian Far East*, pp. 212–213. For a detailed account on the fate of the Koreans in the Far East, see A. Kuzin, *Dal'nevostochnye koreitsy: Zhizn' i tragedia sud'by. Dokumental'no-istoricheskii ocherk* (The Far Eastern Koreans: Life and Tragedy of a Destiny, A Documentary-Historical Essay) (Iuzhno-Sakhalinsk: Dal'nevostochnoe knizhnoe izdatel'stvo. Sakhalinskoe otdelenie, 1993).

[34] Suturin, *Delo kraevogo masshtaba*, p. 100.

[35] By decision of the Military Collegium of the Supreme Court of the USSR of 17 August 1957, the criminal case against V. I. Batmanov was discontinued "for absence of crime" and Batmanov was rehabilitated posthumously. Letter to V. I. Batmanov's son, Anatolii Vasil'evich Batmanov, dated 26 February 1994 and signed by Lavrentsov, Aleksandr Pavlovich, Administration of the Federal Service of Security (UFSB) of the Khabarovsk Region, UFSB-KhK, Arkhivnoe ugolovnoe delo R-80993.

[36] Suturin, *Delo kraevogo masshtaba*, pp. 101–102; Stephan, *Russian Far East*, p. 336.

[37] Suturin, *Delo kraevogo masshtaba*, p. 118.

[38] Ibid., p. 103.

[39] Ian Gamarnik was accused of participating in the alleged Tukhachevskii conspiracy.

[40] Stephan, *Russian Far East*, p. 314; Suturin, *Delo kraevogo masshtaba*, pp. 38–39.

[41] For general figures on the repressions in the Far East, see Stephan, *Russian Far East*, pp. 220–221.

7. The Notebooks of Komsomol'sk

[1] After the general campaign to control the press, in particular the resolution on the journal *Oktiabr'* in August 1939 by the Administration of Propaganda and Agitation, Azhaev's worries were certainly justified. They turned out to be premature: *Na rubezhe* had just reappeared and was not shut down (again) until 1941.

[2] GAKhK, f. 1738 op.1, ed. khr. 35.

[3] Vas. Azhaev, "Tarakany: Povest'. 1938 g.–dekabr' 1939 g. g. Svobodnyi," pp. 1–11, AA.

⁴An. Gai and N. Shalyi, "Vospityvat' pisatelei Komsomol'ska," *Stalinskii Komsomol'sk* (Organ Komsomol'skogo-na-Amure gorkoma VKP[b] i gorsoveta, Komsomol'sk-na-Amure), 26 October 1940, p. 3. Nikolai Shalyi was the literary pseudonym of Nikolai Kirillovich Povarenkin, whose poems and commentary can be found in many issues of *Stalinskii Komsomol'sk*. The former were generally published under his pseudonym, the latter under his real name. Povarenkin, who had come to Komsomol'sk in 1932, following the appeal of the Central Committee of the All-Union Leninist Communist Youth League, was one of the main activists of the city's literary association.

⁵Vasilii Azhaev, "Smert' cheloveka: Rasskaz," pp. 1–9, AA. I was unable to find the published story in *Na rubezhe*.

⁶"O Metode Uskoreniia i Udeshevleniia Bureniia Tverdikh Porod Primeneniem Ponizitelei Tverdosti," AA.

⁷"Vas. Azhaev, 1940 god, gor. Svobodnyi, Dal'nii Vostok, gor. Komsomol'sk-na-Amure," AA.

⁸Both diaries are contained in the same notebook. For the sake of convenience I have introduced page numbers: pp. 1–268 for the diary of 1 February to 31 May 1941, and pp. 1–47 for the diary of 3 March to 28 September 1942.

⁹V. Azhaev, 1941 diary, p. 110, AA.

¹⁰"Pis'ma N. A. Zabolotskogo 1938–1944 godov" (Letters of N. A. Zabolotskii of 1938–1944), *Znamia*, no. 1 (1989): 113. According to these sources, Zabolotskii was detained from February 1939 until May 1943 in the system of the Vostlag NKVD, region of Komsomol'sk-on-the-Amur. Zabolotskii was arrested on 19 March 1938 and sent to the camps after a fabricated trial for "anti-Soviet propaganda." In "Istoriia moego zakliucheniia" (History of My Imprisonment), Zabolotskii describes, among other things, his arrival in the "realm of the BAM" in Komsomol'sk. Nikolai Zabolotskii, "Istoriia moego zakliucheniia," in *Stolbtsy: Stikhotvoreniia. Poemy* (Columns: Verses and [Longer] Poems) (Leningrad: Lenizdat, 1990), pp. 328–344.

¹¹"Khab. otdelenie SSP. Lichnoe delo chlena SSP SSSR Agisheva Rustama Konstantinovicha." GAKhK, f. 1738, op. 1, ed. khr. 99.

¹²Azhaev, 1941 diary, p. 3. Iuliia Shestakova remembers a discussion taking place in the late 1930s or early 1940s, devoted to a play by Azhaev on the theme of a prisoners' construction site. The play was judged weak, and the writer was advised to transform it into a novella. A second discussion was held on the novella, which "lasted until dawn." This time Azhaev was told to transform the novella into a story on a construction site of free laborers. Interview with Iuliia Shestakova, 15 July 1994.

¹³Acronym for Vostochnyi Lager' (East Camp), located in Sovetskaia Gavan' and Vanino on the Tatar Strait. See O. P. Elantseva, *Stroitel'stvo No. 500 NKVD SSSR: zheleznaia doroga Komsomol'sk–Sovetskaia Gavan' (1930–40-e gody)* (Project No. 500 of the NKVD of the USSR: The Komsomol'sk–Sovetskaia Gavan' Railway [The 1930s and 1940s]) (Vladivostok: Izdatel'stvo Dal'nevostochnogo Universiteta, 1995), p. 37.

¹⁴"Unrestricted circulation" (*vol'noe khozhdenie*) meant that a given prisoner could work, unguarded, outside the limits of the camp.

¹⁵The "person-day" (*cheloveko/den'*) was the volume of work each person had to produce in a workday. See Jacques Rossi, *The Gulag Handbook: An Encyclopedia Dictionary of Soviet Penitentiary Institutions and Terms Related to the Forced Labor Camps,* trans. William A. Burhans (New York: Paragon House, 1989), p. 492.

¹⁶Azhaev, 1941 diary, pp. 70–104.

[17] Azhaev, 1941 diary, pp. 36–37. The reference is to G. M. Malenkov's speech at the Eighteenth Party Congress on 15 February 1941, "O zadachakh partiinykh organizatsii v oblasti promyshlennosti i transporta" (On the Tasks of the Party Organizations in the Domain of Industry and Transport). Following the All-Union ritual, Malenkov's speech was reprinted in *Stalinskii Komsomol'sk*, 17 February 1941, pp. 1–4, which was undoubtedly Azhaev's source.

[18] The Eighteenth Congress of the Communist Party (10–21 March 1939), in which only fifty-nine delegates of the preceding congress participated (1,108 of the 1,956 delegates had been arrested). The congress announced new statutes, the end of mass purges, and a new campaign of membership recruitment. It adopted the Third Five-Year Plan and also strengthened centralized party control over various sectors, including economics and culture. One of the outcomes of the congress was the creation, on 3 August 1939, of the Administration of Propaganda and Agitation, attached to the Central Committee and headed by Aleksandr Zhdanov. D. A. Polikarpov, whom we will meet again in later chapters, was appointed head of the Department for Cultural-Educational Institutions. See D. L. Babichenko, *Pisateli i tsenzory: Sovetskaia literatura 1940-kh godov pod politicheskim kontrolem TsK* (The Writers and the Censors: Soviet Literature of the 1940s under the Political Control of the Central Committee) (Moscow: Rossiia Molodaia, 1994), pp. 16–17.

[19] Azhaev, 1941 diary, p. 76.

[20] Azhaev, 1941 diary, pp. 36, 52, 100.

[21] Evgenii Dolmatovskii, *Bylo: Zapiski poeta* (The Past: Notes of a Poet) (Moscow: Sovetskii Pisatel, 1982), pp. 438–450.

[22] Evgenii Dolmatovskii, "Vasilii Nikolaevich Azhaev," *Pesnia moia—Komsomol'sk: Vospominaniia, stikhi, ocherki* (My Song is Komsomol'sk: Recollections, Poems, Essays), ed. L. S. Ovechkina (Khabarovsk: Khabarovskoe knizhnoe izdatel'stvo, 1982), pp. 82–94. The Komsomol'sk version of Dolmatovskii's memoir lacks the poet's recollections on Azhaev's "silence" and "moral crisis" during later years published in the *Bylo* version.

[23] Forty degrees centigrade below freezing.

[24] Gavriil Sergeevich Fedoseev, director of the Gorky Literary Institute at that time.

[25] Dolmatovskii, *Bylo*, pp. 440–442.

[26] Vasili Azhayev, *Far From Moscow*, trans. R. Prokofieva (Moscow: Foreign Languages Publishing House, 1950), bk. 2, p. 155.

[27] The story had been published several months before in the local newspaper. Vas. Azhaev, "Medved': Rasskaz" (The Bear: A Story), *Stalinskii Komsomol'sk*, 5 December 1940, p. 3.

[28] Azhaev, 1941 diary, p. 82.

[29] Azhaev, 1941 diary, p. 145. The roads of Komsomol'sk began to be paved only in the late 1940s, as attested to by a resolution of 4 October 1949: "O stroitel'stve v g. Komsomol'ske-na-Amure asfal'tirovanykh dorog i trotuarov. Postanovlenie Soveta Ministrov SSSR i RSFSR No. 4215" (On the Construction in Komsomol'sk-on-the-Amur of Asphalt Roads and Sidewalks: Resolution of the Council of Ministers of the USSR and the RSFSR No. 4215).

[30] Azhaev, 1941 diary, pp. 134–135.

[31] Vas. Azhaev, "O tom, kak odin Oroch stroil dorogu na nebo: Orocheskaia skazka," *Stalinskii Komsomol'sk*, 24 November 1940, p. 3. The Oroch are natives of the Amur. See Yuri Slezkine, *Arctic Mirrors: Russia and the Small Peoples of the North* (Ithaca: Cornell University Press, 1994), pp. 2–3.

[32] Vas. Azhaev, "Tungusskaia skazka pro lisu," *Stalinskii Komsomol'sk,* 26 January 1941, p. 3. The Tungus (Evenk, Even, and Negidal) are natives of the Amur dispersed throughout Eastern Siberia. See Slezkine, *Arctic Mirrors.*

[33] V. Azhaev, "Nani u partizan: Otryvki iz povesti," *Stalinskii Komsomol'sk,* 23 March 1941, p. 3.

[34] Vas. Azhaev, "Sovest': Rasskaz" (Conscientiousness: A Story), *Stalinskii Komsomol'sk,* 5 May 1941, p. 3; "Zaichikhi: Rasskaz" (The Doe-Hares: A Story), *Stalinskii Komsomol'sk,* 3 January, 1941, p. 3.

[35] Moshe Lewin, *Russia/USSR/Russia: The Drive and Drift of a Superstate* (New York: New Press, 1995), p. 220. See also Lewin's comments on the "cultural revolution" in his introduction to *The Making of the Soviet System: Essays in the Social History of Interwar Russia* (1985; rpt. New York: New Press, 1994), pp. 38–41.

[36] Azhaev, 1941 diary, p. 72.

[37] Boris Gusev, "Stikhi" (Poems), in *Na rubezhe. Literaturno-khudozhestvennyi al'manakh* (Khabarovsk: Dal'nevostochnoe Gosudarstvennoe Izdatel'stvo, 1946), pp. 130–132.

[38] See, for example, *Putearmeets* 5 (August 1936): 40, which identifies one Gusev as "Zav. khudozh. chast'iu" (responsible for the artistic part).

[39] Azhaev probably refers to a series of literary sketches, published by Zhagir in *Stalinskii Komsomol'sk* on 10 April 1941. One of them tells of the difficulties encountered by Komsomol construction workers in trying to lay sewer pipes underwater. They finally succeed by using gas masks (instead of the unavailable diving masks), but only after a fierce competition during which the workers challenge one another in extending the amount of time they are able to remain underwater. P. Zhagir, "Dva epizoda" (Two Episodes), *Stalinskii Komsomol'sk,* 10 April 1941, p. 3.

[40] Azhaev, 1941 diary, pp. 154–156.

[41] Ibid., p. 166.

[42] A story by P. Zhagir was published four days later: "Sluchai s shoferom: Rasskaz" (The Incident with the Driver: A Story), *Stalinskii Komsomol'sk,* 27 April 1941, p. 3. This is a story about a worker who lacks labor enthusiasm but is eventually inspired by learning how to drive a truck. Zhagir's "triumph" was certainly triggered by the fact that his story appeared on the literary page of the newspaper, alongside works by recognized authors of the Komsomol'sk literary scene, including Pavel Andreev, Nikolai Shalyi (N. Povarenkin), and Aleksandr Savitskii.

[43] In *Far from Moscow,* Batmanov's wife is "Anna Ivanovna."

[44] Created in February 1919, the Osobyi otdel VChK (VChK Special Department) was set up "to combat counterrevolution and espionage in the army and the navy." See Rossi, *The Gulag Handbook,* p. 276.

[45] The "third section," also called "operational department," functioned as a "secret police within the domain of the secret police." See Edwin Bacon, *The Gulag at War: Stalin's Forced Labour System in the Light of the Archives* (New York: New York University Press, 1994), p. 67.

[46] Matvei Berman was head of the Gulag at that time, and S. G. Firin was his deputy. L. I. Kogan had been head of the Belomor Canal, but as of August 1936 he was in the Timber Commissariat. See Robert Conquest, *Inside Stalin's Secret Police: NKVD Politics, 1936–1939* (Stanford: Hoover Institution Press, 1985), pp. 19, 56.

[47] The "good news" must have been Genrikh Iagoda's imminent removal (on 26 September 1936) and Nikolai Ezhov's promotion. When Berman was appointed to the post of

People's Commissar for Communications in August 1937, Firin was already under arrest. Conquest, *Inside Stalin's Secret Police*, pp. 21, 43.

[48] Azhaev, 1941 diary, pp. 126–128.

[49] Azhaev, *Far from Moscow*, bk. 2, chap. 10; translation mine. The standard (Moscow 1950) translation omits the reference to the "old Russian tale": "Beridze gazed in admiration at Batmanov standing there tall, broad-shouldered and handsome in his white sheepskin jacket and fur cap, with the sunset reflected in his gray eyes" (p. 378). The original text perfectly illustrates Katerina Clark's chapter "The Sense of Reality in the Heroic Age," in *The Soviet Novel: History as Ritual* (1981; rpt. Chicago: University of Chicago Press, 1985), pp. 136–152.

[50] Azhaev, 1941 diary, pp. 10, 62, 95, 68, 224, 125.

[51] Ibid., p. 124. The article mentioned is S. Mstislavskii, "Masterstvo zhizni i mastera slova" (The Mastery of Life and the Masters of the Word), *Novyi mir*, nos. 11–12 (1940): 264–289.

[52] Azhaev, 1941 diary, pp. 234, 236, 244–245.

[53] Ibid., p. 262. The scene with the Japanese man recalls an episode in Konstantin Iudin's 1939 film comedy *Devushka s kharakterom* (The Girl with a Strong Character). A Japanese man is scared off from the dining car of a train heading to Moscow from the Far East by such sinister-sounding menu items as *shchi krasnoflotskie* (cabbage soup à la Red Fleet) and *okroshka* (cold kvass soup), a delicacy—he is told—*"kogda na melkie chasti rubiat"* (when chopped into tiny pieces).

[54] Evgeny Aronovich [Dolmatovskii]. Azhaev, 1941 diary, p. 263.

[55] Azhaev, 1941 diary, p. 268.

[56] Azhayev, *Far from Moscow*, bk. 1, p. 17.

[57] Azhaev, 1942 diary, p. 1.

[58] Since I could not gain access to various files of "fond 35" in the Khabarovsk archives, I had to rely on the notes of Marina Kuz'mina.

[59] "Shatalinu ot Mikhailova. Spravka o sostoianii rabot na stroike No. 15. 30.6.42 g." GAKhK, f. 35, op. 1, d. 1306 (notes of M. Kuz'mina).

[60] "Akt pravitel'stvennoi komissii po priemke v promyshlennuiu eksploatatsiiu nefteprovoda Okha-na-Sakhaline—s. Sofiiskoe-na-Amure i materialy k nemu. V ispolnenie postanovleniia SNK SSSR No. 1596–756/SS ot 29.9.1942 g." GAKhK, f. 35, op. 1, d. 1306 (notes of M. Kuz'mina).

[61] Ibid.

[62] From a "secret" order signed 19 December 1942 by the plenipotentiary of the NKVD for the Far East, Commissar of the State Security of the Second Rank Goglidze, we learn that Azhaev, "head of the industrial department of the Camp of the Lower Amur of the NKVD," was one of three who were awarded a bonus for "excellent work in the organization of special production and fulfillment of the order of the Army of the Far Eastern Front." The other two recipients were G. M. Orentlikherman, "former head of the Camp of the Lower Amur of the NKVD" (Orentlikherman, as it seems, had already been replaced by I. G. Petrenko; see note 72), and P. I. Fishman, "deputy head of the Camp of the Lower Amur of the NKVD." "Prikaz upoln. NKVD po Buriato-Mongol'skoi ASSR Primorskomu i Khabarovskomu Kraiam i Chitinskoi oblasti. Soderzhanie: O premirovanii sotrudnikov lagerei i kolonii za vypolnenie oboronnykh zakazov. Kopiia. Sekretno," AA.

[63] Leonid Sergeevich Buianov, deputy head of the Main Administration of Railway Construction Camps (GULZhDS). See Appendix.

[64] Azhaev, 1942 diary, pp. 8–9.

[65] Ibid., pp. 13–14.

[66] Fedor Fedorovich Akimov, deputy head of Project No. 15.

[67] Sergei Arsent'evich Goglidze, Commissar of the State Security of the Second Rank, was plenipotentiary of the NKVD for the Far East (see note 62).

[68] Azhaev, 1942 diary, pp. 19–24.

[69] After a first attempt to build the Komsomol'sk–Sovetskaia Gavan' Railway in 1939–1941, which failed, the decision was finally taken on 21 May 1943 by the State Committee of Defense. The NKVD was put in charge of building the 475-kilometer track ("Postanovlenie No. 3407 'O stroitel'stve zheleznodorozhnoi linii Komsomol'sk–Sovetskaia Gavan'"). See Elantseva, *Stroitel'stvo No. 500*, pp. 18–34; V. F. Zuev and P. L. Fefilov, *Serdtse ostanovilos' na perevale* (The Heart Stopped Beating on the Pass) (Moscow: Finizdat, 1995), p. 28.

[70] Dolmatovskii, *Bylo*, p. 440.

[71] Shestakova added the following information: Azhaev divorced his first wife around 1948 to marry Irina Leonidovna Liubimova, but "treated her with honor" and continued to help her financially. Interview with Iuliia Shestakova, 15 July 1994.

[72] Interview with Ivan Panin, 22 August 1995. According to Marina Kuz'mina, Petrenko became the head of the Camp of the Lower Amur, headquartered in Komsomol'sk, on 18 September 1942; a year later, after F. A. Gvozdevskii was appointed head of Project No. 500 (May 1943), Petrenko commanded the camp administration in Khungari (Gurskoe). M. Kuz'mina, *Chernyi kamen' na krasnoi zemle* (Black Stone on Red Earth) (Komsomol'sk-na-Amure: Gorodskoi Komitet "Memorial," 1992), p. 71. According to other sources, Petrenko did not become head of the Camp of the Lower Amur until the fall of 1943. Zuev and Fefilov, *Serdtse ostanovilos' na perevale*, p. 48. Finally, according to Irina Liubimova-Azhaeva (Azhaev's second wife; interview, November 1991), Major-General Petrenko had threatened to arrest Azhaev after the future author of *Far from Moscow* had written a report on the poor sanitary conditions in the camp. To what camp and what time she referred could again not be established. The fact remains that in 1939, Petrenko, then head of the Corrective Labor Camp of the Amur and in charge of the Izvestkovaia-Urgal section of the BAM, had signed a certificate naming Azhaev, head of the TsBRIZ, "best Stakhanovite and shock worker" on the occasion of the twenty-second anniversary of the October Revolution. Yet Petrenko was also one of the supporters of the "right variant" of the pipeline construction in fall 1942. "Vypiska iz Prikaza po Upravleniiu Amurskogo Ispravitel'no-Trudovogo Lageriia NKVD za 1939 g. No. 467. O nagrazhdenii sotrudnikov Upravleniia v oznamenovanie 22 Godovshchiny Oktiabr'skoi Revoliutsii. No. 467 '6' noiabria 1939 g. Nachal'nik Upravleniia Amurskogo Lageria NKVD Maior Gosbezopasnosti Petrenko; Nachal'nik Politotdela Amurlaga NKVD Brigadnyi komissar Korneichuk," AA.

[73] Azhaev, 1942 diary, pp. 29–30.

[74] Ibid., p. 36.

8. Far from Moscow

[1] Gennadii Ivanovich Nevel'skoi (1813–76), Russian explorer of the Far East, admiral. Nevel'skoi, who had directed expeditions in the Tatar Strait and established settlements on the Lower Amur, confirmed the insularity of Sakhalin.

[2] Iuliia Shestakova remembers that she and other friends and acquaintances of Azhaev

repeatedly rejected these rumors during various conferences and discussions that took place after the publication of *Far from Moscow.*

³ Interview with Ivan Panin, 22 August 1995.

⁴ Aleksandr Grachev's literary biography, written by the Komsomol'sk author Gennadii N. Khlebnikov, does not confirm this rumor. G. Khlebnikov, *Khozhdenie za gorizont: Khudozhestvenno-dokumental'naia povest'* (Walking Beyond the Horizon: An Artistic-Documentary Novella) (Khabarovsk: Khabarovskoe knizhnoe izdatel'stvo, 1988).

⁵ Letter from A. Grachev, Khabarovsk (12 August 1954), AA. Grachev's novel was finally published in 1960. A. Grachev, *Pervaia proseka: Roman* (Khabarovsk: Khabarovskoe knizhnoe izdatel'stvo, 1960).

⁶ N. I. Riabov was a historian from Khabarovsk. Several of his articles were published in *Na rubezhe* during the late 1930s and early 1940s.

⁷ Another document, Chkheidze's report on the "left variant," which was requested from Azhaev in 1945 from the NKVD, figures as one of the genuine raw materials of *Far from Moscow.*

⁸ Yuri Slezkine, *Arctic Mirrors: Russia and the Small Peoples of the North* (Ithaca: Cornell University Press, 1994), p. 328. Azhaev is named as one of the authors whose works illustrate this and other postwar themes: "Azhaev's novel is primarily concerned with other matters, but the native Long Journey is an important subplot." Among other authors cited by Slezkine we find two with whom we have become acquainted here: R. K. Agishev and S. M. Bytovoi.

⁹ V. Azhaev, "Materialy k 'Daleko ot Moskvy,'" p. 2: "Po nanaiskim stoibishcham (Ekspeditsiia N. I. Riabova)," AA.

¹⁰ Vasili Azhayev, *Far from Moscow,* trans. R. Prokofieva (Moscow: Foreign Languages Publishing House, 1950), bk. 2, chap. 2, p. 57. Some subsequent citations appear in the text; translations modified.

¹¹ Ibid., pp. 58–60, 101–104, 107, 113; "Po nanaiskim stoibishcham," pp. 2, 3. The operetta *Silva* (1915), by the Hungarian composer Imre Kálmán (1882–1953), enjoyed great popularity in these years, as did the film based on it by Aleksandr Ivanovskii (1945). See Maya Turovskaya, "The Tastes of Soviet Moviegoers during the 1930s," in *Late Soviet Culture: From Perestroika to Novostroika,* ed. Thomas Lahusen, with Gene Kuperman (Durham: Duke University Press, 1993), pp. 104. The Rubezhansk (Khabarovsk) Theater of Musical Comedy regularly came to Komsomol'sk in the late 1930s and early 1940s, as demonstrated by various announcements and reviews on the pages of *Stalinskii Komsomol'sk.* Several of the reviews were signed by Serafima Plisetskaia, Rustam Agishev's wife.

¹² "Po nanaiskim stoibishcham," p. 1.

¹³ Azhayev, *Far from Moscow,* bk. 2, p. 98; translation modified.

¹⁴ "Po nanaiskim stoibishcham," p. 3; Azhayev, *Far from Moscow,* bk. 2, pp. 97, 100; translation modified.

¹⁵ Azhayev, *Far from Moscow,* bk. 2, pp. 19–22; translation modified.

¹⁶ The name also has some historical relevance here: it is well known in Komsomol'sk and the Russian Far East. The Silin were among the settlers who had come to the shores of the Lower Amur to found the village of Permskoe (the future Komsomol'sk) in 1860. Another branch had settled in the Maritime Province (Primor'e). V. I. Remizovskii, "Rudoznatets iuzhnogo Primor'ia—Fedor Andreevich Silin" (The Ore Expert of the Southern Part of Primor'e: Fedor Andreevich Silin), *Vestnik DVO RAN* 4 (1995): 133–138.

¹⁷ Azhayev, *Far from Moscow,* bk. 3, pp. 217–219; translation modified.

[18] V. Azhaev, "Materialy k 'Daleko ot Moskvy,'" pp. 5–26: "Belov Nikolai Maksimovich, byvshii nachal'nik pogibinskogo otdeleniia stroitel'stva No. 15 o svoei rabote na stroitel'stve," AA.

[19] Viktor Ivanovich Kuchera, head of the political department (the party organizer) of Project No. 15. In *Far from Moscow* he is depicted as Zalkind; Gavriil Nikiforovich Bondarenko, head of the Laguri section of Project No. 15 and head of the division; Grigorii Afanas'evich Badiul, commissar of the militarized guard (see Appendix).

[20] Films by I. Savchenko (1941) and S. Eisenstein (1938).

[21] The great difficulties of navigation in the Tatar Strait during the war years are well documented. See A. A. Vostrikova, "Trudovoi podvig transportnikov Dal'nego Vostoka v gody Velikoi Otechestvennoi voiny" (The Heroic Deeds of the Far Eastern Transporters during the Great Patriotic War), in *Dal'nii Vostok za 40 let Sovetskoi vlasti* (The Far East during Forty Years of Soviet Power) (Komsomol'sk-na-Amure, 1958), p. 520.

[22] Acronym for "Ekspeditsiia podvodnykh rabot osobogo naznacheniia." A special organization for the salvaging of sunken vessels and other rescue work, EPRON was founded in 1923 and attached to the OGPU.

[23] Azhayev, *Far from Moscow*, bk. 2, pp. 43–45.

[24] Ibid., bk. 1, pp. 361–362.

[25] Ibid., bk. 2, p. 43. Such a disability was evidently not serious enough to preclude one's being drafted for the Great Patriotic War. Here is a case where the direct reflection of reality (as we already know, Azhaev was blind, or partially blind, in one eye) was unsuitable for being too obvious.

[26] Ibid., p. 43.

[27] V. Azhaev, "Vyskazyvaniia G. D. Chkheidze, glavnogo inzhenera stroitel'stva No. 15 po povodu i v sviazi s romanom 'Daleko ot Moskvy'," and "G. M. Orentlikherman, v sviazi s romanom (razgovor o vtoroi chasti)," both in "Materialy k 'Daleko ot Moskvy,'" pp. 25–29, 53.

[28] V. Azhaev, "Dokumenty. Telegramma ob okonchanii razvozki sektsii po prolivu; telegramma ob okonchanii rabot po morperekhodu," AA, p. 24.

[29] "250e otdelenie. Prikazy. Nachal'nik 250go otdeleniia Belov." ITs UVD Khabarovskogo kraia, f. 74, op. 1, d. 5 (notes by M. Kuz'mina).

[30] "Pervoe otdelenie Stroitel'stva No. 15 Nizhne-Amurskogo ITL NKVD. Prikazy po pervomu otdeleniiu Okha-na-Sakhaline 3. 7. 1941 g. na osnovanii prikaza nachal'nika upravleniia Nizhne-Amurskogo ITL No. 59." ITs UVD Khabarovskogo kraia, f. 74, op. 1, d. 1 (notes by M. Kuz'mina).

[31] L. I. Timofeev, *Teoriia literatury* (Moscow: Uchpedgiz, 1945), p. 28.

9. Borderline II

[1] "Protokol zasedaniia oblastnoi komissii Soiuza Sovetskikh Pisatelei. 18 dekabria 1944 goda. Obsuzhdenie proizvedenii Vasiliia Azhaeva. g. Khabarovsk," AA.

[2] Whether Fedoseev was still the director of the Gorky Literary Institute could not be verified. In his recollections about Fedor Gladkov, director of the Gorky Literary Institute from 1945 to 1948, A. Parfenov writes that "the directors of the institute were changed, during these years, like gloves." A. Parfenov, "Uchitel'" (The Teacher), in *Vospominaniia o Litinstitute, 1933–1983* (Memories of the Literary Institute), ed. Konstantin Vanshenkin et al. (Moscow: Sovetskii Pisatel', 1983), p. 179.

[3] Dmitrii Alekseevich Polikarpov was the "organizational secretary" of the Soviet Writers' Union at that time, that is, the "ideological commissar" of the Writers' Union. On this function and Polikarpov, see John Garrard and Carol Garrard, *Inside the Soviet Writers' Union* (New York: Free Press, 1990), p. 87.

[4] Petr Stepanovich Komarov, who had been editor of *Na rubezhe* from 1939 to 1941, was secretary of the Khabarovsk Branch of the Soviet Writers' Union between 1943 and 1946. From 1946 to 1949 he was editor of *Dal'nii Vostok.* John J. Stephan, *The Russian Far East: A History* (Stanford: Stanford University Press, 1994), p. 321.

[5] *Na rubezhe* ceased regular publication as a journal after the third issue of 1941. It reappeared as an almanac in 1942, 1944, and 1946. See *Na rubezhe. Literaturno-khudozhestvennyi al'manakh* (Khabarovsk: OGIZ. Dal'nevostochnoe Gosudarstvennoe Izdatel'stvo, 1942, 1944, 1946).

[6] "Pis'mo V. Azhaeva poetu P. Komarovu, napisannoe 23 maia 1945 g., rukopis'." GAKhK, f. 1740, op. 1, d. 23, l. 2.

[7] D. L. Babichenko, *Pisateli i tsenzory: Sovetskaia literatura 1940-kh godov pod politicheskim kontrolem TsK* (The Writers and the Censors: Soviet Literature of the 1940s under the Political Control of the Central Committee) (Moscow: Rossiia Molodaia, 1994), p. 112. Polikarpov's career did not end here. By the same order of the Central Committee, he was confirmed as auditor of the Higher Party School. In 1951 Polikarpov graduated with a Ph.D. (*aspirantura*) from the Academy of Social Sciences, attached to the Central Committee; from 1951 to 1955 he headed the Lenin Moscow State Institute of Pedagogy, and in January 1955 he resumed his activities as secretary of the (central) Board of the Writers' Union. In October of that year Polikarpov was promoted to head the Department of Culture of the Party's Central Committee. Ibid., p. 114.

[8] Vasilii Ivanovich Chapaev (1887–1919), hero of the civil war, who was immortalized in a famous novel, *Chapaev,* by Dmitrii Furmanov (1923) and in a film of the same title by the Vasil'ev brothers (1934). Sergei Lazo was a hero and martyr of the Vladivostok uprising in 1920.

[9] In March 1946 the commissariats were renamed ministries; the People's Commissariat of Internal Affairs (NKVD) became the Ministry of Internal Affairs (MVD).

[10] *Kul'tura i zhizn'* (20 August 1946). Quoted from *Istoriia russkoi sovetskoi literatury,* vol. 3, *1941–1957* (Moscow: Izd. Akademii Nauk SSSR, 1961), p. 670.

[11] "Protokol zasedaniia komissii SSP po russkoi literature oblastei i kraev RSFSR, ot 15.IV. 47 g. Obsuzhdenie zhurnala 'Dal'nii Vostok' (NoNo 1–2, 3, 4, 5–6 za 1946 g.). Stenogramma obsuzhd. i pismenn. otzyvy," pp. 99–121, AA.

[12] The fact that *Na rubezhe* was suspended between November 1937 and April 1939 was of course not mentioned.

[13] Anatolii Gai must have forgotten that *Na rubezhe* was suspended in 1938. Both Agishev and Ivashchenko list N. Rogal', *U granitsy* (At the Border) (Khabarovsk: Dal'giz, 1939). R. K. Agishev, *Sovetskii Dal'nii Vostok v khudozhestvennoi literature: Bibliograficheskii ukazatel'* (The Soviet Far East in Literature: A Bibliographical Guide), 2d rev. enl. ed. (Khabarovsk: Khabarovskaia Kraevaia Biblioteka, 1957), p. 63; L. Ia. Ivashchenko, *Khudozhestvennaia literatura o Dal'nem Vostoke: Bibliograficheskii ukazatel'* (Literature about the Far East: A Bibliographical Guide) (Vladivostok: RIO Primuprpoligrafizdata, 1990–91), 1: 62.

[14] Protokol zasedaniia komissii SSP po russkoi literature oblastei i kraev RSFSR, ot 15.IV. 47 g., p. 6.

[15] Gai's view contradicts that found in the memoirs of Israel Emiot, a former Birobidzhan poet, according to whom the immediate postwar years saw important demographic growth as a result of increased immigration to the Jewish Autonomous Region and a "flurry of cultural advances." See Israel Emiot, *The Birobidzhan Affair* (Philadelphia: Jewish Publication Society of America, 1981), p. xvii. In any case, most of the cultural organizations in the Autonomous Region were liquidated in the late 1940s. See L. Ia. Ivashchenko, *Istoricheskie aspekty sozdaniia i razvitiia mnogonatsional'noi khudozhestvennoi literatury na Dal'nem Vostoke Rossii, 1917–seredina 1980-kh godov: Ocherki* (Historical Aspects of the Formation and Development of the Multi-National Literature in the Russian Far East, 1917–mid-1980s: Essays) (Vladivostok: Dal'nauka, 1995), pp. 113–114.

[16] According to Marina Kuz'mina, 61 percent of the work force of Amurstal' came from the Lower Amur Correctional Camp system. M. Kuz'mina, *Chernyi kamen' na krasnoi zemle* (Black Stone on Red Earth) (Komsomol'sk-na-Amure: Gorodskoi Komitet "Memorial," 1992), p. 77.

[17] Protokol zasedaniia komissii SSP po russkoi literature oblastei i kraev RSFSR, ot 15.IV. 47 g., p. 7.

[18] Anatolii Gai, "Iz morskoi tetradi, stikhi," *Dal'nii Vostok,* nos. 1–2 (1946): 109–111.

[19] Protokol zasedaniia komissii SSP po russkoi literature oblastei i kraev RSFSR, ot 15.IV. 47 g., p. 99.

[20] According to the *Short Literary Encyclopaedia,* Fedor Markovich Levin had graduated from the Institute of Red Professors in 1933. He had already published a volume of poetry, *In the Storm of the Days,* in 1928, and a novella for children, *Fedka,* in 1939. During the 1930s and 1940s, he published numerous works of criticism, including articles on F. Gladkov's *Energy* and A. Makarenko's *Pedagogical Poem,* on A. Herzen, V. Belinskii, and other authors. He was known "for the polemical style of his criticism" and the fact that he "posed acute questions about contemporary Soviet literature." *Kratkaia Literaturnaia Entsiklopediia,* vol. 4 (Moscow: Sovetskaia Entsiklopediia, 1967), pp. 85–86; hereafter *KLE. KLE* does not explain the "gap" in Levin's bibliography between 1939 and 1957; as we shall see, it had to do with Levin's "polemical style."

[21] Protokol zasedaniia komissii SSP po russkoi literature oblastei i kraev RSFSR, ot 15.IV. 47 g., p. 17.

[22] Ibid., pp. 19–24.

[23] Ibid., p. 25.

[24] Undoubtedly a reference to B. Polevoi's *We Are Soviet People* (1948).

[25] A. Makarov, "Tikhoi sapoi" (On the Sly), *Literaturnaia gazeta,* 12 March 1949. Cited in Evgenii Dobrenko, *Metafora vlasti: Literatura stalinskoi epokhi v istoricheskom osveshchenii* (Metaphors of Authority: The Literature of the Stalin Era in Historical Context) (Munich: Otto Sagner, 1993), p. 350.

[26] V. A. Gerasimova, "Nenastoiashchie" (Unreal People) (1923), cited in *KLE* 2:130–131.

[27] Protokol zasedaniia komissii SSP po russkoi literature oblastei i kraev RSFSR, ot 15.IV. 47 g., pp. 42–43.

[28] *KLE* 4:989.

[29] Protokol zasedaniia komissii SSP po russkoi literature oblastei i kraev RSFSR, ot 15.IV. 47 g., pp. 52–56.

[30] *KLE* 2:986.

[31] "For the living man in literature" was the principal slogan of "psychological realism," a "dialectical materialist method" in literature advocated by the theorists of RAPP (Russian Association of Proletarian Writers) during the late 1920s. According to this method, the real world should be presented as the struggle of opposites in society and in individual characters. In 1930 and 1931 "psychologism" was attacked and finally rejected for focusing excessively on the spiritual and emotional problems of the individual at the expense of socially significant events. See Herman Ermolaev, *Soviet Literary Theories, 1917–1934: The Genesis of Socialist Realism* (Berkeley: University of California Press, 1963), pp. 61–70, 102–107.

[32] Protokol zasedaniia komissii SSP po russkoi literature oblastei i kraev RSFSR, ot 15.IV.47 g., pp. 62–70.

[33] Ibid., p. 101.

[34] *KLE* 6:237.

[35] An allusion to the discussion of Nekrasov's *In the Trenches of Stalingrad* (1946) shortly after it was awarded the Stalin Prize (second class) in 1947.

[36] Protokol zasedaniia komissii SSP po russkoi literature oblastei i kraev RSFSR, ot 15.IV. 47 g., pp. 83–84.

[37] Ibid., pp. 58–60.

[38] Ibid., pp. 33–34.

[39] Ibid., p. 107.

[40] Ibid., p. 37. Israel Emiot (Israel Yanovsky-Goldwasser; according to Soviet documents, Srul' Natanovich Gol'dvasser) was expelled from the Soviet Writers' Union as a "bourgeois nationalist" in September 1949. The decision was signed by N. Rogal', as it appears on a document found in the Khabarovsk archives: "Vypiska iz protokola zasedaniia Biuro Khabarovskogo otdeleniia Soiuza sovetskikh pisatelei ot 1 sentiabria 1949 g. No. 5." GAKhK, f. 1738, op. 1, d. 109, l. 21a. Emiot was actually arrested in 1948 and shown, during his interrogation, the findings of a special literary commission organized by the MGB from among the Khabarovsk Russian writers. On the basis of literary materials, he was accused of "bourgeois nationalism." Sentenced under sections 10 and 11 of paragraph 58 to ten years at hard labor, he was released from a prison camp in 1956 and repatriated to Poland (from where he had escaped the Nazi occupation in 1939). He finally joined his wife and children in the United States in 1958. He died in 1978. Emiot, *Birobidzhan Affair*, p. 34.

[41] Iuliia Shestakova, "V khorskikh lesakh: Ocherki" (In the Khorsk Forests: Essays), *Dal'nii Vostok*, nos. 1–2 (1946): 112–135.

[42] *Dal'nii Vostok* published two double issues in 1946: nos. 1–2 and 5–6.

[43] Protokol zasedaniia komissii SSP po russkoi literature oblastei i kraev RSFSR, ot 15.IV. 47 g., p. 104.

[44] V. Azhaev to K. Simonov, 12 May 1948, AA.

10. Between Engineers

[1] "Neizdannye proizvedeniia N. G. Chernyshevskogo" (Unpublished Works of N. G. Chernyshevsky), *Literatura i marksizm* (Literature and Marxism) (Moscow, 1928), cited in V. V. Vinogradov, *O iazyke khudozhestvennoi literatury* (On the Language of Belles Lettres) (Moscow: GIKhL, 1959), p. 141.

[2] M. Bakhtin, *Problemy poetiki Dostoevskogo* (Problems of Dostoevsky's Poetics) (Moscow: Sovetskaia Rossiia, 1979), pp. 76–81.

[3] Gayle Rubin, "The Traffic in Women: Notes toward a Political Economy of Sex," in *Toward an Anthropology of Women*, ed. Rayna Reiter (New York: Monthly Review Press, 1975), pp. 157–210. I quote from Eve Kosofsky Sedgwick's discussion of this essay in *Between Men: English Literature and Male Homosocial Desire* (New York: Columbia University Press, 1985), pp. 25–26.

[4] Katerina Clark, *The Soviet Novel: History as Ritual* (1981; rpt. Chicago: University of Chicago Press, 1985), p. 182.

[5] Vasili Azhayev, *Far from Moscow*, trans. R. Prokofieva (Moscow: Foreign Languages Publishing House, 1950), bk. 1, pp. 32–33; translation modified.

[6] Ibid., pp. 33–35.

[7] V. Azhaev, "Daleko ot Moskvy," *Dal'nii Vostok*, nos. 1–2 (1946): 9; V. Azhaev, "Daleko ot Moskvy," *Novyi mir*, no. 7 (1948): 7–8.

[8] Azhayev, *Far From Moscow*, bk. 2, pp. 350, 354, 358.

[9] Azhayev, "Daleko ot Moskvy," *Dal'nii Vostok*, nos. 1–2 (1946): 4; Azhayev, "Daleko ot Moskvy," *Novyi mir*, no. 7 (1948): 4.

[10] Azhayev, "Daleko ot Moskvy," *Dal'nii Vostok*, nos. 1–2 (1946): 10.

[11] Azhayev, "Daleko ot Moskvy," *Novyi mir*, no. 7 (1948): 38.

[12] Title of chapter 14 of book 1. The seventh of November was the day of the October Revolution (25 October old style).

[13] Azhayev, *Far from Moscow*, bk. 1, pp. 421–422; translation modified. The literal translation reads: "Kovshov caught up with Zalkind, already dressed" (*Kovshova v koridore dognal uzhe odetyi Zalkind*).

[14] Ibid., pp. 344–347; translation modified.

[15] Ibid., p. 349; translation modified.

[16] Evgenii Dolmatovskii, *Bylo: Zapiski poeta* (The Past: Notes of a Poet) (Moscow: Sovetskii Pisatel, 1982), p. 442.

[17] This precaution was used against the editor in chief of *Novyi mir* a few years later, when "vigilance" was once again on the political agenda. For details, see Evgenii Dobrenko, "'Pravda zhizni' kak formula real'nosti" (The "Truth of Life" as Reality's Formula), *Voprosy literatury*, no. 1 (1992): 12–13.

[18] Vera Mikhailovna Inber (1890–1972), a Russian writer who was close to the constructivists in the 1920s. She later became known for her diary on the Leningrad blockade, *Pochti tri goda* (Almost Three Years, 1946–47), and the long poem *Pulkovskii meridian* (Pulkovo Meridian, 1942–46), for which she was awarded a Stalin Prize (second class). *Pochti tri goda* was criticized for "naturalism." See Evgenii Dobrenko, *Metafora vlasti: Literatura stalinskoi epokhi v istoricheskom osveshchenii* (Metaphors of Authority: The Literature of the Stalin Era in Historical Context) (Munich: Otto Sagner, 1993), p. 244.

[19] "Obsuzhdenie rukopisi Azhaeva na zasedanii redkollegii zhurnala 'Novyi mir' 27 maia 1948 goda" (Discussion on the manuscript by Azhaev during the meeting of the editorial board of the journal *Novyi mir* of 27 May 1948), p. 3, AA.

[20] "Zamechaniia K. I. Simonova po romanu V. N. Azhaeva—"Daleko ot Moskvy"— 29–go maia 1948 g." (Remarks by K. I. Simonov concerning the novel by V. N. Azhaev *Far from Moscow*, 29 May 1948), p. 7, AA.

[21] This sentence does not figure in the official (Foreign Languages Publishing House) translation, nor does it appear in various other translations—done in Moscow or abroad— that I consulted. Present in the *Novyi mir* edition, it disappeared from all subsequent Russ-

ian reeditions of the novel, including the first book edition of 1949 at Sovetskii Pisatel'. Compare Vasilii Azhaev, "Daleko ot Moskvy," *Novyi mir*, no. 9 (1948): 148; idem, *Daleko ot Moskvy: Roman* (Moscow: Sovetskii Pisatel', 1949), p. 748.

[22] Azhayev, *Far from Moscow*, bk. 3, pp. 465–466; translation modified.

[23] Vasilii Azhaev, "Daleko ot Moskvy: Roman, chast' tret'ia" (Far from Moscow: A Novel, Third Part), *Dal'nii Vostok*, no. 2 (1948): 74.

[24] "Zamechaniia K. I. Simonova po romanu V. N. Azhaeva—'Daleko ot Moskvy'— 29-go maia 1948 g.," pp. 1–2.

[25] Azhaev, "Daleko ot Moskvy," *Dal'nii Vostok*, nos. 1–2 (1946): 19; Azhayev, *Far from Moscow*, bk. 1, pp. 65–66.

[26] "Zamechaniia K. I. Simonova po romanu V. N. Azhaeva—"Daleko ot Moskvy"— 27-go maia 1948 g." (Remarks by K. I. Simonov concerning the novel by V. N. Azhaev *Far from Moscow*, 27 May 1948), p. 11, AA.

[27] Azhayev, *Far From Moscow*, bk. 1, p. 189.

[28] On the myth of mentor and disciple and its realizations in Soviet literature, see Clark, *The Soviet Novel.*

[29] Azhayev, *Far from Moscow*, bk. 1, p. 56.

[30] Vasilii Azhaev, *Daleko ot Moskvy: Roman* (Far from Moscow: A Novel) (Moscow: Molodaia Gvardiia, 1954), p. 21. All editions of the novel published after 1954 contain this passage.

[31] Vasilii Azhaev, "Daleko ot Moskvy. Roman. Chast' pervaia" (Far from Moscow: A Novel, First Part), *Dal'nii Vostok*, nos. 1–2 (1946): 16.

[32] V. Azhaev, 1942 diary, pp. 1–3, AA.

[33] V. Azhaev, "Na sed'moi den'," pp. 1–10, AA.

[34] Mikhail Ivanovich Kalinin (1875–1946), formal head of the Soviet state from 1919 to 1946. As chairman of the Central Executive Committee of the All-Russian Congress of the Soviets, Kalinin supported Stalin, survived the purges, and retained his high party and government offices until shortly before his death.

[35] Janice A. Radway, *Reading the Romance: Women, Patriarchy, and Popular Literature* (Chapel Hill: University of North Carolina Press, 1991), pp. 11, 61.

[36] See n. 21.

[37] L. I. Timofeev, *Teoriia literatury* (Moscow: Uchpedgiz, 1945), p. 28.

[38] Letter from Alla Lubenskaia, Moscow, 16 June 1949, AA.

11. A Thousand and One Nights

[1] "MGB i MVD (Klub im. Dzherzinskogo)—3 fevralia 1949 goda," item no. 38 of "Chitatel'skie konferentsii i obsuzhdeniia po romanu V. Azhaeva 'Daleko ot Moskvy,'" AA. The list is reproduced later in this chapter.

[2] "I look at you, my dear Petr Yefimovich, and simply can't make you out—by what right do you call yourself a Russian? Where's your Russian breadth of scope, your love of the new? What is there Russian left in you?" Vasili Azhayev, *Far from Moscow*, trans. R. Prokofieva (Moscow: Foreign Languages Publishing House, 1950), bk. 2, p. 160.

[3] A few days before the readers' conference, *Pravda* had published its infamous editorial "About One Antipatriotic Group of Theatrical Critics." See *Pravda*, 28 January 1949.

[4] "Chitatel'skie konferentsii i obsuzhdeniia po romanu V. Azhaeva 'Daleko ot Moskvy,'" AA.

[5] "Stenogramma konferentsii chitatelei biblioteki Gor'kovskoi oblastnoi kontory Gosbanka." Enclosure: letter from the chairman of the local trade union committee I. Kolosov and the chairman of the readers' council N. Kirik of 6 June 1951 (city of Gor'kii); "Protokol konferentsii po knige Azhaeva 'Daleko ot Moskvy' v biblioteke peredvizhke zavoda 'Medproborov' 24. VII. 53 g," AA.

[6] "Provedeniia konferentsii chitatelei po obsuzhdeniiu romana Vasiliia AZHAEVA 'Daleko ot Moskvy.' Sostavlen 15 fevraliia 1949 g," AA.

[7] N. Kovalev. Partorg TsK VKP (b) na avtozavode imeni Stalina, "Chitatel'skie konferentsii," Novyi mir, no. 7 (1949): 206-219. For a presentation of Kovalev's article (and his abridged version in the Soviet magazine for export, La littérature soviétique), see Antoine Baudin, Leonid Heller, and Thomas Lahusen, "Le réalisme socialiste de l'ère Jdanov. Compte rendu d'une enquête en cours," Études de lettres (Lausanne), 4 (1988): 69-103.

[8] Kovalev, "Chitatel'skie konferentsii," p. 208.

[9] Ibid., p. 209.

[10] Ibid., p. 216.

[11] Baudin, Heller, and Lahusen, "Le réalisme socialiste de l'ère Jdanov," p. 96.

[12] Evgeny Dobrenko, The Making of the State Reader: The Social and Aesthetic Context of the Reception of Soviet Literature (Stanford: Stanford University Press, 1997). I quote from the Russian manuscript, "Konets perspektivy: Sotsial'nyi i esteticheskii kontekst retseptsii sovetskoi literatury," chap. 8.

[13] Kovalev, "Chitatel'skie konferentsii," p. 215.

[14] "Stenogramma konferentsii chitatelei v tsekhe Motor no. 2 Avtozavoda im. Stalina po obsuzhdeniiu knigi Azhaeva 'Daleko ot Moskvy' 22.IV-1949 g.," pp. 3-5, AA. Muromtsev misspells the name of the "American commentator." Fadeev quoted a book by the demographer and birth control specialist William Vogt, Road to Survival (New York: W. Sloane Associates, 1948). Muromtsev—or the person who typed the stenographic report—must have been from southern Russia, where "g" is pronounced "kh." The editor of Novyi mir corrected the Russian transcription.

[15] See L. Heller and T. Lahusen, "Palimpsexes: Les métamorphoses de la thématique sexuelle dans le roman de F. Gladkov Le Ciment: Notes pour une approche analytico-interprétative de la littérature soviétique," Wiener Slawistischer Almanach 15 (1985): 211-54; Thomas Lahusen, "The Ethnicization of Nations: Russia, the Soviet Union, and the People," South Atlantic Quarterly 94, no. 4 (1995): 1103-22.

[16] "Tsentral'nyi dom literatorov. Stenogramma zasedaniia sektsii prozy Soiuza Sovetskikh Pisatelei SSSR, posviashchennogo obsuzhdeniiu romana Azhaeva 'Daleko ot Moskvy.' 12 oktiabria 1948 goda. gor. Moskva," pp. 27-29, AA.

[17] Ibid., p. 32. Intervention by B(V?)osniatskii.

[18] Ibid., pp. 5-8. Tarasenkov was one of the central figures of the struggle against "cosmopolitanism." See A. Tarasenkov, "Kosmopolity ot literaturovedeniia" (The Cosmopolitans in Literary Science), Novyi mir, no. 2 (1948): 124-137.

[19] "Tsentral'nyi dom literatorov," p. 31.

[20] Ibid., p. 41. Aleksandr Borisovich Chakovskii, author of the "Leningrad trilogy" (1944-1947) and of the four-volume Blokada (1968-1973); secretary of the Soviet Writers' Union since 1962. KLE 8:428.

[21] "Stenogramma konferentsii v Zaporozh'i," AA.

[22] Ibid., pp. 22-29. All quotes from Sobolevskii are drawn from these pages.

[23] Chapaev, a film by the Vasil'ev brothers (1934), emphasized the class nature of the

civil war and the organizing and leading role of the party during the struggle. It became the first experiment with state-sponsored film for the masses, as marked by the lead story in *Pravda* of 21 November 1934, headlined "The Whole Country Is Watching *Chapaev*": "[*Chapaev*] is being reproduced in hundreds of copies for the sound screen. Silent versions will also be made so that *Chapaev* will be shown in every corner of our immense country: in the towns and villages, the collective farms and settlements, in barracks, clubs, and squares." See Richard Taylor and Ian Christie, eds., *The Film Factory: Russian and Soviet Cinema in Documents, 1896–1939* (Cambridge: Harvard University Press, 1988), pp. 334–335.

[24] Aleksandr Matveevich Matrosov (1924–1943) was a much-celebrated martyr of the Great Patriotic War.

[25] "Stenogramma konferentsii v Zaporozh'i," p. 30.

[26] Ibid., p. 33.

[27] Ibid., pp. 36, 37.

[28] Ibid., pp. 41–43.

[29] Ibid., p. 58.

[30] "Kritika i bibliografiia po romanu Vas. Azhaeva 'Daleko ot Moskvy,'" AA. The two-and-a-half-page list is organized according to the following headings: number; place and date of publication of the article or the review; author of the article or the review; title of the article or review.

[31] "V partiinom komitete, reshenie partkoma o konferentsii po romanu, 'Stroitel'" (gazeta Zaporozhstroia) No. 183 ot 2.X.48 g. 'Peredavaia i zaia polosa.'" Quoted from "Kritika i bibliografiia," pp. 1–2.

[32] Vas. Azhaev, "Glavnomu redaktoru 'Literaturnoi gazety' tov. N. [*sic*] V. Ermilovu. 10 aprelia 1949 goda, g. Leningrad," AA. Ermilov was editor in chief of *Literaturnaia gazeta* from 1946 to 1950.

[33] M. Shkerin, "Ob odnom iz glavnykh geroev. Po povodu romanov napisannykh i ne napisannykh," *Oktiabr'*, no. 4 (1949): 174–91.

[34] Azhaev, "Glavnomu redaktoru," p. 3.

[35] "V. N. Azhaevu, Vypiska iz postanovleniia Sekretariata Soiuza Sovetskikh Pisatelei SSSR protokol No. 18 15 ot 9 maia 1949 g," AA.

[36] Interview, 10 November 1991.

[37] V. Azhaev, "Vsesoiuznoe ob"edinenie 'Mezhdunarodnaia kniga.' Direktoru Agenstva po izdaniiu knig za granitsei tov. Koshelevu. 8 aprelia 1949 g," AA. Concerning the organizations "engaged in publishing books by Soviet writers abroad," Azhaev's archive contains a letter of 16 May 1949, addressed to the author by M. Markushevich from the central editorial board of *Sovetskaia literatura* (Soviet Literature), the official foreign-language literary journal. Markushevich asked Azhaev to select and send him "large excerpts" of his novel to be published in the journal. Over the text of the letter, the following (handwritten) lines appear: "Carried out [*Ispolneno*] 25 May. Text of the novel sent to the journal with abbreviations of the second and third books, and a summary of the first book. V. Azhaev." The summary is attached to the letter.

[38] Letter from V. K. Konkin, Tomsk, TAU-"D," 24 June 1950, AA.

[39] Letter from E. F. Pacheena, Zaporozhskaia obl., s. Novo-Vasil'evka, 14 March 1949, AA.

[40] Vorkuta was also the location of the infamous Vorkutlag or Vorkutpechlag. According to Jacques Rossi, about 150,000 prisoners were imprisoned in the Vorkuta Coal Basin in the late 1940s, that is, at the time when this letter was written. Jacques Rossi, *The Gulag*

Handbook: An Encyclopedia Dictionary of Soviet Penitentiary Institutions and Terms Related to the Forced Labor Camps, trans. William A. Burhans (New York: Paragon House, 1989), p. 55. Azhaev's former boss, the head of the Lower Amur Corrective Labor Camp, Vasilii Arsent'evich Barabanov, had worked there during his administrative punishment. Testimony of Barabanov's wife, Aleksandra Ivanovna (see Chapter 7).

[41] Letter from Vasilii Dmitrievich Kuz'min, 1895 goda rozhd., gor. Vorkuta Komi ASSR, poselok Rudnik, 12 May 1949, AA.

[42] Letter from Vasilii Dmitrievich Kuz'min, g. Vorkuta, Komi ASSR, pos. Rudnik, dom 29, 20 June 1949, AA.

[43] Letter from Z. Karateeva, Leningrad, f-ka im. Bebelia, n.d., AA.

[44] Letter from K. O. Wagner, Moscow, 13 December 1951, AA.

[45] Letter from Xie Sutai and Liu Liaoyi, Beijing, 17 December 1957, AA.

[46] Letter from L. Olitskii, Warsaw, 3 August 1957, AA. The publications mentioned in the letter are *Vayt fun Moskve: roman* (Far from Moscow: A Novel), trans. L. Frumkin, 3 vols. (Warsaw: Yidish-bukh, 1951–52); *Vayt fun Moskve: roman,* trans. Leo Frumkin, 3 vols. (Buenos Ayres [*sic*]: Farlag Haymland, 1954). Olitskii seems to have used a pseudonym for his translations.

[47] Letter from Iurii Vadimovich Iurovskii, Pskov, 22 September 1949, AA.

[48] Letter from Grigorii K. Kirii, Chernigov, 23 June 1949, AA. The author of the letter attached his diploma from the Philological Faculty of the T. G. Shevchenko State University in Kiev.

[49] Letter from P. Koksharova, 12 October 1949, AA.

[50] Letter of 26 July 1948, Moscow, Dzerzhinskogo 20, AA. Name of author illegible.

[51] Letter from Nikolai A. Sobolev, Komsomol'sk-na-Amure, 26 July 1949, AA. For Section 39 of the Instruction on Internal Passports, see Rossi, *Gulag Handbook,* p. 294. Sobolev was also the author of an unpublished play, "Put' k okeanu" (The Track to the Ocean). Coincidence or not, Azhaev had published an article with almost the same title two years before. It was devoted to the construction of the Komsomol'sk–Sovetskaia Gavan' Railway (i.e., "Project No. 500"). See Vas. Azhaev, "Doroga na okean" (The Road to the Ocean), *Tikhookeanskaia zvezda,* 12 November 1947. Project No. 500 also became the subject of a film, *Put' k okeanu* (The Track to the Ocean), directed by L. O. Matusevich. See O. P. Elantseva, "Iz istorii stroitel'stva zheleznoi dorogi Komsomol'sk–Sovetskaia Gavan' (1943–1945 gg.)" (On the History of the Construction of the Komsomol'sk–Sovetskaia Gavan' Railway [1943–1945]), *Otechestvennye arkhivy,* no. 3 (1995): 90.

[52] Letter from T. L. Il'inskaia, Podol'sk, 27 September 1949, AA.

[53] Letter from P. Zhagir, Alma-Ata, 19 November 1950, AA.

[54] Letter from P. Zhagir, 11 December 1952, AA.

[55] Letter from P. Zhagir, Stalingrad, n.d., AA.

[56] Letter from Shura Bulgakova, Tania (illeg.), Klava (illeg.) 10 April 1949, AA.

[57] Letter from Boris Dmitrievich Strat'ev, Moscow, n.d., AA.

[58] Letter from Dzhek Lindsei (Jack Lindsay), Halstead, Essex, 7 January 1953, AA. A note at the bottom of the letter reads, "Translated on 19 January 1953." For Lindsay's overall view on the Soviet Union, see Jack Lindsay, *A World Ahead: Journal of a Soviet Journey* (London: Fore Publications, 1950), which relates his impressions from a June 1949 visit.

[59] "Voprosy glavnogo redaktora gazety 'Se Suar' frantsuzskogo pisatelia P'era Deksa–V. Azhaevu," AA.

[60] Letter from Josef Crha, Prague, 3 January 1957, AA.

[61] The name of the letter's sender could not be ascertained (AA).

[62] Letter from Ia. Kokushkin, St. Usta, Gor'kovsk. zh.d., selo 2 Chernoe, Kontora lesorazrabotok zavoda "Krasnoe Sormovo," n.d., AA.

[63] Letter from Vladimir N. Pleshokov, Moskva, 93, v/ch 62128 "Zh," 2 June 1950, AA.

[64] Letter from Iu. M. Novikov, Udmurtskaia ASSR, g. Sarapul, zaton Simonikha, Poselkovyi sovet, Novikovoi T. V. dlia Novikova Iuriia Mikhailova, 28 November 1950, AA.

[65] Letter from Anna Gavrilova, g. Serpukhov, 4 June 1952, AA.

12. The Screen

[1] Maiia Turovskaia, "I moe mnenie ob ekranizatsii" (And My Opinion on the Screening of Literature), in *Kniga sporit s fil'mom* (Moscow: Iskusstvo, 1973), pp. 222–233.

[2] Ibid., p. 226.

[3] "Pravlenie SSP SSSR. Kinokommissiia sektsii dramaturgov s aktivom. Obsuzhdenie plana stsenarnykh zakazov Ministerstva Kinematografii na 1948 g., 9 ianvaria 1948 g." RGALI, f. 631, op. 3, ed. khr. 355.

[4] Therefore, the figure given by the Soviet Catalogue of Feature Films for 1951 is reduced from nine to seven. See Peter Kenez, *Cinema and Soviet Society, 1917–1953* (New York: Cambridge University Press, 1992), pp. 210–211. The United States produced from 356 to 383 feature films per year during this time. These figures refer to feature films of an hour or more in length, including co-productions and feature-length documentaries. See Patrick Robertson, *Movie: Facts and Feats—A Guinness Record Book* (New York: Sterling, 1980), p. 28.

[5] Stolper realized precisely these documentary aesthetics when this again became possible, notably, in *The Living and the Dead* (1966) and its sequel, *Retribution* (1969), adapted from Konstantin Simonov's war novels *The Living and the Dead* and *Soldiers are Not Born*, respectively. The use of black and white and the total absence of background music in these films create a coherent semiotic—and therefore aesthetic—system, which is precisely what his film of *Far from Moscow* lacks. I am grateful to Maiia Turovskaia for this insight.

[6] K. Paramonova, "Daleko ot Moskvy" (Far from Moscow), *Iskusstvo kino*, no. 1 (1951): 9–12.

[7] Ibid. *A Story about a Real Man*, directed by Aleksandr Stolper (Mosfil'm, 1948), is the film adaptation of Boris Polevoi's well-known war novel. Both the novel and the film were awarded the Stalin Prize. Sergei Prokofiev composed an opera based on the novel in 1948.

[8] Paramonova, "Daleko ot Moskvy," p. 11.

[9] Ibid., p. 12.

[10] Ibid.

[11] "Zakliuchenie po stsenariiu M. Papava 'Daleko ot Moskvy' (po odnoimennomu romanu V. Azhaeva), 30 iunia 1949 g." and other documents, RGALI, f. 2453 op. 3, ed. khr. 338, ll. 9–38.

[12] Leonid Leonov's *Russkii les* (The Russian Forest) was published in 1953. Azhaev knew Leonov from his teenage years in the Moscow Zariad'e district. According to his widow, Azhaev had shown Leonov his first literary efforts when he was thirteen years old and had received "encouragements" from the great master of Soviet belles lettres. Interview with Irina Liubimova-Azhaeva, 10 November 1991.

[13] V. Azhaev, "Predsedateliu khudozhestvennogo soveta Ministerstva Kinematografii SSSR tov. Il'ichevu, 4 iiulia 1949 g." RGALI, f. 2453, op. 3, ed. khr. 339, ll. 11–12.

[14] "Vypiska iz protokola zasedaniia Khudozhestvennogo Soveta Ministerstva kine-matografii SSSR ot 21 iiulia 1949 g. Obsuzhdenie literaturnogo stsenariia 'Daleko ot Moskvy.'" RGALI, f. 2453, op. 3, ed. khr. 339, ll. 13–30.

[15] Ibid., ll. 24–26.

[16] Lavrentii Beria had been appointed People's Commissar of the Interior in 1938. He was shot in 1953.

[17] "Vypiska iz protokola zasedaniia Khudozhestvennogo Soveta Ministerstva kine-matografii SSSR ot 21 iiulia 1949g.," l. 14.

[18] "Zakliuchenie po rezhisserskomu stsenariiu 'Daleko ot Moskvy.' Avtor ekraniza-tsii—Papava M. I., rezhisser—Stolper A," n.d. (inscribed by hand; sent to the ministry 18 October 1949). RGALI, f. 2453, op. 3, ed. khr. 339.

[19] "Direktoru kinostudii 'Mosfil'm' tov. Kuznetsovu; Nachal'niku stsenarno-postano-vochnogo otdela Ministerstva Kinematografii SSSR tov. Dulgerovu V. E.; Tekst ob"ekta 'Fanza'; Direktoru Kinostudii 'Mosfil'm' tov. Kuznetsovu S. A. ot 8 iiunia 1950 g." RGALI, f. 2453, op. 3, ed. khr. 339, ll. 5–7, 11, 12–13, 14.

[20] "Vypiska iz protokola zasedaniia Khudozhestvennogo Soveta Ministerstva kine-matografii SSSR ot 27 iiulia 1950g." RGALI, f. 2453, op. 3, ed. khr. 339, ll. 23–25.

[21] "Vypiska iz protokola zasedaniia Khudozhestvennogo Soveta Ministerstva kine-matografii SSSR ot 9 noiabria 1950g." RGALI, f. 2453, op. 3, ed. khr. 339, l. 38.

[22] Three years later Azhaev became a member of the Artistic Council of Mosfil'm. "Prikaz Ministerstva Kul'tury SSSR No. 1358-K, 12 noiabria 1953 g. p/p Ministr Kul'tury SSSR P. Ponomarenko," AA.

13. Borderline III

[1] Vera Ketlinskaia (1906–1976) was the author of *Muzhestvo* (Courage) (1938), a fa-mous novel on the first years of Komsomol'sk.

[2] "Kserokopiia izvlechenii iz stenogrammy utrennego zasedaniia tvorcheskoi konfer-entsii pisatelei Dal'nego Vostoka 15. II.49." GAKhK, f. 1738, op. 1, d. 63, ll. 217–218, 236, 251–258. The Bureia is a river in the Khabarovsk region.

[3] Evgenii Dolmatovskii, *Bylo: Zapiski poeta* (The Past: Notes of a Poet) (Moscow: Sovetskii Pisatel', 1982), p. 446.

[4] Interview with Ivan Panin, 23 August 1995.

[5] The first book edition was published as *Predislovie k zhizni: Povest'* (A Foreword to Life: A Novella) (Moscow: Molodaia Gvardiia, 1962). A new edition of *A Foreword to Life* was published in 1987 with a print run of 200,000: Vasilii Azhaev, *Predislovie k zhizni: Povesti i rasskazy* (Moscow: Sovetskii Pisatel', 1987).

[6] On 6 October 1957 one Boris L. Brainin wrote from Poste Restante, Tomsk, to thank Azhaev for his help in achieving full rehabilitation, AA.

[7] "Fame," in *Boris Pasternak: Poems,* trans. Eugene M. Kayden (Ann Arbor: University of Michigan Press, 1959), p. 173.

[8] Lydia Chukovskaya, *Going Under,* trans. Peter M. Weston (London: Barrie & Jen-kins, 1972).

[9] Cited in Grigori Svirski, *A History of Post-War Soviet Writing: The Literature of Moral Opposition* (Ann Arbor: Ardis, 1981), pp. 220–221.

[10] Ibid., p. 221.

[11] Chukovskaya, *Going Under,* p. 134.

[12] Formerly the Ministry of Internal Affairs, which it became again after Khrushchev's removal. See Jerry F. Hough and Merle Fainsod, *How the Soviet Union Is Governed* (Cambridge: Harvard University Press, 1979), p. 254.

[13] V. Azhaev, "Pamiat' serdtsa," p. 62, AA.

Epilogue

[1] "Snova Daleko ot Moskvy. O tom, kak zhizn' dopisyvaet knigu," P. Kulakov, Komsomol'sk-na-Amure–Tsimmermanovka, AA.

[2] Lazarev and De-Kastri are part of the Ul'ch district of the Khabarovsk Region.

[3] Kliment Voroshilov (1881–1969), marshal of the Soviet Union, vice president of the Council of Ministers of the USSR from 1946 to 1953, president of the Presidium of the Supreme Soviet of the USSR from 1953 to 1960.

[4] See Vasili Azhayev, *Far from Moscow,* trans. R. Prokofieva (Foreign Languages Publishing House, 1950), bk. 2, p. 132.

[5] See Appendix.

[6] This offense was punishable by ten years of forced labor (law of 7 August 1932). See Jacques Rossi, *The Gulag Handbook: An Encyclopedia Dictionary of Soviet Penitentiary Institutions and Terms Related to the Forced Labor Camps,* trans. William A. Burhans (New York: Paragon House, 1989), pp. 167–168.

[7] One Petr Efimovich Zhagirnovskii, "director of the garment factory," figures among those who were awarded a medal "for labor distinction" on 30 October 1942 by decree of the Supreme Soviet of the USSR "On Awards to Construction Workers of Special Projects." See Appendix.

[8] Azhayev, *Far from Moscow,* bk. 1, p. 109; translation modified.

INDEX